EVER AFTER

THE LAST YEARS OF
MUSICAL THEATER
AND BEYOND

BARRY SINGER

APPLAUSE
THEATRE & CINEMA BOOKS

Ever After
The Last Years of Musical Theater
and Beyond

Copyright © 2004 by Barry Singer
All rights reserved

Additional credits can be found on
page 329

Library of Congress Control Number:
2003113110

APPLAUSE THEATRE & CINEMA BOOKS
151 West 46th Street, 8th Floor
New York, NY 10036
Phone: (212) 575-9265
Fax: (646) 562-5852
Email: info@applausepub.com
Internet: www.applausepub.com

Sales & Distribution

NORTH AMERICA:
Hal Leonard Corp.
7777 West Bluemound Road
P. O. Box 13819
Milwaukee, WI 53213
Phone: (414) 774-3630
Fax: (414) 774-3259
Email: halinfo@halleonard.com
Internet: www.halleonard.com
EUROPE:
Roundhouse Publishing Ltd.
Millstone, Limers Lane
Northam, North Devon EX 39 2RG
Phone: (0) 1237-474-474
Fax: (0) 1237-474-774
Email: roundhouse.group@ukgateway.net

For Leah,
who never saw any of these shows.

And for Loretta,
who now feels as if she has.

Yeah, everybody loves musicals. Even people who say they don't, love them. They're either the best thing or the worst. When they're really bad, they're just pathetic and they'll make you throw up. If they're really good, they just take you to another level of humanity or something.

—Randy Courts
Composer/Lyricist [1]

TABLE OF CONTENTS

IS IT DEAD YET?

Talking about musicals is a thing of the past.

Not only don't people do it much anymore, those few who still bother, speak almost exclusively in the past tense.

Books about musical theater's various "golden ages" revisit compulsively the same distant terrain over and over. Books about the quixotic nature of musicals today—or, at the very least, just yesterday? Well, nobody wants to go there.

Nothing more painfully sums up the current state of musical theater than this lack of interest in what is being done now, who has written what lately. And how does it sound?

Hand-wringing we have in abundance. *Where has musical theater gone?* The very question traces its own unspoken, backward-glancing spin: Why isn't musical theater as it once was?

Well, how could it be? Over the latter decades of the last century the whole business was forced to its knees, battered from without by radical shifts of taste in popular music and even norms of literacy, and from within by the decimation of so many creative links to its past and future via attrition and premature AIDS-related death. That musical theater managed to survive at all is, in fact, something of a miracle.

New musicals continue to be written in abundance and produced largely in obscurity. Dead composers dominate Broadway in revivals *ad nauseam*. Living composers generally write far from Broadway for audiences who are not especially interested.

So, is musical theater's troubled present worth anything at all?

In the spring of 1997 the theater editor at the *New York Times* Arts & Leisure section, Andrea Stevens, asked me a similar, if more diplomatically phrased, question: "What's the story about musical theater today?"

My tentative answer, at nearly 3,000 words, ran on the last Sunday in August of that year. Trends—to the extent that they existed at all—were noted, the previous season's musical output was assessed, the forthcoming season's projected productions were itemized and a handful of promising young composers were briefly profiled; most of them, for the first time under the banner: *All the News That's Fit to Print*.

Thereafter on the last Sunday in August, for the next four years, Andrea encouraged me to do it again. And again. And so a snapshot emerged of recent musical theater in microcosm.

So much detail got left out, though, due to the limitations of space in a daily newspaper. A larger canvas really was needed.

Thoughts about expanding these *Times* pieces into a book led to a much more daunting realization: No-one had yet written the history of the last 25 years in musical theater, period.

Now I was in for it.

Taking as a not-in-the-least-bit-arbitrary starting point that moment just before the arrival of British mega-musicals in America when a new generation of young theater composers began to stir Off-Broadway, this book now treads where nobody much strolls anymore.

My focus almost exclusively? Original new musicals. Revivals I have virtually ignored. Let someone else write that history.

As a result of my work for the *Times*, as well as for *The New Yorker* and for *New York* magazine, I seem to have interviewed virtually everyone who has had an impact on musical theater during the past quarter century. And so they are all here, as characters, speaking for themselves. This is, after all, a story and I've tried to tell it that way. Searching, I guess, for a happy ending.

All quotations in this book are from interviews conducted firsthand, with three noted exceptions (see Chapters 12 and 25).

All ages given in this book are contemporaneous with the moment in time covered by the chapters in which they appear. For a person's current age, the reader will have to do the math.

Dispensing with the tedious litany of opening night reviews that dominate so many musical theater histories, all reviews quoted here are in endnotes only, with one exception (see Chapter 1). A complete season-by-season chronology of Broadway musicals is offered in an addendum section called The Seasons, where data on all composers, lyricists and bookwriters is provided, as well as the month of opening and theater for shows lacking that information in the text.

Ever After ends in the early summer of 2003. All "in-the-works" musicals covered have, of course, continued to evolve. The book, however, had to stop somewhere.

"Ever after," we all know, is a fairy tale state, usually involving the word "happily" but preceding the words "The End."

"Ever after" is also how the last 25 years of musical theater seem destined to be viewed by history—an era ever *after* musical theater's many golden ages.

Are these the last years of musical theater?

Yes.

And no.

Let me tell you about them.

AND NOW LIFE REALLY BEGINS

—A Chorus Line

Sixty-five hours after the funeral, came the wake.

Sixty-five hours after the anything-but-funereal final performance of *A Chorus Line* at the Shubert Theater on Saturday night, April 28, 1990, many, if not most of the surviving cast members from the show's 6,137-performance, fifteen-year, uptown run returned to the Shubert for something few of them were comfortable about but, as one, felt compelled nevertheless to attend.

The End of the Line Auction and Tag Sale read hastily printed signs out front along Shubert Alley. Apparently, Broadway's most influential musical, the longest-running of its day, would not simply *cease*. The very sum of its parts would have to be dispersed, sold off in one sweeping fund-raising finale.

It's difficult now, even a relative few years later, to recapture all that *A Chorus Line* represented to the Broadway musical community in 1990. So much has changed so drastically in the very nature of what constitutes a Broadway musical. Long-running hits are now franchises first, their components largely assembled by corporate fiat. Their souls are those of profit machines.

A Chorus Line was both a celebration and summation of the hand-crafted fashion by which musicals once were created, a method refined and passed down generation to generation. Its soul belonged exclusively to its creators and its performers.

5

The show was both deeply traditional in terms of style, music, and movement, and deceptively experimental in subtler ways, especially the innovative process by which it had evolved. As the first Broadway musical developed entirely Off-Broadway in a series of workshops rather than for Broadway directly, through a series of out-of-town tryouts, *A Chorus Line* broke the mold. In its wake few musicals would ever again come into being through trial and error on the road. To this day "workshop" remains the dominant word in the development life of any new musical.

But *A Chorus Line* also was a love letter to the painstaking experience, the sweat, of making a new musical from scratch. Its farewell was a valedictory to a very specific way of doing things.

Entering through the Shubert Theater stage door on this quiet Tuesday afternoon, cast members found themselves, as always, almost instantly onstage beneath the Shubert proscenium, straddling that stretch where *A Chorus Line*'s long white line—the show's signature design element—once had extended. The line now was a furrow. Each individual "line" floor panel had been pried up, to be sold in the next day's tag sale ("like the Berlin Wall," someone remarked) at $100 per segment.

Everywhere, the detritus of *A Chorus Line*'s fifteen year existence loomed up out of the darkness: "light boxes" and "three-sheets," "flying mirrors" and "twinkle lights," all for sale. There were small mountains of mirrored, Mylar-faced signage: *Quote Panels* from the Shubert facade, *Price Scale* boards from the box office, a *Quiet Please—Performance In Progress* sign. Monumental color photo blow-ups commemorated *Chorus Line*'s myriad companies. A complete set of costumes, seventeen sets of rehearsal clothes, hung like flattened cartoon characters from a pipe above the pocked Shubert stage. Even the show's dazzling closing number "Sunburst" set was up for grabs in panel sections strung haphazardly from the flies.

So long as it lasted, *A Chorus Line* had been Broadway's leader, a beacon really. Since the show's first day uptown in July 1975, an entire generation of Broadway "gypsies" had been employed on its line. When *A Chorus Line* first had surfaced downtown as a workshop at the New York Shakespeare Festival in the summer of 1974, musical theater was at a nadir in the wake of the rock and roll revolution of the 1960s. Though the show's success hardly had reversed this downward spiral of pop cultural irrelevance for musical theater, it sure had mitigated it nicely.

As the original producer of *A Chorus Line*, the New York Shakespeare Festival's founder Joseph Papp had reaped on behalf of his theater much of the financial benefit from the show's record-setting run on Broadway. Now his Shakespeare Festival would also be the sole beneficiary of all proceeds from *A Chorus Line*'s auction and tag sale.

Downstage right, Papp could be found at that moment deep in conversation with two *Chorus Line* alums: Donna McKechnie, the show's original lead, as *Cassie*, and Laurie Gamache, the show's final *Cassie*, along with a young man who also looked to be a dancer.

"This is Randy Clements," Gamache announced helpfully. "Randy's gonna be our auctioneer tomorrow. He's played *Zach* a lot too."

"You played *Zach*…?" Papp responded hazily before recovering with impressive impresarial tact. "…You were very good too, weren't you."

"He was!" agreed Gamache.

"Well, I hope you're also one hell of an auctioneer," Papp added quietly. "We're depending on you for next year's income."

"Here Joe, I brought these, I hope they're alright," McKechnie interjected, producing from her bag a pair of autographed dance shoes.

"Are those from your days in the show?" someone asked.

"Actually they're shoes that I still use," McKechnie admitted. "I wanted to give something of myself from right now, a part of me *now*, because that's what we did when we were in the show. You know what I mean?"

More than anyone in the Shubert Theater at that moment, McKechnie seemed to embody all that *A Chorus Line* would now leave behind. The show had made her a Broadway legend. She herself had married Michael Bennett, *A Chorus Line*'s conceiver, director, and choreographer, only to see their marriage dissolve after a very brief run. Bennett would die of AIDS in 1987.

Where Joe Papp seemed to be steeling himself against the magnitude of his show's demise, and Laurie Gamache appeared entirely stunned with sadness, McKechnie projected a more infinite sorrow matured in grief; not in the least a quantitative difference, merely a matter of experience. In a sense, McKechnie was simply the widow of *A Chorus Line*.

Downstairs, in the Shubert Theater lounge, an insider's pre–tag sale was already underway. The lounge bar was piled with every conceivable souvenir *Chorus Line* T-shirt, the lounge itself was lined with rack upon rack of shimmering gold *Finale* tuxedos. A long table displayed posters, lapel pins and programs, plus costume ensembles for every *Chorus Line* character — little heaps of red *Cassie* leotards, pink *Sheila* Danskins. Crowding the floor were twelve laundry baskets overflowing with straw hats, homburgs, derbies, top hats and, of course, dance shoes — satin *Finale* shoes and more prosaic Capezios. For the *Finales*, four bucks. A dollar a pair for the others.

Already the lounge was overrun with *Chorus Line* shoppers. Many members of the original cast were there, pawing through the remains. In an open men's room door Donna McKechnie now loitered with the show's original *Diana Morales*, Priscilla Lopez, laughing as Lopez slipped herself into a *Finale* monkey suit.

Sitting watchfully on a lounge stair step, Alyce Gilbert, the only wardrobe mistress *A Chorus Line* ever had, surveyed the action; a lean, handsome woman in a black blouse with five pens in her pocket and two large safety pins stuck into a lapel.

"I've been here since the first days at the Newman Theater downtown," she said, with a weary gesture toward the racks. "When the costumes were delivered to Michael, I came with them. We've saved just about every costume ever produced for the show; we kept them in this terrible cave-like room underneath Shubert Alley. It had a dirt floor when we first moved in, and the pipes *still* leak."

Gilbert watched Priscilla Lopez come bounding from the men's room, looking so swell in her costume that many in the room began to applaud.

"Now I need some shoes," Lopez announced.

"It was pulling the costumes out of the cave that really got to me," Alyce Gilbert went on. "All of them have many, many names inked into their collars. It's really the history of the show right there, and as I was laying them out I realized I recognized at least fifteen boys' names who were dead now. Young, healthy boys. It shocked me. I don't just remember their faces, you see, I remember their bodies."

Nearby, Laurie Gamache was buying one of each costume article, "so that when I get home to Des Moines one day, I can stage the whole show myself," she explained.

Gilbert shook her head. "They all keep trying to restage the thing," she muttered affectionately. "They get the precise lighting cues, they take the costumes, but they can never get it to look the same. They'll never get it to look the same, I'm afraid, because Michael designed *A Chorus Line* with Theoni Aldredge and Tharon Musser—the costume and lighting designers—to look the way he saw it in his head. No matter where you do it again, the lights don't look as good, the costume colors don't quite read as they should because Michael painted with them *in here*, in the Shubert Theater.

"That's the tragedy," Gilbert concluded. "It's the last Michael Bennett show that will ever look like Michael saw it."

All around the room snatches of conversation floated up like dialogue fragments from the show itself; dancers among themselves:

"...Quick, before they sell it!"

"...Just gives you an empty feeling."

"What the hell was I gonna do with it anyway?"

Did Gilbert think Bennett would have approved of *A Chorus Line* ending this way, with a tag sale and an auction?

Gilbert remained silent for a moment.

"Michael was very astute about business," she said finally. "I think he would have understood and accepted all of this. But I also think he would have come up with a way to stage it all so that people would have remembered. I'm quite sure he would have created something memorable for the closing. Michael would have known how to make this end right."

CHAPTER I

WE'RE BITCHING

I'm bitching. He's bitching.
They're bitching. We're bitching.

— March of the Falsettos

One day in 1977, a 21-year-old musical theater nut from Washington Heights named Ira Weitzman turned west at the outlying border of the Broadway theater district and kept on walking.

Throughout the history of the Broadway musical tradition that he doted on, the theater district literally had reached no further west than this — Eighth Avenue. Weitzman however, had heard talk of a new theatrical neighborhood taking shape farther west, beyond the limits of Broadway's once-glamorous 42nd Street hub.

In an effort to rehabilitate a particularly tawdry slab of 42nd Street blockfront between Ninth and Tenth Avenues, New York City had recently undertaken a well-publicized urban renewal project: turning a grim strip of low-rise porn shops and massage parlors into a bunch of small theaters. One of these spaces was now home to Playwrights Horizons, an ambitious six-year-old troupe founded out in Queens by Robert Moss, a visionary character; in fact, an instigator of 42nd Street's current redevelopment.

None of this was a secret. What sent Weitzman west that day was inside news that Moss at this moment was looking to hire an assistant.

"I don't know where exactly my fantasy of working in the theater came from," Weitzman would later admit, "Not just the theater —

musical theater specifically. My parents had a lot of original cast albums and I pretty much used to wear them out; it's kind of a cliché, but I was inspired."

Weitzman had gotten his first job at fifteen working for WBAI, New York's famously flaky, longtime left-leaning, non-profit radio station. "I did a number of jobs for them, including running something called the 'Free Music Store,' mounting two or three concerts per week, live, from a studio big enough to seat 300 people," recalled Weitzman. "Which taught me how to produce and make artistic decisions, essentially. I also put together a fairly substantial on-air tribute to Richard Rodgers, who was my idol in the theater. He was still alive then, he heard it, and I actually got to meet him."

Earlier in 1976 Weitzman had left WBAI after the station's transmitter was stormed by its own striking staff, shutting the place down for a week. Now, months later, he went to work for Bob Moss and Playwrights Horizons on 42nd Street's newly dubbed "Theater Row."

For a year he worked practically free.

"I finally approached André Bishop — until-then Playwrights' literary manager, who'd just taken over as artistic director while Bob retained the title of producing director. I asked him: 'Can we do musicals?' Under Bob, Playwrights had never seriously done anything in musical theater. Andre had the same obsession with Richard Rodgers, Mary Martin, Ethel Merman, and musicals that I did. He was completely receptive."

Word soon went out that Playwrights Horizons was now interested in musicals. Which changed next to nothing at all. Except that Weitzman did find himself getting bombarded with phone calls from some guy named Bill Finn and various friends of Finn.

A composer (formally untrained), lyricist, and bookwriter from Natick, Massachusetts, by way of Williams College (alma mater of

Stephen Sondheim), the 26-year-old Finn was presenting a musical he'd been working on; just a few performances at his apartment. The piece was called *In Trousers*.

"So one of the first things I did in my new job as a developer of musicals for Playwrights Horizons," recalled Weitzman, "was to go to see *In Trousers* at Bill Finn's apartment."

As an epiphany, the evening proved memorable but imperfect.

"There was no book. There was no structure. There were just these marvelous, sort of stream of consciousness songs. It was gutsy. It was adult. It was emotional. It was different. It was all of these things that were my fantasy of what contemporary musical theater might be. I had goose bumps! I thought that everyone in that room was going to run up to this man and say, 'I must work with you.' It just cried out to be worked on. The minute it ended I ran up to Bill myself and said, '*Please* come to Playwrights Horizons and we'll work on this.'"

In Trousers essentially was a confessional revue, a string of analyst couch songs delivered by a deeply neurotic Finn-manqué named Marvin. The musical—almost entirely sung-through—coyly traced the married Marvin's shaky romantic evolution from a spoiled fourteen-year-old student lusting after his high school English teacher, through Marvin's fateful first tryst with the lovable, insecure woman who was now his wife and the mother of his child, to the climactic revelation that Marvin was about to leave his family for a homosexual lover.

The subject matter—for musical theater, of course—was revolutionary; homosexuality had rarely before figured so overtly in any musical ostensibly conceived for a mass audience. In retrospect, though, it was the dramatic scale of *In Trousers* that proved to be the show's most influential innovation. Parsing one man's personal emotional minutiae with the kind of narcissistic focus that would soon define the "Me Generation" of the 1980s, Finn gave self-involvement musical form—a disjunctive, simultaneously self-effacing yet operatic, seemingly unmediated yet tightly wrought, undeniably adult yet disingenuously childlike, sing-song musical style that was, above all else, really accessibly small in scale.

"It was a mess," acknowledged Weitzman. "A brilliant, brilliant, brilliant mess."

In Trousers made its first appearance at Playwrights Horizons directed by Finn himself, who also played Marvin, at an 11 PM quasi-workshop in an upstairs stage space, inaugurating what was dubbed Weitzman's "Musical Theater Workshop" series. But barely.

"Playwrights Horizons was just beginning to have subscribers," explained Weitzman. "So initially they said, 'Oh, great, we'll use musicals to get more subscribers.' They gave me this slot at 11 PM on the set of whatever show was then playing, for what they called musical 'cabarets,' which they offered to subscribers as 'premiums.' Of course this really didn't sit right with me but I've always tried to make use of whatever I'm given; I am a completely self-educated person theatrically and my way of learning what there was to learn about the theater was to just delve right in."

In Trousers—again directed by Finn, with a cast of four superlative performers—Alison Fraser, Joanna Green, Mary Testa, and Chip Zien as Marvin—re-opened on December 8, 1978 downstairs at Playwrights Horizons' Main Stage, where it ran for just 28 performances.

"Still, it re-defined my job," insisted Weitzman. "Because Bill Finn demanded to be treated like an artist; like a playwright. He was not interested in creating little musical cabarets at 11 o'clock. He expected rehearsal time. He expected artistic respect."

A year later Finn was back with the next chapter in his life of Marvin, *Four Jews in a Room Bitching*. "More great material," noted

Weitzman ruefully, "within the sketchiest shell of a story. I was let go from Playwrights Horizons after that reading. It was expensive to maintain a musical theater series and Playwrights just decided it wasn't worth it."

In the wake of Weitzman's dismissal, James Lapine—a young Yale-educated playwright whose own play, *Table Settings*, had work-shopped at Playwrights Horizons around the same time as *In Trousers*—stepped in as a bookwriter and as a director to work with Finn on his unwieldy mess of a musical.

The fully revamped results opened at Playwrights as *March of the Falsettos*, a legitimate production with its own 8 PM curtain, on the 21st of May, 1981. A far more lucid rendition of Marvin's socio-sexual odyssey, *March of the Falsettos* commenced with Marvin (Michael Rupert) happily in the arms of his male lover, Whizzer Brown (Stephen Bogardus). Marvin's ex-wife, Trina (Alison Fraser), mean-while had found her way into the bed of Marvin's psychiatrist, Mendel (Chip Zien). All four—parents and surrogate parents—then labored touchingly to do what was best for Marvin and Trina's ten-year-old son, Jason (James Kushner), ultimately imparting to him Finn's fundamental message that being brave enough to be yourself is life's greatest challenge and greatest reward.

As ever, Finn's craftsmanship as a lyricist and as a composer remained spasmodically uneven; his musical palette, an appealing if often-frantic amalgamation of old-school musical theater tics updated with rather middle-of-the-road contemporary pop flourishes. His lyrics, rapid-fire, conversational laundry-lists of self-help-caliber personal observations, were fashioned into daffy, often Brechtian-style odes with titles like, "Marvin at the Psychiatrist," "My Father's a Homo," and "Four Jews in a Room Bitching." Still, the idiosyncratic neurotic energy of Finn's musical and dramatic meanderings gave *March of the Falsettos* a breathless frisson. And few were more stimulated by this jolt of neurotic juice than the *New York Times'* reigning drama critic, Frank Rich.

"When the best two musicals of the season (*The Pirates of Penzance*, *Sophisticated Ladies*) are both the work of dead songwriters," began Rich in his review of *March of the Falsettos*, "you know that the American musical theater is in trouble. Indeed, I can't even remember the last time I attended a musical—on Broadway or off—that introduced a new composer or lyricist of serious promise. And that's why I had trouble believing my ears at a new show with the unlikely title of *March of the Falsettos*."

> This one-hour, musical, which is now running in the small upstairs space at Playwrights Horizons, tells its story through 20 songs by William Finn. The songs are so fresh that the show is only a few bars old before one feels the unmistakable, revivifying charge of pure talent.
>
> However slight and predictable the raw materials, Finn has transformed them into a show that is funny and tender on its own contained, anecdotal terms... *March of the Falsettos* is that rare musical that actually has something to be cocky about.

"Suddenly Playwrights Horizons was recognized for musical theater," marveled Weitzman. "Which allowed me to come back and reclaim my job. *March of the Falsettos* legitimized Playwrights, as the theater's first big hit, and it legitimized me. All I knew now was I wanted to make more musicals with new writers like Bill Finn. I didn't know exactly what that meant or how, because frankly there was no model. But that became my mission. I would go everywhere, see everything, and try to meet everyone. My goal was to develop at least one new musical each season that I could be excited about."

The Broadway musical theater mindset that Weitzman's nascent alternative community of new writers now hoped to contravene was, as Rich's review suggested, disproportionately necrophilic.

"Broadway was dominated by what I would call 'dead composer

shows,'" Weitzman himself put it, "shows like *Ain't Misbehavin'*, a really nice celebration of the dead jazz pianist and composer, Fats Waller. *Sophisticated Ladies*—Duke Ellington. Gilbert and Sullivan's *Pirates of Penzance*. There was very little support of any *living*, let alone new, young writers. There was no model, though, in the non-profit Off-Broadway arena either for developing new musicals. So, I was filling a void."

Alongside Broadway's "dead composer" shows were endlessly derivative revivals and retro-shtick-fests like the burlesque salute *Sugar Babies* (1979) and the clever Golden Age of Hollywood homage *A Day in Hollywood/A Night in the Ukraine* (1980). Yes, there were still new, original book musicals. The 1977–1978 season had *On the Twentieth Century*, a pseudo-operatic romp composed by Cy Coleman with book and lyrics by Betty Comden and Adolph Green adapting the beloved stage and screen classic *Twentieth Century*. The season also had *The Act*, a gerrymandered star turn for Liza Minnelli, with music by John Kander and lyrics by Fred Ebb, directed by an unsung musical auteur named Martin Scorsese. Additionally, it had *Working*, an uneven adaptation of the Studs Terkel oral history compendium by Stephen Schwartz and an assembly line of musical collaborators. *Ain't Misbehavin'* nevertheless took the Tony Award that year.

The ensuing 1978–1979 season had been elevated by Stephen Sondheim and Harold Prince's Tony Award–winning epic of Grand Guignol excess, *Sweeney Todd*, a towering achievement of literate, gutsy, musical theater inventiveness. *Sweeney Todd* was, however, an anomaly for Broadway. This same season also brought wheezing flops from such titans as Jerry Herman (*The Grand Tour*), Burton Lane, and Alan Jay Lerner (*Carmelina*), Lee Adams, and Charles Strouse (*A Broadway Musical*), and Richard Rodgers, offering Broadway his final score, *I Remember Mama*.

Even Michael Bennett, directing and choreographing a musical called *Ballroom*, appeared stymied that year, disoriented by his own recent success with *A Chorus Line*. One Off-Broadway transfer, *The*

Best Little Whorehouse in Texas, did trumpet the arrival of Bennett's pupil, Tommy Tune, as a stage director of fearless imagination. In terms of content, the show also trumpeted a half-baked crudity that seemed the antithesis of Tune's sly wit.

Since the latter 1960s the once reliable musculature for Broadway musical form had continued inexorably to atrophy. What the veteran talents offered now seemed largely a withered accretion of gestures. What relatively young talents, like Marvin Hamlisch, with *They're Playing Our Song*, had to say that same season seemed similarly canned and stale.

Broadway in 1979–1980 would generate just two original musicals of quality, both of them biographies of sorts: *Barnum* and *Evita*. *Barnum* was the story of America's favorite carny-barker/showman, P. T. Barnum. Its untraditional staging and ultra-traditional music by a wily pair of veterans, Joe Layton and Cy Coleman, respectively, proved both clever and quaint. Michael Stewart's lyrics and Mark Bramble's book unashamedly underlined the fact that this musical was all about Broadway prestidigitation, the kind where reassuringly familiar melody and brazen directorial ingenuity made a gaping lack of substance virtually disappear.

Andrew Lloyd Webber's *Evita* by contrast was essentially the same magic trick in reverse: an empty-headed lump of pomposity palmed off as something substantial. A sung-through semi-operetta in what would soon be recognized as Lloyd Webber's definitively dysfunctional style, *Evita* (along with the composer's *Cats* two years later) heralded Broadway's new money-making model: the mega-musical—a crass and bombastic phenomenon, sleek and flabby all at once.

Lloyd Webber was then just 32-years-old. As an Oxford educated Englishman, his sense of Broadway musical theater was somewhat limited and secondhand—rooted in Richard Rodgers's more ponderous, hymn-like, late–Oscar Hammerstein period, with youthful touches derived from '70s pop as filtered through the English music hall. Working with another Oxford escapee, named Tim Rice, as his lyricist, Lloyd Webber in the late '60s had fashioned out of familiar bible stories a pair of "rock operas" (more rock cantatas actually, which is to say these musicals loudly signified far more than they dramatized): *Joseph and the Amazing Technicolor Dreamcoat* in 1968, followed by *Jesus Christ Superstar* in 1971.

Both had sung with a contemporary musical voice, one that essentially belonged to Galt MacDermot, the revolutionary composer of *Hair*, who'd brilliantly and eclectically homogenized the backbeat of rock and roll with musical theater tradition. In swiping MacDermot's sound, Lloyd Webber added one note to MacDermot's innovation: portentousness. "I Don't Know How To Love Him," *Superstar*'s big hit, was a sweet folk ballad with strenuous intimations of grandeur. It was Lloyd Webber's title tune, though, for *Superstar* which proved *the* model for future, infernally repetitive Lloyd Webberian bombast.

Still, both songs together returned musical theater to the pop charts in 1971.

Which was no mean feat.

"Nothing could be more conventional than the idea of Jesus Christ as a story," acknowledged Rice. "Everybody has one bad Jesus work in them. But if you lay onto that *most* conventional of stories what was then contemporary rock music, you have something very interesting."

In 1975, in London, the team followed their bible successes with *Evita*. María Eva ("Evita") Duarte Perón had been the mistress and, later, wife of Argentina's venal 1950s dictator, Juan Perón. Still notorious for her tarnished (purported) saintliness, though long deceased, she was an oddly original focus for a musical, both fresh and frivolous at once.

Lloyd Webber tackled Evita's inherent trashiness with operatically ennobling pop-rock arias like "Don't Cry for Me, Argentina". The subject had little to do with the music; the music, little to do with its subject. Rice's lyrics, though acute and evocative, were often awkwardly set, a function of Rice's own carelessness as a craftsman and Lloyd Webber's insistence that his musicals be sung-through virtually down to the last line of dialogue. Smartly deployed scenic projections and crowds of swarming company members (directed by veteran Sondheim collaborator Harold Prince) helped to distract audiences from the tarted up lugubriousness of the proceedings.

So much so, in fact that *Evita* ended up a Tony Award–winning hit. Abetted by terrific star turns from two young musical theater up-and-comers — Mandy Patinkin as Che Guevara and Patti LuPone as the title character — *Evita* was a hit big enough to herald Lloyd Webber's future dominance on Broadway. It was also troubling enough musically to suggest that this dominance would inspire considerable aesthetic loathing.

Were Broadway's biggest new musicals at this time all biographies of sorts? Or did it only seem that way? *Woman of the Year* in 1981, with music by Kander and Ebb, sketched the biography of a fictional international newspaper correspondent, as derived from the Tracy and Hepburn 1940s Hollywood flick of the same name. *Dreamgirls*, also in 1981, with music by Henry Krieger, was the semi-fictionalized biography of The Supremes, as triumphantly directed and co-choreographed by Michael Bennett. *Nine*, in 1982, with music by Maury Yeston and spectacular staging by Tommy Tune, was the abstract impressionistic biography of a nominally fictional Italian film director, as adapted from the classic Frederico Fellini film, *8½*. Lloyd Webber's *Cats*, also in 1982, was T. S. Eliot's poeticized biography of an entirely fictional pack of alley cats.

Cats, when it first appeared, was at least a flight of fancy. No other musical had ever before quite looked as director Trevor Nunn, designer John Napier, and choreographer Gillian Lynne made *Cats* look. These innovations were, however, nearly entirely cosmetic. The show's be-whiskered painted faces, its calculatingly frolicsome façade grew more irritating by the instant. So did its super-sized trash dump of a set. As for Lloyd Webber's predictably operatic-pop-rock score, as defined by the Puccini-inspired hit, "Memory," its sound already had crossed the cusp of cliché. Despite this musical's future history-making box office longevity, *Cats* in the end had little aesthetic staying power at all

Dreamgirls was another story entirely. Initiated by the composer Krieger and the lyricist-librettist (and initially the director) Tom Eyen, as a musical about the world of black pop/soul backup singers, the show would only deepen with age. Krieger, a Westchester boy, largely self-taught as a musician, had been a press agent for black soul singers like Jerry Butler, who, as Krieger later put it, "taught me about the physics of songwriting." Krieger had evolved into a composer with a gift for operatic, pop/soul theater arias, a variety of show stopper that he virtually invented in *Dreamgirls* with the searing "And I Am Telling You, I'm Not Going," as shouted out by Jennifer Holliday.

It took *Dreamgirls* at least four or five different workshops plus a nine-week, out-of-town tryout in Boston to find its final explosive shape and thinly veiled subject, the backstage Supremes saga. Bennett only signed on as director late in the show's workshop evolution. His fluid choreographic and directorial invention, in tandem with scenic designer Robin Wagner and lighting designer Tharon Musser's expressively shifting light tower formations, made *Dreamgirls* a huge critical hit.[2] Still, it was Krieger's pastiche-Motown score that decisively separated *Dreamgirls* from its Broadway peers. Here, at last, was a successful theatrical reimagining of fairly recent pop music. Though, admittedly, the moment that it captured was already a good 20 years in the past.

It was not *Dreamgirls* but *Nine* that won the Tony Award for Best Musical of 1981–1982. *Nine* had stagecraft by Tommy Tune that legitimately contended with Bennett's brilliant *Dreamgirls* work. It also had a stultifyingly uneventful book by Arthur Kopit and a score by Maury Yeston full of grandiose, largely unconsummated, musical gestures. How it managed to eclipse the truly timeless *Dreamgirls* remains an enigma.

Off-Broadway, the years preceding Finn's 1981 *March of the Falsettos* breakthrough at Playwrights Horizons were littered with original mis-fires and more "dead composer" revues (some of them quite good) like *One Mo' Time* (1979), *Blues in the Night* (1980) and *Tintypes* (1979). The latter two, in fact, transferred to Broadway for brief runs.

Elizabeth Swados was the period's singular exception. Swados tends today to be entirely overlooked. During the years just preceding *March of the Falsettos*, however, she was a truly innovative voice. An unregenerate child of the '60s, Swados possessed an original sensibility and, even better, an adventurer's spirit. Her run of works presented at the New York Shakespeare Festival from 1978 to 1981 was as exhilarating as just about any enjoyed by any one composer since; four imaginative new musicals: *Runaways*, about abused teenagers in 1978, which ultimately moved to Broadway, receiving a Tony nomination for Best Musical; *Dispatches*, derived from the Vietnam War memoir by Thomas Herr, in 1979; *The Haggadah: A Passover Cantata* in 1980; and *Alice in Concert* in 1981, her take on Lewis Carroll's *Alice in Wonderland*.

Swados' musicals were always raucously free-wheeling but self-consciously so, often suggesting some hippie kid with a face painted just a little too perfectly, tripping out at the Be-In but steering clear of the actual acid. A strong whiff of self-righteousness also colored her work. Yet, no musical theater creator of the period better conjured the sounds of the moment within a theatrical frame.

The only other ray of originality to pierce the clouds of nostalgia and mediocrity that predominated at this time was *Little Shop of Horrors* in 1982. Insouciant, cheeky, even just a little deliciously rude, the show, derived from the camp 1960 Roger Corman film about a man-eating plant named Audrey, had music by 33-year-old Alan Menken and book, staging, and lyrics by his 32-year-old collaborator, Howard Ashman.

Menken and Ashman combined heartfelt musical theater traditionalism and craft with raucously sardonic contemporary smarts. After breaking in as a team three years earlier with an adaptation of the Kurt Vonnegut novel, *God Bless You, Mr. Rosewater*, Off-Off-Broadway at the WPA Theater where Ashman was artistic director, the pair next wrote *Little Shop of Horrors*, a musical with a sensibility that managed to celebrate musical theater tradition while also tweaking it. Musicals that camp-illy laughed at themselves for being musicals would become something of a vogue and increasingly a blight in our own time. *Little Shop of Horrors*, though, while certainly presaging this trend, did not grossly succumb to it. After opening at the WPA, the show copped most of the 1982–1983 musical theater season's significant awards, everything except the Broadway Best Musical Tony Award, of course (which went to *Cats*).

Ashman and Menken should have been the Broadway musical's future. Ashman possessed refreshing musical theater savvy. Menken's pop/rock melodic sense was nevertheless steeped in musical theater history. Both had studied the form voraciously, internalizing its essentials while maintaining a youthful and very healthy skepticism about its hidebound essence. *Little Shop of Horrors*, however, never transferred to Broadway. Though optioned after its successful debut by a rarified producing triumvirate—the media mogul David Geffen, the British mega-musical impresario Cameron Mackintosh, and Broadway's dominant theater landlord and producer, the Shubert Organization—*Little Shop of Horrors* was only transported so far as the Orpheum Theater downtown on Second Avenue, where it opened in July 1982.

"As far as I know, Howard was the one who opposed a transfer to Broadway," said Menken. "He felt that our production would lose too much of its hip veneer in a Broadway house. What burst at the seams in a tiny, funky theater like the Orpheum would get lost in a larger theater at a higher ticket price; our tiny band and tacky look might just seem a little tacky, not smart and fun. I think the producers understood Howard's logic. I'm not at all sure, though, that they agreed."

Menken and Ashman would soon be swept out to Hollywood, wooed by the Walt Disney Company, for whom they would help resuscitate the animated movie musical with witty, hugely popular, Broadway-infused scores for *The Little Mermaid* and *Beauty and the Beast*. Both Broadway and Hollywood would tragically be deprived of Ashman's gifts, though, with Ashman's death from AIDS in 1991.

As for André Bishop and Ira Weitzman, far Off-Broadway at Playwrights Horizons, their desire to discover and champion new, young musical theater talent was about to take an unexpected turn.

CHAPTER 2

ALL IT HAS TO BE IS GOOD

All it has to be is good.
And George you're good.
You're really good.

—Sunday in the Park with George

It could be argued that Stephen Sondheim still could pass as a new voice in musical theater right now. Over a career spanning more than half-a-century, every one of his musicals has differed intrinsically and often profoundly from its predecessors, as if each actually had been written by someone new, someone ever eager to test the form. And yet, Sondheim's ties to the once-changeless Broadway establishment also define him. As the protégé of Oscar Hammerstein, he has been, since his teens, a long-running Broadway insider.

Into the 1980s, Broadway was where Sondheim musicals lived. Then in 1981 he and Harold Prince brought their newest, the musical *Merrily We Roll Along*, to Broadway, as they had brought *Company* and *Follies*, *A Little Night Music*, *Pacific Overtures*, and *Sweeney Todd* before it. The results were catastrophic.

Adapted from a 1934 Kaufman and Hart play about the disillusionments of age, *Merrily* offered Sondheim numerous technical challenges beginning with the fact that the play's narrative ran backward in time, beginning at the end and ending ultimately at the beginning. Sondheim rose to these challenges, composing a score that effected surreptitious innovations while returning him to his deepest Broadway musical comedy roots. Marshalling traditional

Broadway musical blare and sass for a sophisticated new purpose, Sondheim managed to diagram the contours of the confusing plot *and* define each leading character's sometimes cloudy dramatic essence by deploying a series of vivid musical motifs in a manner that was deceptively operatic, given the music's seeming old-school Broadway accessibility. The results proved phenomenally satisfying.

This success was not matched, however, by director Prince's attempt at an audacious staging conceit. Hoping to capture conceptually *Merrily*'s over-riding message that youth's dreams easily go astray, Prince cast the show entirely with very young, inexperienced kids. What he wound up with, though, was a production that simply felt awkward and even amateurish, alienating many ticket buyers and most critics.

Merrily We Roll Along closed after sixteen performances, leaving Sondheim confused about his own future in musical theater. The show's fall came in the midst of a transitional moment for the business of Broadway musicals. *Merrily* had been developed without backers' auditions or an out-of-town tryout—the two staples of nearly every Broadway musical's creative journey up to that time.

"Not being able to go out of town was a terrible problem," acknowledged Sondheim. "It's very important to do one's work away from the Broadway vultures and gossips. *West Side Story* was exposed in New York only once before we got out of town. We did one backer's audition in some rich lady's apartment and didn't raise a cent. That was the first time Lenny [composer Leonard Bernstein] and I heard the score performed. I think Arthur [book writer Arthur Laurents] told the story, and Lenny and I and some actors sang it. For *Anyone Can Whistle*, Arthur did one or two backers' auditions with me but he was so hostile toward the audience because he resented doing them so much that I eventually did the rest all myself. I think I did over 30 auditions for *Anyone Can Whistle*. But you didn't read the script at those things. You just summarized it. And the purpose was to raise money. Not to hear what you'd written. That was for out-of-town."

Out-of-town tryouts had simply become too expensive by the 1980s. The alternative, though: Opening a show on Broadway after a number of very public preview performances, could result in a catastrophe along the lines of…well, *Merrily We Roll Along*. (Though sometimes it worked. *Sweeney Todd*, for example, had been developed without an out-of-town tryout, too.) Still, there had to be a better way. But Sondheim and most of his peers, for that matter, remained unsure what that way might be. Michael Bennett's protracted workshop method with *A Chorus Line*, despite its indisputable success, still struck many as too much of a hothouse approach for creating a commercial musical.

"Workshops were the only way that *Chorus Line*—which is in many ways a revue as much as it is a musical—could have been put together," insisted producer Cameron Mackintosh. "Basically Michael and his assistant Bob Avian sifted through months and months of material, got Marvin Hamlisch to write dozens and dozens of songs, and then over a long period of time slowly collaged the show together. It wasn't two authors, as usually happens in the musical theater, taking a subject, having their own interpretation and then presenting it to a producer who went, yeah, now we need to get to work on this.

"I don't think it's always appropriate to do a workshop," Mackintosh concluded. "I've seen a number, particularly in America, where a half-a-million or a million dollars is put together for a workshop and basically after the first couple of weeks they're trying to stage the thing before it's ready in half the time you would normally, in order to attract the money to go to the next stage. Seems to me to defeat the purpose."

"I believe Jerry Robbins really began the workshop process as we know it with *A Funny Thing Happened on the Way to the Forum*," Sondheim reflected. "Hal was producing the show and we asked Jerry to come in as director[3] but he was skittish and asked me to play the songs for him, with actors playing the parts. Some of the cast from that first reading actually wound up staying with the piece. That really was the first workshop, to my knowledge, for a Broadway musical.

"Every show I've done with Hal, though, we've had a series of closed readings," added Sondheim. "You've got to. There's a huge difference between the page and the stage, even if it's just a stage in someone's office; the difference between what you've written and how it sounds aloud is night and day. If you're just sitting around a table, you hear the thing bald. I can remember vividly sitting there with [the book writer] George Furth listening to Hal read *Company*'s first act for the first time. You really hear where scenes work and don't work. Of course you're fooled sometimes without an audience. But one of the fatal statements in the theater is: 'Wait till we get an audience.' That has sunk many a show and continues to do so. It's a myth that you need an audience to hear what you've written. Audiences tend to respond to toe-tapping songs and comedy numbers. And at readings they bring an awful lot of good will. You really need to listen yourself, without an audience encouraging you to perhaps paste over the flaws.

"For most of our shows we did two or three readings, just for office staff and friends, in Hal's office or at a table; no staging at all. The first reading was usually after we'd finished the first act and I'd play two or three songs while Hal read everything himself. Next we'd get some actors to sit around a table and read a re-written first act and I would play five or six songs or whatever; I think I always sang the songs. Sometimes we'd do one more reading but never more than three. And we never, ever, did a workshop with the public invited because that, to me, is all a vanity act, it's not done to effectively reshape a show but rather to show it off. There's a real danger of losing your purpose working like that. Workshops today are almost always for show—very little work gets done, that's just what happens, there's no reality in the room. Oscar Hammerstein taught me that if you can't be critical toward your own work, you're lost. And workshops, to me, never are about being critical towards the work."

It was James Lapine, the young director/playwright responsible for saving William Finn's *March of the Falsettos*, who delivered Stephen Sondheim over to Bishop and Weitzman at Playwrights Horizons. During the year immediately following *Merrily*'s demise, Lapine had been brought together with Sondheim by Broadway producer Lewis Allen to work on a project that both Sondheim and Lapine soon decided was not right for them. Sondheim, however, had seen some of Lapine's plays and liked one particularly, a rather experimental and especially visual piece called *Twelve Dreams* at the New York Shakespeare Festival. He invited Lapine to meet with him weekly for a series of brainstorming sessions. What emerged was a decidedly unconventional notion for a musical — an exploration of the life and character of the pioneering, fin de siècle, French pointillist painter, Georges Seurat, specifically through the prism of his most famous painting, "A Sunday Afternoon on the Island of La Grande Jatte."

"Lapine had received a commission from us to do something of his choice at Playwrights, anything at all," recalled Weitzman. "To our amazement and delight he brought in Stephen Sondheim, who was, without any exaggeration at all, our idol — *all* of us — our god of musical theater.

"The whole thing was very secretive," Weitzman recalled. "We called it 'Project X.' We had no idea what it would be like to work with Sondheim. We had no idea what it would be like to work on a project of this scale. In the end, all writers are the same, though. They all need the same things, want the same things: support and a safe environment to create. And that's what we provided."

The process could not have been more gently nurturing. First, late in 1982, a small cast was engaged to read Lapine's fragmentary script (tentatively titled *Seurat*) to the authors, absent any music at all. This, Sondheim later acknowledged, helped him realize more concretely the sound that his score should pursue. In May of 1983 the musical, now formally titled *Sunday in the Park with George*, was read again — at O'Neal's restaurant — two relatively complete acts with five relatively complete songs from the first act (all of them sung by Sondheim): "Yoo Hoo," "No Life," "Color and Light," "Gossip," and the title song. It was at this reading that Mandy Patinkin played Georges Seurat publicly for the first time.

The results were encouraging enough to warrant scheduling a full workshop for *Sunday in the Park* at Playwrights: three weeks of performances in July with a cast that now would include Bernadette Peters as Seurat's model and muse, Dot.

Despite his reservations about workshops, Sondheim agreed to give it a shot.

"It really was a highly produced workshop," remembered Weitzman. "Perhaps too highly produced; it had a very expensive set, for what we were used to at Playwrights, and a high profile cast."

Still, it was very much a workshop, not a backer's audition and definitely not an out-of-town tryout.

Writing creatively remained an unchanging pursuit, of course, for Sondheim. The work was the work, no matter the setting or auspices. Yet, here he was Broadway's quintessential musical theater composer, lured Off-Broadway by his new collaborator to be reborn there as an artist of the not-for-profit world.

"I think working with us became kind of an antidote for him," observed Weitzman, "an antidote for what he'd just gone through on Broadway with *Merrily*. I mean, when you're *on Broadway* there are always millions of dollars on the line, with everybody watching. *Sunday*, I think, was liberating for him. It was relatively pressure-free. And clearly he was writing something from the heart, about the creation of art itself."

Some argued, not illegitimately, that developing the work of a hyper-established Broadway composer like Sondheim Off-Broadway in a non-commercial setting was a miscarriage of justice somehow.

"'Why are you doing the Broadway tryout for Stephen Sondheim's new musical in your non-profit theater?' some people asked," acknowledged Weitzman. "We got a lot of knocks for that, despite the fact this was a distinctly appropriate piece to be working on in that environment."

Sunday in the Park was a very venturesome musical. Whether it would have been produced at all on Broadway without its initial development at Playwrights Horizons remains an open question. "The fact is," said Sondheim, "I don't think if we just presented *Sunday in the Park* to some Broadway producer it would have gotten on. I'm not sure of that. But I don't think so."

Commercial Broadway producers did, however, monitor *Sunday in the Park*'s evolution on the western outskirts of 42nd Street as intensively as any actual out-of-town tryout.

Perhaps the most liberating aspect of the workshop process for Sondheim proved to be its indulgence for his procrastinating writing habits. *Sunday in the Park*'s 25-performance run at Playwrights commenced with an incomplete first act, musically, and no performable second act at all. Only toward the end of the second week did Sondheim turn in the balance of his first-act songs, including the unforgettable "Beautiful" and the landmark "Finishing the Hat." The show's second act would ultimately be performed three times only, at the tail end of the run, with but two finished songs—this to nightly paying audiences of Playwrights Horizons subscribers and the curious New York theatrical elite.

Was this liberation an altogether good thing? Certainly in terms of music, *Sunday in the Park* cannot be faulted. Reinventing himself as radically as he ever had before, Sondheim created a sound and compositional structure for *Sunday* that reflected perfectly Seurat's own pointillist painting method, a sound that brilliantly combined facets from French composer contemporaries of Seurat's, like Debussy's liquid harmonies, with those of American post-modernist composer contemporaries of Sondheim's, like Philip Glass and Steve Reich's rigorous minimalism.

Dramatically, though, *Sunday in the Park* remained something of a flawed work, with a dislocated and often unconvincing second act. Leaping forward chronologically to more or less reimagine Seurat living as an artist today, the act functioned far better conceptually than as coherent theater.

Can one actually blame the indulgent workshop process for this seemingly self-indulgent coda to one of musical theater's otherwise more superbly realized experiments?

"No," Sondheim insists. "Because we did change *Sunday in the Park*'s second act a lot as a result of the workshop. You can't ask any more from a workshop. We learned a great deal from it."

Even with its flaws, *Sunday in the Park* easily seduced two significant commercial producers—the Shubert Organization and Emanuel Azenberg—who moved it to the Booth Theater on Broadway the following spring. Still, some of the most effective re-writing of the piece apparently only came in response to this anticipated move cross-town. At the eleventh hour, under Broadway-opening night deadline pressure, rather than Off-Broadway laissez faire workshop conditions, Sondheim birthed two songs, "Lesson #8" and "Children and Art," that together supplied *Sunday in the Park*'s second act with its essential missing pieces.

Sunday in the Park with George would go on to win the Pulitzer Prize for Drama in 1984 but not the Tony Award. That trophy would go to Jerry Herman for his anthemic salute to cross-dressing, *La Cage aux Folles*. Many still gripe that Sondheim and *Sunday* were jobbed by the Tonys that year. Herman's score was proficient where Sondheim's was revolutionary. One could say, however, that this only would be the case if *Sunday* was first a Broadway musical. Despite the Broadway address, in its heart *Sunday in the Park with George* no longer belonged to Broadway at all.

CHAPTER 3

OH, THERE'S A CAST OF THOUSANDS

And oh, there's a cast of thousands
Making a scene.
Oh, there's a cast of thousands
Filling the screen.

— *Three Postcards*

Sunday in the Park's success meant one thing to Bishop and Weitzman at Playwrights Horizons. "Now," said Weitzman, "in terms of musical theater, we could really do just about anything we wanted."

The question, though, remained: Precisely what was that?

In *Sunday in the Park*'s immediate wake there were no answers at all. Playwrights had mounted a charming little two-character musical called *Herringbone* in 1982, just prior to Sondheim's arrival, with a book by Tom Cone, music by Skip Kennon and lyrics by Ellen Fitzhugh. The theater had, however, so concentrated its energy and resources on the Sondheim workshop that few new musical projects were waiting to follow in the pipeline.

Sunday in the Park aside, Broadway generated very few musicals of any significance during this period. Henry Krieger followed *Dreamgirls* with *The Tap Dance Kid* in December 1983 at the Broadhurst Theater, a show that danced mightily to the raw vitality of Krieger's music without ever quite working dramatically. *Baby*, which also opened in December 1983, at the Ethel Barrymore

Theater, managed to sweetly capture in music by David Shire and lyrics by Richard Maltby, Jr. the wild journey of pregnancy for three expectant couples; from conception to birth. *Big River: The Adventures of Huckleberry Finn* at the Eugene O'Neill Theater was a Tony Award winner in 1985 as Best Musical, with a score by country-western's "King of the Road," Roger Miller.

Despite its seeming straightforward essence as an uncomplicated adaptation of an American literary classic, *Big River* was actually something of a concept musical—the concept being the introduction of country music into the Broadway musical mix, via Miller's roguish musical charm. This notion was the brainchild of *Big River*'s lead producer, Rocco Landesman, who'd pursued Miller for years. "I thought Roger was a great songwriter; in fact, he was just about my favorite," Landesman later explained. "And I figured Broadway needed his sound, something accessible and very American."

In a sense, Landesman was right. Tapping the popularity of country music was nearly as important—and as difficult—for Broadway to accomplish as connecting with contemporary pop and rock. Landesman and his partners in Dodger Productions had already tasted success Off-Broadway with an original country music revue called *Pump Boys and Dinettes*. *Pump Boys and Dinettes* had opened at the Colonnades Theater in October 1981, with music and lyrics supplied by members of its cast. The show had become a modest hit, ultimately transferring to Broadway's Princess Theater in February 1982 and running there for over a year.

Revues were one thing, though. Constructing an original book musical with an integrated country music score was another. Miller pulled off the trick with seeming ease, wisely emphasizing country music's gospel roots in songs that rose to the demands of Broadway emotionalism via a projection of heightened spiritual fervor. It all may have seemed perfectly amiable on the surface and an estimable cast led by Daniel Jenkins as Huck and Ron Richardson as Jim, sang Miller's deceptively easy-going ditties admirably. But Miller's music never condescended either to its Broadway musical aspirations or to its country music essence. Though his songs rarely advanced plot in a traditional sense, they did underline story developments with an organic simplicity that worked beautifully. While *Big River's* "good old boy" sound could only be considered new in the catatonic context of the Broadway musical, the score was nevertheless an unpolished jewel, widely under-appreciated to this day.

Off-Broadway remained a wasteland for musical theater at this time. Over the course of nearly two seasons, no more than three productions even remotely represented new creative talent: the hugely popular revue, *Nunsense*, by Dan Goggin, which opened at the Cherry Lane Theater in December 1985; an ambitious little book musical called *Olympus on My Mind*, based on Heinrich Von Kleist's *Amphitryon*, with music by Grant Sturiale, book, lyrics and direction by Barry Harman, which transferred to the Lamb's Theater for a six month run after opening at the Actor's Outlet in May of 1986; and another revue, called *Diamonds*, which celebrated the game of baseball.

Despite its dusty subject, *Diamonds*, presented at Circle in the Square Downtown in December 1984, did seek out a surprising number of young songwriters as contributors for its score. This becomes much less surprising when one realizes that *Diamonds* was directed by Harold Prince (with musical direction by Stephen Sondheim's longtime conductor, Paul Gemignani). Prince had, with *Merrily We Roll Along*, certainly proved his almost suicidal willingness to take chances on the young and relatively untested.

Diamonds featured one nifty song, "In the Cards" (about baseball cards, logically enough) by *Little Shop of Horrors'* composer Alan Menken, with a lyric by David Zippel, a young ex-lawyer turned lyricist who would soon be heard from on Broadway. The revue offered another charming number, "Hundreds of Hats," with lyrics by Menken's *Little Shop* collaborator Howard Ashman, here working with an ambitious young composer named Jonathan Sheffer, whose immediate future would prove to be as a writer of film scores. (Sheffer is perhaps equally known today as the founder and artistic director of Eos Orchestra.) Three songs were supplied by the team of Larry Grossman and Ellen Fitzhugh, who later in the 1985 season would provide music for the unfortunate Broadway musical *Grind*, also directed by Prince. Still, Grossman and particularly his lyricist, Fitzhugh, had talent worth encouraging. Lastly, *Diamonds* featured a superbly elegiac song, "What You'd Call a Dream," by a young lyricist and composer of craft and imagination named Craig Carnelia.

Diamonds nevertheless closed in a little more than three months, a total of 122 performances.

In September of 1985, Playwrights Horizons' search for new musical theater talent at last yielded a preliminary payoff with *Paradise!*, a new musical by a graduate of the recently-created graduate program in musical theater writing at NYU, a 31-year-old African American librettist and lyricist named George C. Wolfe.

Born in Frankfort, Kentucky, Wolfe was omni-talented, with a BA in directing from Pomona College complementing his NYU theater writing MFA. More significantly, Wolfe had a penetrating and decisively encompassing point of view as a budding theatrical artist. His writing and even his stage directing were consumed with sending up the stereotypes of race in America. Wolfe, however, did not have an agenda so much as he had a gift, a sure instinct for fiercely theatrical stagecraft. A year later his play, *The Colored Museum*, would shock and delight audiences across the racial, theatrical and political spectrum after being presented under Wolfe's own direction at the New York Shakespeare Festival. His career would be launched.

Unfortunately for Playwrights, *Paradise!* was a lesser work. With music by Robert Forrest, the piece garnered little attention and closed inside of a month. Still, Weitzman and Bishop were on target. Wolfe's talent was major and Playwrights had noticed.

"*Paradise!* was George's first show in New York," Weitzman later said. "And that was good for all concerned."

Another new voice was heard from for the first time publicly in 1985 at the tiny Vineyard Theater. Opening in October, *Goblin Market*, adapted from the poem by Christina Rossetti, introduced a young musical theater performer–turned–composer-lyricist named Polly Pen.

Pen was originally from Chicago but her aesthetic was anything but Midwestern. An English major at Ithaca College, her determinedly self-conscious literary sensibility was rooted in centuries other than the 20th. After moving to New York City, she'd sustained a successful acting career while writing music privately for her own pleasure. It was the Vineyard Theater's artistic director, Douglas Aibel, who finally cornered her; when Pen told Aibel she could only audition her music for him if he turned his back to her while she played, Aibel obliged, then responded by commissioning *Goblin Market* on the spot.

Pen's musical style could best be described as monastically spare, her lyrics, co-written with Peggy Harmon, rigorously understated. Though the *New York Times* described *Goblin Market* as an "entrancing expedition," others found its miniaturizing aesthetic monochromatic. Still, Pen had a voice of her own. Noisy it wasn't. But she definitely did have a niche that was new.

The balance of the 1985–1986 season was numbingly routine. On Broadway, at the Royale Theater, Andrew Lloyd Webber's *Song & Dance* was a shotgun marriage between a Lloyd Webber/Don Black one-act musical called *Tell Me on a Sunday* and dances built around Lloyd Webber's *Variations* on a musical theme by Paganini. Blessed with Bernadette Peters' solo voice and superb supporting dance talent—choreography by the New York City Ballet's Peter Martins, and an assemblage of Broadway's very finest gypsies—*Song & Dance* remained fatally burdened by a simpering lead character in the first act and a stultifying lack of melodic imagination all around.

The Mystery of Edwin Drood was at least an original musical with an original slant—audience participation—as devised by the composer, lyricist and bookwriter, Rupert Holmes, adapting Charles Dickens' famously unfinished novel of the same name. Holmes invited *Drood* audiences to vote at each performance for the murderer of poor unfortunate Edwin Drood. After opening to strong reviews at the New York Shakespeare Festival's Delacorte Theater in Central Park in the summer of 1985, *Drood* transferred to Broadway's Imperial Theater in December, ultimately winning the Tony Award for Best Musical.

The show was pleasant. It also was thoroughly conventional if not altogether predictable musically. In a theatrical environment touched by even a modicum of originality or adventure it would have seemed retrograde. In the Broadway musical theater climate of 1985–1986 it was a breath of air, hardly fresh but at least marginally oxygenated.

Nothing more sadly captured the defeated spirit of the Broadway musical that year than *Big Deal* at the Broadway Theater in April, a last hurrah for one of Broadway's greatest musical theater innovators, the director and choreographer, Bob Fosse, who would die of a heart attack in September 1987. Dispensing with living songwriters for his *Big Deal* score altogether, Fosse fashioned what would prove to be his own farewell out of a patchwork of recycled Tin Pan Alley chestnuts. He deployed the tune "Life Is Just a Bowl of Cherries" for his curtain raiser, then knowingly reprised it as he rang the curtain down for the last time.

The 1986–1987 Broadway musical season that followed Fosse's farewell yielded a very different sort of devastation. Two all-American musicals appeared that year written by some of the more adept writers in the medium.

Rags, about the American immigrant experience, had a book reminiscent of *Fiddler on the Roof* by Joseph Stein (whose previous book-writing credits included *Fiddler on the Roof,* among many others). It also had a richly textured, sadly under-appreciated score by the composer Charles Strouse (*Annie, Bye, Bye Birdie*), and the lyricist Stephen Schwartz (composer and lyricist for both *Godspell* and *Pippin*), along with a volcanic starring performance by the opera diva, Teresa Stratas.

Smile was the saga of an American beauty pageant, with book and lyrics by Howard Ashman (*Little Shop of Horrors*) and music by Marvin Hamlisch (*A Chorus Line*).

Both shows failed ignominiously. In their stead, at season's end, stood two new European-derived mega-musicals that embodied not just Broadway's present but its long-term future: *Starlight Express* and *Les Misérables.*

The former, which opened in March at the Gershwin Theater, was the latest imported work from the now-ubiquitous Lloyd Webber, this time delivering a ponderously cartoonish morality tale for animistic model trains robotically brought to life by singing actors on roller skates. The latter—at the Broadway Theater, also in March—was a first, in a sense, an homage to the Lloyd Webber musical model by a French writing team: composer/bookwriter Claude-Michel Schönberg and bookwriter/lyricist Alain Boublil, as produced by Cameron Mackintosh.

Growing up in North London, Mackintosh had been a child obsessed with musicals. Pursuing this obsession into his early twenties as a backstage worker and occasional chorus singer, Mackintosh had finally begun producing musicals himself, partly out of fear that the form had fallen so far out of touch with contemporary culture musically that it was in danger of dying out altogether.

Though Mackintosh hoped to pursue musicals directly descended from *Hair*, Stephen Schwartz's *Godspell* and, most particularly, Andrew Lloyd Webber's *Jesus Christ Superstar*, his early career in the West End, ironically enough, was solidified by his shepherding the landmark revue *Side by Side by Sondheim* into a hit, first in London and then on Broadway. It was this success that induced Lloyd Webber to offer Mackintosh the opportunity to produce, in 1980, his latest musical, *Cats*. Mackintosh initially had little enthusiasm for "this musical about pussycats." In time, though, his feelings changed.

Mackintosh's early reticence about *Les Misérables* had followed a similar trajectory.

"If you'd said to me, 'Cameron, have you read *Les Miz* lately, why don't we turn this into a musical?' I'd have probably given you a cup of tea or a large gin depending on the time of day—thank you very much but no," Mackintosh later said. "What got me excited about *Les Miz* was hearing, even in French, what these fellows had done to it.

"Funnily enough, Alain Boublil told me that *Les Miz* came to him while he was watching a revival of *Oliver!* in 1978 that I produced at the Aubrey Theater in London. He said that as he watched the Artful Dodger sing 'Consider Yourself,' the character of Gavroche from *Les Miz* suddenly just jumped into his head. By the end of the show he had worked out roughly what he wanted to do with all the characters and afterward he immediately telephoned Claude-Michel in Paris and said, 'I've got the subject for our next musical.'"

Schönberg, 42, had started out as a singer before becoming an accomplished writer and producer of French pop songs. Born in Tunisia, Boublil had emigrated to Paris at the age of 18, working in music publishing and writing lyrics for French pop as well. Their first musical collaboration, *La Revolution Française*, was produced in 1973. Boublil met Mackintosh in 1983 after *Abbacadabra*, his musical based on ABBA songs, had opened in London. The team's musical adaptation of Victor Hugo's *Les Misérables*, had premiered at Paris' Palais des Sports in 1980, then London in 1985.

As a composer, Schönberg was nearly as enthusiastic about reprises and gargantuan flourishes as Lloyd Webber himself. His strongest suit was the power ballad; two of the show's biggest hits, "I Dreamed a Dream" and "Bring Him Home," were brawny, brazen examples of this 1980s pop radio–inspired song form. Each contained quite a bit more heartfelt spark than Lloyd Webber's inflated, rote exercises in songwriting. Still, the overall impact of *Les Miz* resided largely in its brand of musical totalitarianism, a mindless march-time that stormed the ramparts with ever-louder choral reprises. As patrons in Paris and then London had before them, though, Broadway audiences meekly bowed beneath *Les Misérables'* heavily booted heel.

Why? Director Trevor Nunn's staging and set designer John Napier's shape-shifting set rendered *Les Miz* as a series of near-religious Old Master–style tableaus, inviting audiences to give themselves over to a coercive, parochial kind of musical theater passion. *Les Miz* also spewed its emotions with zeal. Though what was being invoked here most resembled the emotionalism of fascist political rallies (absent the hate content), audiences related easily to these outpourings. *This*, they believed, was real feeling.

Off-Broadway one intriguingly diaphanous musical floated to the surface in contrast to the overwhelming weight of *Les Miz*. *Three Postcards*, presented at Playwrights Horizons, was a delicately filigreed one-act of private musings set to music. Written by Craig Lucas, also a former musical theater performer–turned–playwright (an alumnus, in fact, of Sondheim's 1979 *Sweeney Todd* cast), with music and lyrics by Craig Carnelia, *Three Postcards* simply and often poignantly captured the emotionally scarred internal world of three women friends reuniting over dinner at an upscale New York restaurant, as well as the contrapuntal thoughts of the waitstaff that served them.

Like William Finn, Carnelia's subject really was the self in the '80s and, as with Finn, his lyrics set a good deal of psychoanalytic chat to music. But there the resemblance ended. Where Finn was exuberant, Carnelia was reticent. Where Finn was indelicate, Carnelia was refined. Where Finn was raw and often unfocused, Carnelia was meticulous. His songs were near-perfect miniatures, and they sang of the prosaic with transcendence.

A 38-year-old Long Island native, Carnelia, too, had been a musical theater performer briefly. His song contributions to the scores of two short-lived Broadway flops, *Working* in 1978, and *Is There Life After High School?* in 1982 (as well as his one song for *Diamonds*) were all accomplished formative efforts that projected an already singular voice. Carnelia's writing for *Three Postcards* constituted not just a collection of songs but a true musical score—intricately woven, cunningly executed. The songs were full of wistfulness, a ruminative space of mind entirely unlike the in-your-face here and now of the traditional Broadway musical. Yes, there was a preciousness to it all. For better or worse, though, the chamber-scale moods and chamber-music-sized aesthetic of *Three Postcards* offered an escape from Broadway bombast. At least for a moment, anyway.

CHAPTER 4

MUSIC OF THE NIGHT

One night in Bangkok makes a hard man humble
Not much between despair and ecstasy.

— *Chess*

Then all those people who scream night and day
"Poor prayin' Carrie!"
They'd see me with him, and they might even say
"Look! It's Carrie!"

— *Carrie*

Broadway took little notice of *Three Postcards*. Instead, as if spurred by *Les Misérables'* roaring success, the mainstream Broadway musical seemed to rouse itself the following season with an effusion of splashy new efforts. In the end, though, from a dollars and cents perspective, only one show finally mattered: the Andrew Lloyd Webber juggernaut, *The Phantom of the Opera*.

So much has been said about the symbiosis of simplistic melodies, stage spectacle and marketing that characterized the musicals promoted during the '80s by Cameron Mackintosh (often in tandem with Andrew Lloyd Webber's Really Useful Group), like *Cats* or the (strategically) imitative *Les Miz*. *Phantom*, however, was an apotheosis. As of this writing, it is still running at Broadway's Majestic Theater, a good sixteen years and counting.

Since its 1986 debut in London's West End through its January 1988 opening in New York (and on beyond the shelf-life of this book, no doubt), *Phantom* has remained an accretion of clichés—nearly

45

impossible to strip clean for purposes of analysis. Suffice to say that Lloyd Webber's ersatz-operatic pop score, set to pedestrian lyrics by the previously unknown Charles Hart, was rife with inspiration from Puccini. The monolithic staging (by Prince again) was colossal in the same sense that maulings in the Roman Colosseum must have been. And the performances by *Phantom's* original leads, Michael Crawford and Sarah Brightman (at the time, Lloyd Webber's wife), were not merely ghoulishly vivid but memorably hilarious, as sung by two of the odder voices any Broadway musical will ever hear.

The show also dropped on its audience the most talked about chandelier in Broadway musical history. Which must be acknowledged in any discussion of *Phantom of the Opera*. And now has been.

So why the fuss? That answer would seem to reside more within the diminished taste of Broadway audiences than with any intrinsic aesthetic criteria. These ticket buyers by the year 1988 were increasingly dominated by tourist-novitiates rather than theatergoing regulars. The sensibilities of this constituency had been shaped by fiercesome quantities of mediocre mass-media entertainment—from their televisions, their radios, their phonographs, their local movie screens. The poor folks had simply grown too insensate to defend themselves. And the producer/composer tandem of Mackintosh and Lloyd Webber had figured out fairly precisely how to stimulate their poor, worn-out nerve endings.

There was an additional factor to consider. Mackintosh's productions were now very much exercises in conspicuous consumption.[4] At $8 million, *Phantom of the Opera* tied *Starlight Express* as the most expensive musical produced (to that time). Having charged ticket buyers extravagantly for admission ($50 top!), Mackintosh could at least reassure them that their money was visibly up there onstage. This was particularly true during the 1980s for Wall Street's high-rolling elite, who viewed their very presence at these extravaganzas as direct confirmation of their own over-valued net worth. Since then,

Phantom of the Opera has metastasized into must-see theater for anyone and everyone in between; the greatest audience leveler of all time.

With *Into the Woods*, Stephen Sondheim did not so much attempt to awaken audiences as to infiltrate their dreams. A psychosexual deconstruction of selected Grimm fairy tales, *Into the Woods*—which preceded *Phantom* on Broadway by two months, opening at the Martin Beck Theater in November 1987—hardly pandered to the lowest common denominator that *Phantom* did. Yet, it was not entirely *Phantom*'s opposite either. In the nursery rhyme underpinnings of many of its songs, *Into the Woods* could even be viewed as a grab for some Sondheim-lite, the great musical theater iconoclast's tentative, perhaps even unconscious, attempt at reaching a tiny bit larger, ever-so-slightly less discriminating crowd. Which is not to say that the show's score in any way lacked Sondheim's usual penetrating and sophisticated musical and verbal artistry. Commercially, it simply wasn't the tale of Sweeney Todd this time. Or even Sunday in the park with George Seurat.

Written and directed by James Lapine, *Into the Woods* had received its first readings under André Bishop and Ira Weitzman's auspices at Playwrights Horizons in November, 1985, followed in June 1986 by a pair of fully-staged readings at 890 Broadway, the rehearsal studio building that Michael Bennett had created with some of his profits from *A Chorus Line*. The show then had premiered at the Old Globe Theater in San Diego in December, thus gaining for itself an out-of-town tryout in the traditional sense. This 50-performance run proved a creative boon, with Sondheim delivering the second act's 11 o'clock number, "No One is Alone," during the last days of rehearsal. "I remember him sitting down at the piano in our rehearsal room and singing this song he'd just written," recalled Ira Weitzman, "and all of us just cried."

Having the benefit of a tryout out of town did not spare *Into the Woods* a fairly brutal preview period on Broadway with premature sniping in the press and frantic rewrites nearly up until opening night. The authors never did quite solve the show's second act Giant problems. *Into the Woods* proved, nevertheless, a delight on many levels, particularly during a first act filled with charming melodies, disarming lyrics and a comedic classic in the song, "Agony." When in the second act things turned willfully darker, Sondheim — exploring the aftermath of "happily ever after" — offered three of his most poignantly heartfelt expressions, "No More," "No One is Alone," and "Children Will Listen," all songs of consolation and hope for fathers and sons, mothers and daughters. *Into the Woods* went on to enjoy what, for a Sondheim musical, constituted a very healthy Broadway run, 764 performances.

Sarafina! was the season's wildcard, an anti-apartheid musical set in a South African high school. Conceived, written and directed by a South African, Mbongeni Ngema, who'd also composed the music in collaboration with the South African jazz legend, Hugh Masekela, this import from Johannesburg's Market Theater was initially produced by Lincoln Center Theater at its intimate Mitzi E. Newhouse space in October 1987. The show then transferred with its exuberant cast of predominantly young South African schoolchildren to Broadway's Cort Theater the following January, where it lingered for a surprisingly healthy run. *Sarafina!* was certainly a pleasant anomaly on Broadway, its success ascribable to nothing more complicated than the buoyant lyricism of its music, the irresistible effervescence of its youthful performers, and the politically correct specter of the imprisoned Nelson Mandela.

Yet another rollicking anomaly that year was *The Gospel at Colonus*, a soulful re-rendering of Sophocles' *Oedipus at Colonus* that spotlighted a host of storied black gospel singers, most particularly Clarence Fountain and The Five Blind Boys of Alabama. With its roots-derived score by a pair of (white) downtown veterans of the avant garde Mabou Mines theater troupe, Bob Telson (music) and Lee Breuer (lyrics, as well as book and direction), *Gospel at Colonus* was a gimmicky hybrid that largely worked. Like *Sarafina!*, it enjoyed a Broadway run, lingering for a couple of months at the Lunt-Fontanne Theater after transferring in March following its presentation at the Brooklyn Academy of Music's Next Wave Festival.

Both musicals did reach out to a non-white Broadway audience in a very positive sense, without resorting solely to nostalgic and/or stereotypical clichés about race. Unfortunately, the two also proved less a trend than a pleasant aberration.

Chess, Carrie, and *Romance Romance* bookended the final weeks of Broadway's 1987–1988 season; three mediocrities occupying varying frequencies along the same spectrum. Where *Chess* and *Carrie* were huge, *Romance Romance* was wee. From a musical theater point of view, though, all three were similarly inadequate.

Built around a pre-existing hit studio album released by the Swedish pop group ABBA's resident singer-songwriters, Benny Andersson and Björn Ulvaeus (with lyrics by Tim Rice), *Chess* compensated for its inability to tell its entwined political and romantic stories musically by assaulting audiences with coarse, relentless volume. *Romance Romance*, by Barry Harman and Keith Herrmann, conversely failed to animate its over-refined double-sided romantic tale—part fin-de-siècle Vienna (derived from a short story, *The Little Comedy,* by Arthur Schnitzler), part late-1980s East Hampton (adapted from the Jules Renard play, *Pain De Menage*)—by pitching its own musical voice at such a cloyingly coy volume nearly no sound emerged at all.[5]

Carrie, of course, was an instant classic, a monument in the pantheon of failed Broadway musicals. Adapted by Michael Gore (music) and Dean Pitchford (lyrics) from the notorious Stephen

King novel (and even more notorious film), this $7 million musical celebration of prom vengeance and bad taste materialized at the Virginia Theater on the 12th of May, 1988 and was gone by the 15th, touching all who saw it with a timeless reverence for its indelible, monumental ineptitude.

Chess did possess one tragic note of significance. *Chess* had first been handed to Michael Bennett for development as a stage piece. Despite misgivings about the project's merits, Bennett apparently had attempted to make a musical of it by re-imagining the thing as a high-tech media exercise with an essentially balletic core, utilizing numerous television screens, sleek, uncluttered stage lines and top-drawer dance talent. Bennett's hope was to make the show's culture clash premise — Iron Curtain meets Western Democracy in an all-defining chess match — his focus, rather than the book's banal romantic triangle of a plot. In January 1986, though, three months before performances were to begin in London, Bennett suddenly withdrew, citing an attack of "angina pectoris" brought on by stress. This fictive affliction would in time be revealed as the onset of Bennett's doomed battle with AIDS. He never worked again, dying on the 2nd of July, 1987.

Michael Bennett did not live to see *Phantom of the Opera* open on Broadway but he could have caught the show during its initial year in London. The cinematic fluidity of *Phantom*'s staging certainly owed Bennett an obvious debt but in nearly every other respect, *Phantom of the Opera* bore little relation to anything that Bennett had stood for as a director and choreographer.

It was Trevor Nunn, artistic director of the Royal Shakespeare Company and the directorial hand behind *Cats* and *Les Miz*, who stepped in to complete Bennett's work on *Chess* in time for the show's London opening. Nunn could be such a gifted director. His stagecraft for the R.S.C.'s epic adaptation of *Nicholas Nickleby* in 1981, for example, had approached perfection. Nunn, however, endowed *Chess* with all the elements of ponderous self-importance and lumbering anti-musicality that he'd brought to *Cats* and *Les Miz*, qualities that now sadly seemed to dominate the Broadway musical in the wake of *Phantom of the Opera*'s birth and Michael Bennett's premature death.

CHAPTER 5

YOU'RE NOTHING WITHOUT ME

You're nothing without me
A no one who'd go undefined
You wouldn't exist
You'd never be missed.
— *City of Angels*

Playwrights Horizons had quietly made another discovery.

"I heard Lynn Ahrens and Steve Flaherty at an ASCAP songwriters workshop," Ira Weitzman recalled. "I just walked up to them and said, 'You're great. Please come work at Playwrights Horizons.'

"I then went out and got a National Endowment for the Arts grant that, originally, before George got so big, was intended for the three of them—George C. Wolfe, Lynn, and Steve—to work on something together. After *The Colored Museum*, though, it became just Lynn and Steve."

Flaherty, 27, and Ahrens, 39, had been together since meeting in 1983 at Lehman Engel's BMI Musical Theater Workshop in New York, a veritable crash pad for aspiring musical theater writers looking for artistic sustenance and career direction. Flaherty, a Pittsburgh native, was fresh out of the Cincinnati College Conservatory. Ahrens, New York–born but raised in Neptune, New Jersey, had been something of an ad-agency phenom as a copywriter, a producer, a writer of children's television programs, and a jingle-ist for clients like Chevrolet and Bounty before making the leap from jingle-writer to musical theater lyricist.

"Lynn's practice had been to browse book bins all over town looking for potential projects," noted Weitzman. "That's how she found *The Man Who Broke the Bank at Monte Carlo*, this British black comedy by Michael Butterworth."

A meek English shoe salesman learns he will inherit six million dollars from an American uncle he has never met—on one condition: that he take the uncle's corpse for one last vacation to Monte Carlo. This was the daft premise behind *The Man Who Broke the Bank at Monte Carlo*, as well as the musical *Lucky Stiff* that Ahrens and Flaherty created from it. Weitzman and Bishop brought *Lucky Stiff* to Playwrights Horizons where it opened in April of 1988. The plot was a giddy, slapstick throwback, and Ahrens and Flaherty's score unapologetically reflected this. Flaherty's music was zestfully traditional, with a pronounced Sondheim influence, particularly rhythmically. Ahrens' lyrics were nicely crafted and often funny. There was nothing revolutionary about Ahrens and Flaherty. They were just good.

"I tend to be interested in musicals with a social or humanitarian conscience," Weitzman later said. "But in the case of Ahrens and Flaherty's *Lucky Stiff*, farcical entertainment seemed enough."

Unfortunately, *Lucky Stiff* did not quite entertain onstage at Playwrights Horizons as it had promised to when first viewed in workshop. Critics were not especially impressed and the show was not extended beyond its initial fifteen performance run. Still, the careers of two genuinely promising musical theater talents had been kicked into gear. Ahrens and Flaherty would be heard from again.

From Broadway's point of view this certainly couldn't happen fast enough. The 1988–1989 musical season proved a near non-event. It was as if all the oxygen necessary for creativity had been sucked from the atmosphere by those long-running, really big musicals from across the ocean.

Legs Diamond, a dreary star vehicle for the Australian pop personality Peter Allen; *Welcome to the Club*, a desolate divorce musical about alimony jail by the esteemed Broadway composer Cy Coleman; *Chu Chem*, a far-fetched Chinese-Jewish fairy tale with music by *Man of La Mancha*'s Mitch Leigh; and *Starmites*, a miniscule science fiction musical, were the sum of Broadway's original contributions to musical theater that year. The choice offered to Tony Award voters was so dismal that *Jerome Robbins' Broadway*, a snippet collection of highlights from Robbins' incomparable career, was deemed eligible as the season's best new musical and won, despite the fact that, however filled with brilliance, the show was a revival composite.

Nothing remotely interesting opened Off-Broadway either. For more than a year, the world of musical theater seemed to idle in neutral.

City of Angels momentarily shattered that torpor. Opening in December 1989 at the Virginia Theater, it was a funhouse of imaginative spins on familiar musical theater rides. The score, composed by Cy Coleman, re-visited expertly the big-band-driven musical universe of the 1940s in an impressive demonstration of what used to be called "tunefulness," abetted enormously by the musical arrangements supplied by a jazz veteran of the period, Billy Byers. The show's book, by Larry Gelbart, was easily the production's most original element, a backstage-in-Hollywood yarn crossed with a noir-detective-potboiler as seen, almost simultaneously, through a bifocal lens. Scenes with Stine, the screenwriter, were presented in color, scenes with Stone, his fictional detective alter-ego, were presented in black and white; the two universes tied together by the pseudo-bebop hipness of Coleman's music and director Michael Blakemore's geometrically elegant staging.

"I think what's more important than the subject of a musical is what you do with it," said Coleman. "I used to perform in jazz clubs a lot as a pianist and there's this old jazz tune that goes 'It Ain't What You Do, It's the Way That You Do It.' Producers like to go with a popular property that they think, 'This will make a great musical.' But what really matters is: What's your take on it? Usually I don't get involved in something until I know what I want to do with it musically. Take *On the Twentieth Century*. *On the Twentieth Century* had a wonderfully amusing script by Comden and Green who wanted me to do the score very much. I knew that what everybody expected was a 1920s-sounding score. But selfishly, as a composer, I wasn't interested in doing that. To write what's expected — you can get a college kid to do the research and write that. Well, I couldn't make up my mind what I wanted to do; I drove Comden and Green crazy. And then this idea of a comic opera came into my head, from my childhood days of playing Rossini. *That*, I thought, I can have fun with. The characters were so much larger than life. I had a ball doing it. If you've got a take that's different, that's what makes a show interesting. You gotta have fun first."

The only relatively new face, creatively, in *City of Angels* was that of David Zippel, as lyricist. Zippel, 34, out of Easton, Pennsylvania, had a law degree from Harvard and a nascent career as a lyric writer for some well-received Off-Broadway revues, including *It's Better With a Band* in 1983 and *Just So* in 1985, along with his aforementioned contribution to *Diamonds* in 1984. None of this quite prepared listeners, though, for the efficiency and wit of his wordplay on *City of Angels*. Zippel outdid himself, turning out lyrics that effectively matched the cunning of Gelbart's book and Coleman's music.

The balance of Broadway's musicals that year were hardly in *City of Angels'* Tony Award–winning class. *Aspects of Love*, even by Andrew Lloyd Webber's derivative standards, was a particularly empty exercise, a collection of musical vignettes about love's various aspects, set to lyrics stocked with romantic banalities by Don Black and Charles Hart. The show opened in April at the Broadhurst Theater and posed no threat to the longevity of either *Cats*, *Starlight Express*, or *Phantom*.

Grand Hotel opened in November at the Martin Beck. Derived from the Vicky Baum novel, as filtered through the legendary 1930s Hollywood screen version, the show possessed pedestrian music by two generations of songwriters. The team of Robert Wright and George Forrest had made a name for themselves on Broadway in the 1940s and '50s by reworking popular classical music into musicals like *Song of Norway* and *Kismet*. They supplied one chunk of *Grand Hotel*'s score, utilizing music they'd first composed as far back as 1958 for an unproduced version of the same project, then called *At the Grand*. Maury Yeston, composer of *Nine*, among other musicals, supplemented their work with a few new songs of his own.

What distinguished *Grand Hotel* and in the end saved it was the inspired staging and choreography supplied by Tommy Tune. Tune managed to make the comings and goings of *Grand Hotel*'s myriad guests matter not in what they sang but in how they came and went. His artistry masked what was otherwise a pretty barren enterprise.

Clearly, Tommy Tune was at this moment Broadway's preeminent stager of musicals, a decisive link to Tune's own mentor, Michael Bennett, and the choreographer/director giants, like Bob Fosse, whom Bennett, in turn, was descended from. Admittedly there was a facileness to Tune's gift. His taste, unlike Bennett's, seemed to run toward mediocre shows that he could dominate and thereby improve. Still, his grasp of Broadway musical stagecraft was touched by genius. As the largely disappointing musical theater decade of the 1980s drew to a close, Tommy Tune was the medium's lone hope for anything approaching an inspired creative future. This point was underlined, in passing, by the closing of Bennett's masterwork, *A Chorus Line*, in April of 1990.

CHAPTER 6

WHY WE TELL THE STORY

Hope is why
We tell the story.
Faith is why.

— *Once on this Island*

It would have been nice if the closing of *A Chorus Line* had also marked a new beginning for musical theater on Broadway. It would have been nice if musical theater creators had grabbed this opportunity to shed the cant of Broadway musical history and get on with creating something new, something for their own moment in time. It would have been nice if Broadway producers had encouraged them to do this.

Well, it would have been.

If there is one constant in the history of musical theater on Broadway — beyond the inescapable necessity for at least a little music and a little theater in each and every show — it's that musicals on Broadway are firstly enterprises of commerce and secondarily enterprises of art. In any of Broadway's so-called Golden Ages, from the 1920s through the mid-1960s, this division generated a kind of frisson that frequently produced artful results. The imbalance between pleasing one's muse and pleasing an audience often prodded creators positively. And the culture at large eagerly paid attention.

Or maybe it was the other way around. Maybe, because the culture at large *was* paying attention, the creators of musicals were inspired to synthesize the inequities of commerce and art more productively.

Perhaps better musicals were created simply because the Broadway musical, as a centerpiece of American musical life before television and rock and roll intervened, actually mattered.

Certainly by the time *A Chorus Line* departed Broadway, this centrality was long gone, along with an eager and engaged audience. Musicals had moreover come to cost more than they had any right to. During the 1977–1978 season, with production costs for musicals just beginning to spiral toward $1 million, the top ticket price on Broadway (for *The Act*) was $25. By the 1990–1991 season, the cost of capitalization for *Miss Saigon*, at $10 million, had outdistanced the record of $8 million recently held by *Phantom of the Opera. Miss Saigon's* producer, Cameron Mackintosh, therefore saw fit to raise his top ticket price to $100.

With so much money on the line, producers increasingly lost their nerve altogether, betting only on what seemed to them sure things: revivals, plus the occasional Lloyd Webber entry.

Why did Lloyd Webber thrive? Stephen Sondheim once defined "melodies that you leave the theater humming" as "melodies you also enter the theater humming." The sense that one has heard a song before often helps make a new song memorable. Lloyd Webber clearly possessed a skill for creating melodies, like "Memory," that many people found very easy to remember; songs that were endlessly reminiscent. In the world of musical theater—as, for that matter, in the world of pop—this skill translated into success.

Lloyd Webber musicals now arrived pre-sold. Backed up by Cameron Mackintosh's marketing, they promised audiences branded commodities, packaged and relatively predictable. As ticket prices, along with production costs, climbed to unspeakable dollar figures, audiences grew as timid as the producers who serviced them. Name recognition was everything. And the name Andrew Lloyd Webber (or even the suggestion of that name) came to possess the same relative market value as any revived classic.

The result was a Broadway creative climate of such stultifying predictability that the culture at-large paid almost no attention whatsoever.

Or maybe this too went the other way around.

The 1990–1991 season did nevertheless offer glimmers of possibility, on Broadway and off. An impressive number of genuinely original musicals somehow still broke through the glacial darkness.

Predictably, three of them turned up at Playwrights Horizons.

The first was by Ahrens and Flaherty—*Once on this Island*, which formally opened at Playwrights Horizons in May of 1990.

Adapted from a slim novel entitled *My Love, My Love* by a Caribbean novelist named Rosa Guy (a book that Ahrens had in fact uncovered in an out-of-the-way bookshop), *Once on this Island* evolved virtually as a blueprint of the workshop process at its best. Ahrens and Flaherty took nine months to complete their first draft, immersing themselves in the music and culture of the Caribbean to tell the tale of an island peasant girl who saves the life of a young mulatto aristocrat after his car crashes near her village. Pledging her own life to the god of death to keep the boy alive, the girl also inevitably falls in love, only to discover that the boy's parents already have arranged for their son's marriage to someone from his own class. Goaded by the god of death, the girl tries to kill her lover, but cannot. Instead she fulfills her promise to the gods by giving her life for his.

"*Once on this Island* was a show about racial differences in Haiti, where class and race went hand-in-hand; a subject that was not written about often," said Ira Weitzman. "It showed how a light-skinned black aristocrat of the wealthy class and a dark-skinned peasant girl could never be together, at least not on earth. Musical theater has the ability to convey messages like that through stories and songs without necessarily being heavy handed."

The director-choreographer Graciela Daniele, a close former associate and dancer alumnus of Michael Bennett's, was engaged to stage the piece. A four-week workshop in the fall of 1989 without costumes, sets or lighting helped the musical to find its form and choreographic shape, tightly constrained by the simplicity of the folk fable being told and the fact that Playwrights Horizons' tiny mainstage had no stage-right wing space at all.

The workshop culminated in three invitation-only run-through performances, followed by a winter of rewrites.

The score that Ahrens and Flaherty wound up devising was a tidy amalgamation of lilting island melodic motifs and rhythmic figures accessorized by accessibly contemporary pop inflections. The score was not really compelling so much as it was gently inviting, It also was very, very polished.

Fleshed out by Daniele, *Once on this Island* also became the through-dance piece Ahrens and Flaherty from the first had intended it to be. With handsome costumes by Judy Dearing and primitive painted sets by Loy Arcenas, the finished product finally premiered at Playwrights in April 1990 to strong reviews. And then, extraordinarily, the Shubert Organization, abetted by Capital Cities/ABC, Inc., James Walsh and Suntory International Corp., stepped in to transfer *Once on this Island* to Broadway, the Booth Theater, in October, where the musical enjoyed a run of 469 performances and received eight Tony Award nominations, including Best Musical, Best Score and Best Book.

Its competition that year on Broadway places the uniqueness of *Once on this Island* in perspective. *Shogun: The Musical* was a horrifically bloated adaptation of a best-selling James Clavell oriental potboiler. It vanished mercifully in a matter of months. *Miss Saigon* was a majestically bloated oriental potboiler swiped from Puccini's *Madama Butterfly* and reset in Vietnam by the music men of *Les Misérables*, Boublil and Schönberg, assisted by the American lyricist

Richard Maltby, Jr. Tumultuously staged, complete with onstage helicopter, by the director Nicholas Hytner, *Miss Saigon* was another anvil-like smash from Cameron Mackintosh. After opening at the Broadway Theater in April 1991 it instantly established itself as the newest Mackintosh musical theater franchise.

The Will Rogers Follies arrived in May, an inane biographical revue that thinly sketched the life of the great American humorist while parading as many scantily-clad chorus girls as possible across the expansive stage of the Palace Theater. With a disingenuously countryish-westernish-tinged score by Broadway veterans Cy Coleman, Betty Comden, and Adolph Green, the proceedings were preserved from unmitigated dopiness by the expansive choreography and staging of Tommy Tune who made nothing from nothing once again look so good that *The Will Rogers Follies* actually captured the Tony Award for Best Musical of 1991.

Finally, there was *The Secret Garden*, based on the popular children's novel by Frances Hodgson Burnett, a show that arrived in April at the St. James Theater boasting many very positive attributes. For starters, it was a commercial Broadway musical with a few actual artistic pretensions. For another, it was written, designed, and largely produced entirely by women (a seemingly unprecedented phenomenon on Broadway), with music by Lucy Simon (sister of Carly), a book and lyrics by Marsha Norman (the Pulitzer Prize–winning playwright of *'Night Mother*), direction by the clever Susan H. Schulman, and exquisite scenery by Heidi Landesman (who also was the show's lead producer).

The most radical element of *The Secret Garden* was its scenic design, a riot of ornate Victoriana that enveloped the show like some florid, vintage pop-up book. The story-telling was a bit disjointed, the lyrics effortful, the music rather too period-appropriately musky. The cast was strong across the board, from the powerhouse leads, Mandy Patinkin and Rebecca Luker, through a fine supporting ensemble that included Alison Fraser, Robert Westenberg, and John

Cameron Mitchell. Ultimately, the sum of *Secret Garden* added up to just a bit more than its disparate elements. The overall effort was eminently worthy. In fact, in the context of the Broadway musical moment it was almost heroic.

Of course, *Miss Saigon* overawed all comers at the box office that season. The presence, though, of *Once on this Island* and *Secret Garden* seemed a moderately encouraging sign. Playwrights Horizons was meanwhile not nearly finished for the year. In June of 1990, William Finn returned with *Falsettoland,* a new installment in his Marvin saga. Overtly anchored this time by the trauma of AIDS, *Falsettoland* proved the least glib and most affecting piece Finn had yet produced. His music was still often an overly exuberant mishmash, his lyrics were as sloppy as ever. But the poignancy of Finn's message was this time impossible to resist. Populated by many actors from the same stellar cast that had so effectively animated *March of the Falsettos* some nine years before, *Falsettoland* was such a triumph at Playwrights Horizons that after ending its run the show re-opened at the Lucille Lortel Theater in September for another 161 performances.

Four months later, Stephen Sondheim also returned to Playwrights Horizons with a new project that perhaps no theater other than Playwrights would have touched.

Almost ten years earlier Sondheim had come across a script entitled *Assassins* while serving as a judge for applicants to a musical theater lab run by producer Stuart Ostrow. The title had struck him, though the script itself, about a fictional presidential assassin, did not. When, in 1988, his *Pacific Overtures* collaborator, John Weidman, proposed that he and Sondheim write a musical about Woodrow Wilson, Sondheim found himself reminded of that title again. He contacted the author and received permission to pursue his own idea, an epic musical about what it meant to kill a political figure.

The potential panoply of assassins was soon narrowed to American presidential assassins only. A couple of initial private readings at

Playwrights in the summer of 1989 led to a widely anticipated month-long mainstage subscription production for *Assassins* in December 1990.

Few musical ideas could have been inherently less commercial. Moreover, the opening of the show actually coincided with the onset of the Gulf War. Amid widespread patriotic fervor, Sondheim and Weidman offered up a musical that non-judgmentally examined the character of America's supreme outlaws.

Yet, night after night, Broadway producers again made their way west to see what Sondheim was up to, passing lines that snaked from Playwrights Horizons' front door, down 42nd Street—hordes of desperate, ticketless Sondheim fans hoping for cancellations. Here was the absurd beauty of Sondheim's new Off-Broadway, non-profit status. His *Assassins*, as a limited run on a forbidden topic, gained a kind of cachet it might never have achieved with a traditional Broadway production.

In fact, when *Assassins* closed in January, talk of moving the show for a commercial run on or off Broadway faded away. Despite another challenging Sondheim score, this time composed as a thrillingly warped catalogue of American patriotic song, *Assassins* remained a troubling work; a celebration of America, as sung by America's outsiders. In that sense, *Assassins* really did belong exactly where it was, on the westernmost theatrical fringe beyond Times Square.

Chapter 7

SOMETHIN' MORE

Forget the old us, "Out in the Cold" us,
Forget what we ain't had before,
Time to hustle us somethin' more!

—*Jelly's Last Jam*

It's entirely possible that Jelly Roll Morton and George Gershwin once met in Harlem. Gershwin, as a young man, lived in Harlem and, throughout his brief life, regularly haunted Harlem nightspots in search of musical enlightenment. Morton periodically turned up in Harlem during his own peripatetic performing years, even settling there for a time in 1928.

Gershwin was a white composer who used black music as a launching pad for his own singular compositional genius. Morton, a New Orleans-born mulatto, was a pianist and composer of commensurate genius who claimed to have invented jazz (and probably to some extent did).

When Gershwin died in 1937 at the age of 38 he was internationally famous and wealthy. Morton's death came in 1941 at 51. He died forgotten and, for the most part, impoverished.

Clearly the two never crossed paths downtown on Broadway, where Gershwin thrived as a composer. Morton, for all we know, may have never even set foot in a Broadway house, given that most Broadway theaters during his lifetime observed a de facto policy of segregation.

George Gershwin and Jelly Roll Morton did confront one another posthumously, though, on Broadway during the 1991–1992 season. In doing so they also parenthetically figured in a different sort of segregation that by now separated Broadway musicals into two camps: Those many projects shamelessly thrown together by producers to draw an audience attracted by revivals, versus those rare few that strove to create something new.

The 1991–1992 season marked a negative milestone in Broadway history. It was the first season in which revivals outnumbered original new musicals—by a margin of four to two (excluding three that placed themselves in a creative no-man's land between the two categories). Quality, for the moment, is not even the point. Fear and philistinism among producers had grown so pronounced that backing an original musical, something written from scratch by a living composer and lyricist, was coming to be perceived as an act of almost aberrant rashness.

Unfortunately, the two original musicals produced during that 1991–1992 season bloodily demonstrated why. *Metro* was an oddity, an original Polish musical from Warsaw presented in translation for what turned out to be thirteen performances in April at the Minskoff Theater. *Nick and Nora*, however, had a nice local pedigree. Its score was by Charles Strouse, an under-rated veteran, with lyrics by Richard Maltby, Jr. Its book, peopled by Dashiell Hammett's *Thin Man* characters, was by Arthur Laurents, who also served *Nick and Nora* as director. Laurents was one of the Broadway musical's finest librettists, best known for his books to *West Side Story* and *Gypsy*.

Still, *Nick and Nora* proved an unsalvageable disaster. By the time it opened at the Marquis Theater in December 1991 it had been in previews far longer than the single week it would actually run. Lots of money and much Broadway musical experience and wisdom were flung at *Nick and Nora* to no effect. Despite all that was said and sung and danced onstage, nothing much ever seemed to happen up there.

To some, *Nick and Nora* was one more powerful argument for the economic efficiency of what might best be described as revivals in disguise or "non-revival revivals." Non-revival revivals were the musical theater equivalent of "non-denial denials," the phrase famously coined by Watergate investigative journalists Carl Bernstein and Bob Woodward to describe the evasiveness of the Nixon White House. Perfected, in a sense, by producer David Merrick and director Gower Champion with their Tony Award–winning musical augmentation of the movie *42nd Street* in 1980, non-revival revivals plundered (with permission) the catalogues of classic songwriters to manufacture musicals that could be touted as new, but in fact were ground from very old pulp; musicals that were and were not new.

Dissecting the pedigrees of these shows could only amuse an intellectual property attorney. Imagine, though, how much better *Nick and Nora* might have been if its somnolent proceedings had included, say, some beloved George Gershwin songs. Or even something by Jelly Roll Morton.

This is precisely how the creators of *Five Guys Named Moe*, *Crazy for You*, and (in a wildly different way) *Jelly's Last Jam* saw things.

Five Guys Named Moe, which opened in April 1992, was a revue constructed from the greatest hits of the jump-jazz legend, Louis Jordan. Producer Cameron Mackintosh poured plenty of promotional dollars into *Five Guys Named Moe*, even opening an on-site themed bar alongside the show's Eugene O'Neill Theater home, hoping to replicate the bonhomie as well as the commercial success of *Five Guys Named Moe*'s long-running London West End precursor. His payback, however, was negligible.

Crazy for You opened at the Shubert Theater in February 1992, advertised by its producers as "the new Gerswhin musical comedy," but with a primary story line and score from the landmark 1930 Gershwin hit, *Girl Crazy*; said score sweetened with additional songs from the Gershwin catalogue; said story line somewhat rewritten for *Crazy for You*'s late-20th-century audience.[6]

Crazy for You's precursor and role model was *My One and Only* which had done...well, the very same thing back in 1983, manipulating in that instance the 1927 Gershwin musical *Funny Face* under the very jolly direction of Tommy Tune and his choreographic associate Thommie Walsh.

Needless to say, it took very little producing fortitude and only a certain kind of imagination to tout George Gershwin as something new. This creative marketing was nevertheless well-rewarded. *Crazy for You* actually was handed the Tony Award as Best Musical for 1991–1992.

On the surface, *Jelly's Last Jam* would seem to have been just another such case, with a score assembled almost entirely from Jelly Roll Morton's existing song catalogue. Bringing Jelly Roll Morton to Broadway, however, did require significantly more producing brass and creative chutzpah than remounting George Gershwin. *Jelly's Last Jam* was also a wholly original construct, with an original book by George C. Wolfe that attempted to tell the story, more or less, of Jelly Roll Morton's life. The show's use of music was rather innovative, deploying Morton's essentially non-theatrical jazz riffs in traditional, plot advancing, musical theater fashion through the savvy of musical director Luther Henderson's virtuosic cut-and-paste skills.

Henderson pieced together a coherent Morton score with the help of lyricist Susan Birkenhead's proficient craftsmanship. Those Morton songs that already possessed (often delightfully raw) existing lyrics, like "Michigan Water" and "Doctor Jazz," Henderson unobtrusively retooled for the stage. For those that didn't, Birkenhead wrote (often delightfully raw) new lyrics. The results were...virtually new.

Underwritten by the producers Margo Lion and Pam Koslow, in association with (among others) Rocco Landesman's Jujamcyn theater chain, *Jelly's Last Jam* opened in April at Jujamcyn's Virginia Theater under the direction of Wolfe, whose interest in Morton's life story was self-evident. Ferdinand LeMenthe Morton had been a seminal voice in African American music. Yet, throughout his life, he'd sometimes loudly denied that he was black at all. Whether this bluster actually meant something to Morton (a notorious loud-mouth and a self-avowed con man) is impossible to say. Wolfe, however, seized on this seeming self-abnegation as the dramatic hook for his Jelly Roll Morton musical.

Topping an absolutely sensational cast, including Keith David, Tonya Pinkins and Savion Glover, *Jelly's Last Jam* starred the tap dancer Gregory Hines as Morton. Tailoring the Morton story to Hines' dancing strengths proved something of a dramatic liability; Jelly Roll Morton had not been known for his dancing. Still, this lack of verisimilitude also liberated Wolfe and Hines to present Morton's life less literally and more metaphorically through the prism of dance.

In the end, *Jelly's Last Jam* proved to be an original piece of musical theater, one that stumbled at times dramaturgically but frequently one that soared musically and choreographically. Though a non-revival revival in the narrowest sense, it at least blurred the boundaries between original and revival with a sense of aesthetic aspiration. And it did finally manage to bring Jelly Roll Morton and George Gershwin together on common ground.

Three days after *Jelly's Last Jam* opened, yet another revival of sorts landed on Broadway at the John Golden Theater: *Falsettos*, a melding by director and bookwriter James Lapine of William Finn's *March of the Falsettos* and *Falsettoland* musicals into a single evening of theater. Here was a milestone — Off-Broadway's definitive out-sider musical *on* Broadway, an insider, at last. The show that had helped certify Playwrights Horizons' pioneering pursuit of new musical theater voices in 1981 now helped win a Tony Award for the first among those new voices, William Finn, as composer of the season's best musical score in 1992. His collaborator, James Lapine, also won the Tony for Best Book. Broadway had at last managed to revive something original.

CHAPTER 8

MAYBE IT BETTER SOON NO

What if it happened but maybe it better soon no
But it globbidged and rubbidged me now till it's dofting
And nothing there
Try again

— *Wings*

"Once you've established that people are talented," insisted Ira Weitzman, "then the fact that they're talented is maybe 10 percent of the effort to make a successful piece of musical theater. The other 90 percent is the technical expertise, the ability to carry out the work, the *personality*—to get along, to interact, to be part of a very sophisticated form of collaboration.

"I think that our greatest contribution at Playwrights Horizons was to enable people to function in that sort of collaboration, to facilitate it. We were in the non-profit world where our only goal was art, thank God, and André and I were very much like-minded, both in our taste and in that one objective. That was the only pressure: to live up to the author's vision of any piece. That pressure was tremendous. And it never changed."

"At Playwrights Horizons we produced," André Bishop emphasized. "It wasn't just readings and workshops, we were able to produce a number of early and not so early works by all these writers. It was our belief that it was really through production that writers grow and develop. And that's what we did. Our whole notion of musicals were all of these chamber works with casts of six and five instruments. Because that was all we could do there. At some point, though, you start to think about what it would be like to work on a bigger canvas."

In January 1992 André Bishop announced that he was leaving Playwrights Horizons after ten years as its artistic director to assume the same post at Lincoln Center Theater. With decidedly mixed feelings, Ira Weitzman soon followed him.

Like Playwrights Horizons, Lincoln Center Theater was a non-profit enterprise. Similarities pretty much ended there, however. Lincoln Center Theater was also a mammoth arts institution, kin to its neighbors in the Lincoln Center complex: the New York Philharmonic Orchestra, the Metropolitan Opera, the New York City Opera and the New York City Ballet. Its resources were vast, its subscriber base far larger, far older and far less adventurous than Playwrights Horizons'.

"The stakes, the money? Yeah, I did feel that, a little bit," Weitzman would later admit. "Theirs was a way bigger budget. It was a way bigger theater. Working there was a very high profile job."

Lincoln Center Theater's primary space, the Vivian Beaumont Theater, had upward of 1,000 seats. Now it was Bishop's responsibility (in tandem with Lincoln Center's hold-over executive producer, Bernard Gersten) to fill them.

Predictably, he looked to do so almost immediately with a musical.

My Favorite Year was adapted from the nostalgic and very funny 1982 film about a young comedy writer's first gig working for a thinly disguised Sid Caesar–type variety show during the live, early years of television. It had originally been commissioned from the team of Ahrens and Flaherty, along with bookwriter Joseph Dougherty, as part of a short-lived venture called *New Musicals* that in 1990 had attempted to provide a laboratory for new works at the State University of New York–Purchase. When *New Musicals* collapsed following its inaugural season, *My Favorite Year* was picked up by Lincoln Center Theater.

The show was, of course, by definition, a throwback. Its plot was shticky, its jokes broad. Ahrens and Flaherty's score was bouncy and brassy in the most traditional Broadway sense, an exercise in 1950s-style musical comedy.

For Weitzman and Bishop, who'd spent their Off-Broadway careers shaping forward-thinking alternatives to the traditional Broadway musical, this choice still seems something of a cop out.

Perhaps if *My Favorite Year* had been better. The show was not so very bad. But it wasn't so very good either. Where upstanding intentions, ground-breaking innovations, previously forbidden subject matter or sheer oddness could perhaps carry a new, experimental musical downtown, presenting an old-fashioned Broadway musical uptown at Lincoln Center really demanded one thing only: old-fashioned quality. *My Favorite Year*'s melodies just weren't memorable enough, its lyrics just weren't clever enough, its onstage business just wasn't funny enough and its stars just weren't luminous enough. Carried for a time by Lincoln Center's captive subscription audience, the show closed after 34 performances.

"*My Favorite Year* was a victim of bigness," reflected Weitzman in the end. "Big theater, big Broadway musical expectations, big pressure to succeed on a very different level. A number of mistakes were made along the way, things I'd have done differently if I could go back. But I can't. So you move on."

Another musical survivor from the SUNY Purchase *New Musicals* debacle (*The Secret Garden* actually had been one, too) also re-surfaced on Broadway during the 1992–1993 season with far different results. *Kiss of the Spider Woman* was the Purchase program's most high-profile undertaking. Directed by Harold Prince, its score was by John Kander and Fred Ebb, one of Broadway's marquee songwriting teams, whose work together included *Cabaret, Zorba,* and *Chicago.* Why a Kander and Ebb project should have been presented in a laboratory for new musicals is a good question; Kander and Ebb were the quintessence of mainstream Broadway commerciality. Their presence at Purchase confirmed something the series founder, Marty Bell, in fact never denied, that under the guise of encouraging new work *New Musicals* was also a means for circumventing the staggering cost of developing new commercial musicals for Broadway.

And yet, *Kiss of the Spider Woman* was no easy sell. Adapted from a Manuel Puig novel, its subject was the imagination as a means of survival; its plot, the story of two political prisoners locked away in an unnamed Latin American country, trying to survive confinement, even torture, and still remain sane.

The 1990 Prince production at Purchase proved a morass, tedious and confusing. Unsurprisingly, though, given the all-star creative players involved, *Kiss of the Spider Woman* did not die. Picked up for his Toronto theater by a Canadian former film executive (and as yet not-indicted theatrical entrepreneur[7]) named Garth Drabinsky, *Kiss of the Spider Woman* was endlessly reworked by Prince and company before proceeding on to London's West End in 1992, where it won several significant prizes.

"*Kiss of the Spider Woman* was damned to permanent hell by the *New York Times,* among others, when we did it up at Purchase," insisted Prince.[8] "Drabinsky had the guts to put it on again and see it fly."

It was this heavily revised version — led by Chita Rivera in a sensational star turn as the Spider Woman, and Brent Carver and Anthony Crivello beautifully matched as the prisoners — that landed at the Broadhurst Theater in May and took away the Tony for Best Musical of 1993.

Was the show actually so much improved? No. True, it had some terrifically characteristic Kander and Ebb numbers. These songs, though, could have fit into just about any of the many Kander and Ebb shows down through the years. The team's glitzy Broadway musical voice was ill-suited to an ambitious story that existed on two levels: the reality of prison, pain and political conscience, versus the cinematic escape of the imagination. In Kander and Ebb's score there was virtually no differentiation, and so both stories ultimately were trivialized rather than elevated by the addition of music. In the end, what looked like an adventurous bit of musical theater on paper, really *was* so in synopsis only.

Wings, on the other hand, was the genuine article. Written by two 35-year-old New York theater novitiates, Jeffrey Lunden (music) and Arthur Perlman (book and lyrics), *Wings* was derived from a one-act play by Arthur Kopit that gave voice to the life of a once-vibrant older woman, now silenced by a devastating stroke.

The subject was both eloquently musical and poignantly theatrical. Perlman's disjointed lyrics and Lunden's Sondheim evocative score were inventive, particularly in their handling of the often mono-syllabic, painfully nonsensical near-poetry that the damaged woman spoke. In an odd way, what the very earnest *Wings* lacked was a bit brasher touch, maybe even a little Kander and Ebb–style esprit. Still, it was refreshingly new. Its two-month run at the New York Shakespeare Festival's Public Theater was deservedly well received.

Though Off-Broadway generated nothing of consequence musically beyond *Wings*, Broadway that year was almost shockingly flush with book musicals. Unfortunately, none of them were very good.

Blood Brothers, a 1950s British re-telling of the age-old separated-at-birth story, *Anna Karenina*, a straight-faced musicalization of Tolstoy, and *The Goodbye Girl*, adapted from the Neil Simon film, were each dreadful in their own distinct ways, though all three also shared a few fundamental negative qualities. Where *Karenina*, which opened in August 1992 at Circle in the Square Theater, was mildly pretentious and musically inert, *Blood Brothers*, a huge hit in London, which opened at the Music Box in April 1993, was loudly, grimly, unrepentantly *un*pretentious, and musically inert. *The Goodbye Girl* meanwhile, which opened in March at the Marquis, was so desperately inert despite its heavy hitter lineup of creators — bookwriter Neil Simon (adapting his own film script), composer Marvin Hamlisch and lyricist David Zippel — that no one even noticed whether it had pretensions at all.

Finally, there was *The Who's Tommy*, a non-revival revival that hit the St. James Theater in April like a blast from some cosmic rip in time — which it pretty much was. A super high-tech mounting of The Who's legendary 1968 rock opera by the director Des McAnuff, *Tommy* was a feverish glimpse into Broadway's financial future. It was a show that bridged the nearly unbridgeable gap between contemporary pop music culture and musical theater by reaching back to the pop music of now-aging baby boomers. And why not? This virtually untapped, lost generation of potential ticket buyers were the Broadway musical's best hope. There would be increasingly more musical appeals made to their taste and pocketbooks in the years to come.

CHAPTER 9

THE RED SHOES

The line dividing Jule Styne's present tense on Broadway from his glorious past essentially ran down west 51st Street during the winter of 1993. On the south side of the block sat the Gershwin Theater (formerly the Uris), a 1970s-vintage office tower/parking garage-cum-playhouse. The Gershwin was home that winter to the 88-year-old composer's soon-to-be-unveiled 21st Broadway musical, *The Red Shoes*, adapted from the ubiquitous 1948 ballet film. To the north, almost directly across 51st but a lifetime removed from the Gershwin, was the former Mark Hellinger Theater where Styne for more than 40 years had kept an office.

In 1990 the Nederlander Theatrical Organization, owner of the Hellinger, had bailed on the theater, selling the under-booked Hellinger outright to an evangelical church. Within the year, the theater's 60-year-old marquee was emblazoned: *Times Square Church* in heavenly blue light. Window cards announcing: "God Comes To Broadway!" lined the theater's outer walls. Inside, Styne packed up a career's-worth of his own window cards, framed photographs, posters, scripts, and music scores. He'd been evicted.

A dingy wedge-shaped, cave-like aerie with a tiny window on 51st Street overlooking the Hellinger Stage Door, Styne's office really had been more of a parlor sitting room for Styne and his pals despite the presence of a handsome art-deco standup Steinway buried in one corner and at least three desks. When *My Fair Lady* was in residence downstairs, for example, in 1956, its star, Rex Harrison, often would climb the iron stairs on matinee days to rest between shows on Styne's couch, languidly requesting show tunes from the composer seated at his piano. Judy Holliday, Ethel Merman, Carol Channing, Barbra Streisand, Mary Martin, Dolores Gray, Bert Lahr, Nancy Walker, Phil Silvers, all had dropped up at one time or another. The deli takeout bills, Styne liked to recall, were enormous.

"I knew Mark Hellinger very well before they named the theater after him," Styne announced, seated in his new five-room institutionally faceless office up the block at 1560 Broadway. "He was quite a guy; very bright, a newspaper writer. Spelled the dignity of Broadway, not the *Guys and Dolls* Broadway. Though there was *that* Broadway too. Anyhow, the theater was called the Warner's then. It was a movie house and the entrance was on Broadway. I'd come to New York from Hollywood around 1947 and I'd written *High Button Shoes*, which was a big hit. Tony Farrell, who owned the Warner's, was a good friend of mine. I told Tony to change the theater's entrance.[9] You see, in the legitimate theater a house *on* Broadway was no good. It was good for movies, for revues, for girlie shows but not for theater; for theater you needed a side street—a theater is a gentle place with a side street entrance; what a church is to a church, a theater should be to a theater. I mean, have you been in the theater in that new hotel on Broadway?" Styne interjected suddenly. "The Marriott's Marquis— with the escalators and the corridors and the *walk*?! That walk is the longest on Broadway! That's not a theater—it's one long hallway!

"Anyhow, I said to Tony Farrell, 'Your marquee's on Broadway but your audience has to walk half a block before they actually get into your theater. There's so much space out front, there's room enough for a big store.'

"I had a tailor shop that I went to up on 51st, off Seventh Avenue, tiny little shop, good friend of mine—Cy. I only knew his first name. Still don't know his last name. It was a gold mine. But he couldn't carry enough stock, the place was too small. So, I put him in touch with Tony Farrell and Cy came away with a store on Broadway and Tony moved the entrance of the Warner's around to 51st Street. It opened with a show of mine, *Hazel Flagg*. Critics treated it as a big event, like it was a new theater. Tony was thrilled. In fact, when he retired from show business, he gave me his office. Yeah, that one.

"Anytime I wanted to hear somebody I'd take them right down to the stage," Styne remembered. "Judy Holliday learned a lot of *Bells Are Ringing* in that office and on that stage. Streisand learned some of *Funny Girl* in that office. I went down to see her in a club after reading Walter Kerr's notice on *I Can Get It for You Wholesale*, where he said, 'If they ever do the story of Fanny Brice, they should get this kid.' Thank you, Walter Kerr.

"Stephen Sondheim I never worked with in that office, when we were writing *Gypsy*. Steve, I had come where I lived then, on East 63rd Street. Steve was a loner so I figured I'd make him feel like he was coming into a home; I had warm lunches and dinners cooked for him. We had a great time." [10]

Styne looked pensive for a moment. "Frankly, in the last years it became a bit of a hardship for me to go to that office. Honestly, I felt a little bit in jail. The theater industry has gone away from this neighborhood; there used to be rehearsal halls, dance studios; writers had offices all up and down Broadway. So now the theater's a church. Such a pity. It was a good-size house but always handled wrong. It wasn't the theater's fault. Bad shows ruined the Hellinger; the owners, the Nederlanders, killed it with bad shows. At least the Shuberts hire people to tell them whether a show is good or bad. The Nederlanders ought to be ashamed of themselves for selling. Now the Hellinger's gone to sleep and I'm in an office that at least has an elevator."

Styne's return to 51st Street with *The Red Shoes*, a show he'd been laboring over for most of his eighth decade, had not been painless.

Long before opening, *The Red Shoes* already had run through its original director, its original lyricist, one leading man and a couple of featured actors. Not all that unusual for a major musical on Broadway at any time, but definitely not a cozy conjoining of creative forces.

Styne, Broadway's veteran of veterans, had been persuaded early on to go with three-quarters of the comparatively youthful, all-female creative trio mostly responsible for *The Secret Garden*—respectively, the book writer and lyricist, Marsha Norman, the director, Susan Schulman and the set designer, Heidi Landesman.

Norman was the first to feel the heat, stripped by Styne of her lyric writing chores in favor of Bob Merrill, Styne's lyricist partner on *Funny Girl*. (Merrill would wind up credited pseudonymously as Paul Stryker in *Red Shoes* programs alongside Norman).

Schulman was next, fired outright in August, to be replaced by another old Jule Styne associate, the legendary Hollywood director Stanley Donen, in his Broadway debut.

"Ah, I wouldn't trust a show where everybody got along," Styne growled. "So we fired some people. Do you know how many directors and actors and songwriters have been fired over the years from great shows and not so great shows?"

"I never would have believed it was possible to work under these conditions," Landesman, the lone surviving *Secret Garden* alumna, would later maintain. "I come from a not-for-profit world in which, because everyone basically is not paid, we all have an obligation to treat each other with at least a degree of decency. There is always a feeling that we are not there for profit, we're doing it for art or something. But here, clearly, those pretenses were dropped. To those of us who came out of the non-profit theater movement it was a big shock."

Then again, Landesman conceded, this pre-historic brand of Broadway ruthlessness had added something to *The Red Shoes*.

"We definitely acquired a kind of toughness, a real masculine sense that was good," she remarked. "I always saw our audience as ladies who'd seen the movie as girls, who always wanted to be ballerinas, and who now would take their daughters to see our show. But Jule, the producer Martin Starger and Stanley, being older men, believed that the story was about the middle-aged impresario who falls in love with the girl, doesn't know how to deal with that and consequently destroys everybody in his path. Susan wanted to work a radical feminist revision on the film and I think that freaked Jule out. Heck, it freaked me out! I still believe, though, that those guys were all sexists of the old school. Let's face it, Jule simply had problems with Susan being in charge."

"It's a collaboration," Styne would roar back. "You think Jerry Robbins and I always got along? You gotta tell people what you think and fight for what you want. The bottom line is: Does the show work?"

Styne could not then have suspected that *The Red Shoes* would open and close in four nights. Or maybe he did. Peers in the business already were referring to *The Red Shoes* as "Jule's last jam."

"It's the best work I've ever done," he insisted that day, a little less than a year before his death in September 1994. "It's the ballet music nobody ever thought I could write. It's 28 pieces, the largest Broadway pit orchestra since *Porgy and Bess*. It's a big, big show. The kind nobody writes anymore."

CHAPTER 10

TURN THE BLOOD TO BLACK AND WHITE

Turn the blood to black and white.
It sings with all its might.
—"Over Texas"
from *First Lady Suite*

Michael John LaChiusa was born in Chautauqua, New York, about 75 miles south of Buffalo, a notably cultured town with an arts festival, a symphony, a theater, and even an opera company. His father was a football coach, his mother, a cheerleader-turned-housewife with a love for Broadway musicals.

"We didn't get a chance to go to New York very often; she'd been a couple of times, but she was hooked, absolutely hooked on Broadway shows," LaChiusa would recall. "It's strange, she had every album. You would think she was one of those musical theater queens."

LaChiusa knew from a very early age—four- or five-years-old, he claimed—that he wanted to write musicals.

"I was putting neighborhood kids into musicals, doing my own version of things I'd seen on TV. I did my own *Once Upon a Mattress* in the backyard; I had the sheet music and everything. I learned very early to read music. I had this blind piano teacher, which was great, I could get away with murder—I didn't have to worry about fingering and stuff, so long as it sounded okay."

LaChiusa hesitated and then smiled. "No, she knew," he muttered. "She knew when I was doing the right fingering."

After high school LaChiusa didn't quite know what was next for him. He didn't want to act. He did want to write. He wasn't sure if he was up for entering a conservatory. He tried to get into Juilliard, but his family couldn't afford it and he didn't win a scholarship. For a while he worked at nearby Fredonia State University in the opera program, playing the piano for singers.

"Then I talked my parents into sending me to a TV school where all we did was watch TV all day. It was so strange, aside from theater and writing music, the other thing I loved doing was watching TV. It was this junior college kind of place in Boston, Graham Junior College, right in the heart of Boston, Kenmore Square; two years and you got a degree in TV watching. Oh, it's gone now. All we did all day was watch TV and write about it."

LaChiusa came to New York in 1980 at the age of eighteen, gravitating immediately to the downtown club scene. He played the Bowery club where punk rock was born, CBGB, and worked as an accompanist for new vaudeville comedians like Jeffrey Essmann far off Broadway at theaters like La Mama in the East Village. Soon, though, he began writing musicals in earnest, attending the ASCAP and BMI workshops.

"Those workshops can be good," LaChiusa observed. "A lot of good writers have come out of them. They also can be the worst, for some people. I used to go to Lehman Engel's BMI workshop just to hear him be nasty. He really knew how to deliver the bad news. He was very funny."

In 1984, LaChiusa completed his first full-length musical, based on the Carson McCullers short story, *Ballad of the Sad Café.*

"That's how I met Ira Weitzman over at Playwrights Horizons. I did a couple of songs at the BMI workshop and Ira took me under his wing. The not-for-profit world was really hitting its stride and the musical department at Playwrights was really coming into full flower under Ira's leadership. He was the one you went to, to say, 'Ira, I have a new idea for a new musical; hear my songs for this project?' And Ira would then go, either: 'Gee, that's good,' or, 'That's bad.' If he liked it, if he thought it was interesting, his first goal was to find financing, funding; what kind of grants can be gotten so you can continue your work? For me, that was always the case, how could I proceed to fund the writing of this thing, to get to a reading? Once you got to a reading, the piece could begin to develop momentum and other people would get involved, like the artistic director at Playwrights, André Bishop."

LaChiusa, in 1984, was making money as an accompanist and musical director, while working at Tower Records. *Ballad of the Sad Café* would remain unproduced. LaChiusa had naïvely neglected to secure the rights.

"I think everybody's first piece winds up that way," he shrugged. "Lynn Ahrens and Steve Flaherty made the same mistake with their first, an adaptation of the movie *Bedazzled*. But through those pieces, your whole world begins."

LaChiusa next turned out a couple of wildly offbeat one-act musicals: *Agnes*, about a wheelchair-bound woman who persuades a thief to set her free by killing her, and *Eulogy for Mister Hamm*, in which the residents of an S.R.O. hotel, on line for the one available bathroom, come to fear that their superintendent may be dead. The two pieces helped LaChiusa win his first grant, a Richard Rodgers Development Award for a staged reading in 1986. They would not, however, be produced formally until Playwrights Horizons presented them for fourteen performances in December 1991 on a program with two additional LaChiusa one-acts: *Lucky Nurse*, about a pediatric hospital nurse and the unknowable links between herself, one newborn and a cast of random strangers; and *Break*, wherein two construction workers on lunch break high above the city are visited by the Virgin Mary.

The one-act form revealed LaChiusa's voice. His work as a miniaturist was quick-witted and sophisticated, both musically and dramaturgically. His dramatic situations, however outlandish, were grounded in empathy for his characters. The conversational ease of his lyric-writing and the melodic conciseness of his music made for clean story-telling, no matter how elliptical the story.

LaChiusa next wrote *Over Texas*, the first in a new series of one-acts about a subject that obsessed him: presidential first ladies; what he would call his *First Lady Suite*.

Over Texas proved a masterpiece in miniature, a taut, frequently comic mood piece full of unspoken pathos. Its conceit was terrific, a peek inside Air Force One on the 22nd of November, 1963, winging its way toward Dallas and John F. Kennedy's date with destiny. The characters: Kennedy's devoted personal secretary, Evelyn Lincoln, his wife's personal secretary, Mary Gallagher, the vice president's wife, Lady Bird Johnson, and of course, the first lady herself, Jacqueline Kennedy.

LaChiusa's slanting take on history, his focus on mundane moments as shadowed by future titanic events, proved hauntingly affecting. There was the excited innocence of Gallagher, traveling on Air Force One for the first time; the glimmers of Lincoln's unmistakable infatuation with her handsome boss; the mutual distaste of the two working women for the first lady's seeming frivolousness. All of this combined to suggest, with glancing understatement, the innocence of the nation at that moment in time; the country's own heady infatuation with its handsome young president; and the impending tragic transformation of the dilettantish Jackie into America's First Lady of Sorrows.

Over Texas was really a 20-minute opera, with limpid arias and vivid vocal motifs. Its fleeting appearance as part of a yearly "marathon" of one-acts at the Ensemble Studio Theater, Off-Off-Broadway in the early-summer of 1991, was remarked upon by only a handful. Still, it constituted a major statement.

Through Ira Weitzman's intercession, LaChiusa had begun to get commissions in opera as a librettist. He wrote *Desert of Roses* with the composer Robert Moranon for the Houston Grand Opera, and *Tania* with Anthony Davis, both produced in 1992. The gigs helped pay some bills and taught him a lot.

"I had to learn how to write my own librettos because there were very few good librettists out there," said LaChiusa. "Many of the great librettists throughout history have been rather crummy playwrights. There's just some magic about it, some gift of collaboration, allowing your ego to be absorbed by the music."

LaChiusa wrote a few songs (and also got to play keyboards bare-chested as part of the onstage band) for *Bella, Belle of Byelorussia*, a broad farce by his old collaborator, Jeffrey Essmann, produced by the WPA Theater in January 1992. The 1993–1994 season, though, would be his breakout year.

Predictably, it was Weitzman who set things in motion. After the bitter disappointment of *My Favorite Year*, Weitzman seemed to have regained his footing at Lincoln Center Theater in two ways. He agreed to work on his first revival—the stellar revisionist revival of Rodgers and Hammerstein's *Carousel*, first staged by Nicholas Hytner at the National Theater in London, imported and largely recast by Lincoln Center Theater for its 1994 season. And he turned to Michael John LaChiusa with an idea.

"I called Michael John and said, 'Have you read *La Ronde* by Arthur Schnitzler?'" remembered Weitzman. "He said, 'No,' and I said, 'Read it.' Two days later Michael John called and said, 'Well, I wrote the opening scene.' 'Yeah?' I said. 'Okay, come and play it for me.'

And it was exactly the same opening scene that ended up in our production. 'Keep going,' I said.

"We kept talking about different ways to do it. At first he wanted to put everyone in a different country; he wrote a second scene set in Nicaragua during some insurrection and that's when I think we both decided his best idiom was America.

"In about five days Michael John wrote four scenes out of ten. That's very fast. That's when I told him, 'Well, you'd better play this for Graciela Daniele because this is her idea.' So he played it for Graci and she just flipped out and said, 'Yes, this is exactly what I've been hearing in my head,' and she hugged him and it was sort of born. *Hello Again*, Michael John called it, and very shortly thereafter we did a quick reading to see if we felt *Hello Again* was viable to produce, because a lot of things you read on paper that seem like they may be good, stink when you put them out on a stage."

"It shouldn't take that much time to write a musical," insisted LaChiusa. "It shouldn't take much longer than a year. Musicals should be here and now and that's that. Musicals have to have spontaneity. When you hear it, sitting there in the audience, it has to catch you, as if it's being created in that moment. I think if you keep working and working on a musical, it loses that spark, and an audience registers that, whether they know it or not.

"I read *La Ronde* and just sat right down at the piano with the play and my legal pad. For me, usually my very first step is sitting at the piano with the script over here, the legal pad over here, the piano in front of me, some manuscript paper on top, and a sharpened pencil. I love pencil shavings all around. I love the filth of it."

Hello Again opened in January 1994 at Lincoln Center Theater's basement space, the intimate Mitzi E. Newhouse Theater, as part of a festival of three new American plays. It remained there for three months. Sixty-four performances. The critics were not wildly taken overall with what they saw and heard. Weitzman's suggestion of *La Ronde* to LaChiusa had been right on target, though, the piece was essentially a short-story collection, or rather, a collection of one-acts—ten seemingly unconnected scenes revolving around ten nameless characters, each of whom resurfaces in a roundelay of sexual partnerings. The structure played beautifully to LaChiusa's proven strengths as a miniaturist, while offering him an opportunity to write a full-length work.

Perhaps inevitably, the writing in *Hello Again* was uneven. Some of the songs were aimless, others strained for maximum shock value. But there were many riveting moments both musically and theatrically. The show, moreover, broadened the artistic wingspan of a new, young musical theater writer who already liked to stretch and reach. From its organizational form to its sound, a nice crossbreeding of pop music and tampered-with musical theater traditionalism, *Hello Again* was a defiantly *new* musical.

Weeks earlier, at the Public Theater, LaChiusa had also been afforded the opportunity to at last present his *First Lady Suite* in its entirety—to date.

"I'd still like to do Nancy Reagan," said LaChiusa. At the Public, though, *First Lady Suite* consisted of four first ladies and their plays: Mamie Eisenhower's *Where's Mamie?*, Bess Truman's *Olio*, Eleanor Roosevelt's *Eleanor Sleeps Here* and Jackie Kennedy's *Over Texas*.

Though none of the other three worked quite as brilliantly as *Over Texas*, *First Lady Suite* further displayed LaChiusa's strengths: his wit, his imagination, his craftsmanship, and his willingness to challenge an audience, to disorient, and even discomfit them, without ever neglecting to entertain them too. *First Lady Suite* was a fever dream of radiant awe and disrespect. In tandem with *Hello Again*, it earned LaChiusa an Obie Award for his work in 1993–1994. More importantly, it made him a player to be reckoned with.

CHAPTER 11

A KIND OF HAPPINESS

Some say happiness
Comes and goes.
Then this happiness
Is a kind of happiness
No one really knows.

—*Passion*

The 1993–1994 season actually amounted to more than the escapades of one frisky young composer.

First, *Cyrano: The Musical* arrived, pungent and pasteurized as cheese, from Holland of all places, for a fairly brief stay at the Neil Simon Theater in November, 1993. *Cyrano* brought with it producer Joop Van Den Ende, a Dutch media magnate ("a multi-biljonnair," in the words of one of his press releases), determined to play a Cameron Mackintosh–style role in Broadway's flashier (and trashier) musical theater future. ("If they want cauliflowers, give them cauliflowers," Van Den Ende, back in Holland, had once famously crowed.)

On Van Den Ende's heels came the Walt Disney Company with similar empire-building aspirations and a slightly firmer grasp of the English language. Disney's 1991 animated feature film, *Beauty and the Beast*, delightfully scored by Alan Menken and Howard Ashman, had rung up one of the biggest box office successes in the annals of cartoon cinema. It also had been anointed at the time with a review in the *New York Times* by Frank Rich citing it as superior to just about any musical then running on Broadway.[11]

This constituted an implicit invitation, one that Disney simply could not refuse. Mustering all of the theme-park caliber artistry at its disposal, the company dutifully delivered a live-action *Beauty and the Beast* to the Palace Theater in April, 1994, horrifying many critics, terrifying many long-time Broadway producers and delighting many (admittedly under five foot tall) theatergoers with its synthetic, seemingly bottomless, industrial strength lavishness.[12]

Off-Broadway in June of 1993, at the tiny Actors' Playhouse, the flip-side of this over-the-top, Disney-style plasticity had been strangely anticipated by *Howard Crabtree's Whoop-Dee-Doo!*, a hilarious, low-budget Ziegfeldian girlie revue in drag, partly performed and entirely outfitted by the wildly imaginative Crabtree, whose sartorial concoctions, entirely home-sewn, made the evening a must-see, backed with some clever songs by an assortment of songwriters, but especially Dick Gallagher (music) and Mark Waldrop (lyrics).

Avenue X, produced in February 1994 by Playwrights Horizons absent André Bishop and Ira Weitzman, was an all doo-wop *West Side Story* variant about racial tensions in 1963 Brooklyn. In its vigorous but ultimately endless a cappella harmonizing, *Avenue X* mostly reminded listeners that *West Side Story*, among its many wonders, had somehow managed to tell its own late-1950s teen gang story without resorting to a single note of doo-wop.

Also opening Off-Broadway in February, at the Orpheum Theater, was *Stomp*, an all-percussion thud-fest from England by way of the Edinburgh Festival that snagged a significant slice of the younger ticket-buying demographic Broadway so pined for simply by making a lot of noise. *Stomp* continues to be remounted worldwide, in every conceivable venue for every conceivable audience. It remains a phenomenon—hardly inexplicable, but not all that easy to explain either.

At the Vineyard Theater in May, Polly Pen, a writer for whom the word "stomp" did not exist, offered another of her—for some, charming, for others, arid — musical theater aesthetics exercises with *Christina Alberta's Father*, based on the H. G. Wells novel.

"*Christina Alberta's Father* was my very favorite show that I've ever done at this theater," said the Vineyard's Douglas Aibel. "It was almost an opera, very ambitious, passionate, eccentric — a wonderful piece of theater. And it was way beyond our means. I mean, it was this epic British historical fantasy, tons of characters, tons of plot, tons of music. And we just did it. It was not the Metropolitan Opera production, we used a six-piece orchestra rather than a twenty-piece orchestra and no big chorus. It took us a couple of years. But we found a way."

Finally, triumphantly, there was Stephen Sondheim's *Passion*, perhaps the most naked personal expression of the great composer's career and certainly one of his most rigorously demanding musicals.

Another collaboration with James Lapine, *Passion*, like the previous two Sondheim-Lapine projects, began with a workshop organized by André Bishop with Ira Weitzman; the first away from Playwrights Horizons — at Lincoln Center Theater.

"Part of me wishes *Passion* had stayed at Lincoln Center in an intimate setting," remarked Weitzman, in retrospect, "where it might have avoided some of the issues that followed it to Broadway. But we were not able to offer them a slot right away, and the Shuberts jumped in and offered money and a theater fast."

Unlike *Sunday in the Park* and *Into the Woods*, which were wholly original constructs, *Passion* was an adaptation, derived from the Italian-language film, *Passione D'Amore* and the novel upon which *it* had been based, *Fosca*, by I. U. Tarchetti. Unlike *Into the Woods*, though, *Passion*, did not go out of town before previewing on Broadway.

This, of course left it rather exposed.

A story of obsessive, possessive, compulsive love, *Passion*, was anything but a conventional Broadway romance. The intense unattractiveness of its central character, Fosca, brilliantly, if disconcertingly embodied by the actress Donna Murphy, had an unfortunate effect on many preview audience members. Fosca made them so uncomfortable with her desperate protestations of love that many laughed right out loud.

Here was a nutty predicament emblematic of the level Broadway patrons had reached by the '90s. Audiences could readily weep at the sight of a prosthetically outfitted Walt Disney beast in love or a masked phantom in romantic torment. A real woman, however, with a mole (admittedly planted) and a very plain face pleading for love just got laughs.

Watching Sondheim and Lapine wrestle with *Passion* preview audiences became almost as dramatic as anything occurring onstage; two musical theater pros reconfiguring and re-deploying speeches and songs in an effort to defuse mood-shattering derision. In the end, Sondheim and Lapine more or less won out. The last-minute addition of a new song, "Loving You," in which Fosca heart-rendingly explains herself to the object of her obsession, Giorgio, turned the tide. Audiences stopped laughing, mostly. And *Passion*, after opening at the Plymouth Theater in May, actually went on to win the Tony Award for Best Musical of 1994.

Despite the hope, if not the expectations generated by what actually had been an abundance of new musical activity in 1993–1994, the following season proved a disastrous non-event. Shockingly, only one new book musical opened on Broadway that entire year. Off-Broadway, the promising uniting of composer Michael John LaChiusa with director Harold Prince in *The Petrified Prince* stumbled badly at the Public Theater. A very elaborate political fairy tale with a big budget and a big cast, the musical never managed to master its over-reaching ambitions and simply sing.

Broadway's lone new musical in 1994–1995 was another Andrew Lloyd Webber mega-spectacle, the maestro's mangling of Billy Wilder's gothic Hollywood classic, *Sunset Boulevard*. *Sunset Boulevard* opened in November 1994 at the Minskoff Theater. Its only competition for the Best Musical Tony would be from *Smokey Joe's Café*, a dead composer revue for two still-living songwriters, the rock-and-roll/R&B team of Jerry Leiber and Mike Stoller. The other relatively new musical produced that year was Charles Dickens' *A Christmas Carol*, an effort underwritten by the Madison Square Garden Corporation and Nickelodeon to challenge the unrestricted Christmas franchise of the Radio City Music Hall's ageless Christmas Show. *A Christmas Carol* did have some effective songs by a new teaming: Lynn Ahrens with Alan Menken. It also had an impressively large cast fleetly set in motion by choreographer Susan Stroman. Still, the stifling corporate imprint on this *Christmas Carol* was unmistakable.

Sunset Boulevard collected its uncontested Tony. Banking a bravura performance by Glenn Close as Norma Desmond, a mammoth, gilded set by John Napier, and a pre-sold song, "As If We Never Said Goodbye," that Barbra Streisand had put on the charts well before the show opened, *Sunset Boulevard* seemed yet another over-sized Lloyd Webber hit. And it was. For a time. Once Close left, though, in July of the following year, *Sunset Boulevard*'s grosses began to slip. By its closing in March 1997, *Sunset Boulevard* had failed to recoup its reported $13-million investment.[13]

In this sense, *Sunset Boulevard* proved a very significant milestone. A shift in the Broadway musical landscape was implicit in its failure. The age of the English mega-musical had begun to wane. Though no one could yet say precisely what was next, it seemed clear that somewhere, something had to be.

CHAPTER 12

GLORY

One song.
Glory.

— *Rent*

For a community dismissed as moribund, the American musical theater in 1994 still generated an impressive quantity of cassettes. Most arrived by mail, though a few came hand-delivered, usually with scripts, in fat envelopes that crowded the desks of Broadway producers and non-profit institutional theaters all over town. On average, each tape represented a minimum of three years work. All proffered someone's dream of a newly-minted musical.

Beyond the sheer quantity of music and invested man hours there was something encouraging about the vast number of aspirants these tapes attested to. Despite the chasm still separating musical theater from mainstream popular culture, from commercial recording success, from hip, from cool, from *now*, lots of people still apparently wanted in on the great American musical. This fact inspired hopeful questions. If there was to be life at all for musical theater in the next millennium, what form would that life take? And how? And, most intriguingly, *who*? Who would get this dauntingly irrelevant job done?

Jonathan Larson believed the answer to that question was *him*. His belief was absolute and unshakeable. And so, he submitted tape after tape of the musicals that he wrote to the powers of the musical theater business, tapes that he agonized over in his ragged tenement apartment on rugged lower Greenwich Street in Manhattan. Like virtually every one of his many peers in this strange, fruitless competition, Larson spent nearly as much time packaging his songs and his scripts for submission as he did writing them; printing out well-designed labels for his cassette cases, pulling together the most enticing presentations possible for his shows.

It was a losing game. Even Larson knew it, though he refused to surrender to this knowledge. The odds were ridiculously long that your tape, out of literally thousands, would transcend the pile, to be listened to and, more importantly, *heard*, by anyone.

Yet, Larson persevered, working as a waiter at a diner near his home for almost ten years, writing music during the day and late at night.

Actually, he quite liked his life, fancied its bohemian grit as if it were art rather than an increasingly real poverty that ground him down. Born into the suburban middle class in Mount Vernon, New York, on February 4, 1960, Larson was a good boy who'd discovered musicals, like so many others, listening to his parents' cast album collection. After performing in plays and musicals at White Plains High School, Larson had pursued his passion to a full acting scholarship at Adelphi University, where he wound up writing the music (and an occasional lyric) for ten shows in four years, most of them cabarets.[14]

Of course he moved to Manhattan after graduation, indulging his fantasy of grungy artistic grandeur while auditioning for parts as an actor and singing in a cabaret vocal trio.

Unlike nearly every other person his own age, Larson made no distinction between the music of his time — rock and roll mostly — and the antiquated music of the Broadway musical. Not only did he listen to everything and anything that sounded good to him, he actively sought to incorporate all of that music into his musicals.

"I am striving to become a writer and composer of musicals," he wrote in a letter in 1985.[15] "I am 25 and am faced with a dilemma.

"Although I am a sentimental romantic who loves old fashioned musicals, I am a member of a very unsentimental, unromantic generation who basically think musicals are too corny.

"I feel that if I want to establish myself with 'the powers that be' in the theater, I must compose music that appeals to the older ears in the production houses and audiences.

"But if I want to try to cultivate a new audience for musicals, I must write shows with a score that MTV ears will accept.

"If you were me, which audience would you write for?"

Anticipating the then-impending anniversary of George Orwell's futuristic novel, *1984*, Larson had spent two years brashly adapting the book as a musical, sending a demo tape and script to the Orwell estate, as well as to the director Harold Prince, before discovering, like Ahrens and Flaherty and LaChiusa before him, that he could not get the rights.

Larson remained characteristically undaunted. He rewrote the *1984* musical as *Superbia*, "my own dystopia," he later described it, "*1984* crossed with the scene at this super-hip club, Area, which was right down the street from my apartment at that time. I imagined a futuristic, bottom-line oriented society that was much more user friendly than Orwell's, much more like our own Madison Avenue world."

Early drafts of *Superbia* told the story of a young man who yearned to awaken a benumbed futuristic dictatorship with music. Later drafts would present this hero as someone who never gets his chance to sing. Over the next five years, Larson presented songs from *Superbia* everywhere, including the ASCAP and BMI musical theater workshops.

Somehow, one of these appearances actually caught the ear of Stephen Sondheim. Larson had met Sondheim while still a student at Adelphi. It had been Sondheim, in fact, who'd encouraged Larson to make a choice: either act or compose full-time.

"I heard Jonathan play some songs from *Superbia* at one of Charlie Strouse's ASCAP workshops," recalled Sondheim. "I was not just impressed with the music, I was impressed with Jonathan's *ideas* for songs. I thought they were very original. And good. I decided to Oscar Hammerstein him, by which I mean, do for him as Oscar had done for me: mentor him."

Ira Weitzman also noticed Larson's work at that workshop. "I liked the music," he remembered, "partly because, over the course of the previous ten years, I'd slowly but surely been weaning myself away from show tunes and trying to find other ways of expressing theater with music. I mean, it had just gotten too boring. Sondheim had defined, redefined, redefined again, and redefined *again* what a show tune was. To find an original voice was so hard when there was this living master looming over everything.

"I became interested in Jonathan's sound. I thought he had a great gift for melody. Which I told him. But I also told him how wonderful it might be for him to collaborate with other people because I didn't always think his scriptwriting or his lyric writing were as sophisticated as his aspirations. How did he respond?" Weitzman smiled. "He was understandably resistant."

In 1988, at Sondheim's urging as Chairman of the Richard Rodgers Production Award Committee, Larson won a $14,766 development grant for *Superbia*. The money would fund one rehearsal and two staged readings of the show at Playwrights Horizons.

"We did those readings with a very good cast," recalled Weitzman. "It went well enough. I did not think the piece was producible though, because I just didn't think it was mature enough. I didn't really pursue it."

"*Superbia* was simply unsolvable," said Sondheim. "I became convinced that the book could not be fixed."

Larson was devastated but, again, entirely unbowed, turning his disappointment into another musical, one which went through at least three different titles—first *30/90* (because he'd be turning 30 in 1990), then *Boho Days*, and finally the cruelly prophetic, *tick, tick... BOOM!*

An at times embarrassingly autobiographical rock monologue admittedly influenced by the work of Spalding Gray, Eric Bogosian, and Laurie Anderson, *tick, tick... BOOM!* consisted of twelve varyingly angry songs about thwarted musical theater dreams and the tribulations of waiting tables and growing old. A childhood friend of the protagonist at one point discovers he is HIV-positive—which indeed had occurred to Larson's closest childhood friend not long before. A girlfriend presses the composer to give up writing musicals and get a real job—also painfully close to reality.

"*Tick* was my attempt to come to grips, like others of my generation, with the diminishing opportunities all around us," Larson later said, "to deal with what our burden to bear was; like all generations. There were no characters, no Rodgers and Hammerstein plot, no sets, no costumes; just me, my piano, and a band, the Well Hungarians, telling my story. I'd never had a band of my own. That was cool. *tick, tick... BOOM!* was also about my turning 30. Which was really not cool."

Larson performed *tick tick... BOOM!* (as *Boho Days*) briefly at Second Stage Theater and at the Village Gate. His expectation that these showcases would yield an open-ended run for the piece, or at least a record deal for himself, failed to materialize.

"I went to all his subsequent readings and whatever else he did," Ira Weitzman remembered. "I tried to be very loyal and supportive."

In 1989, the American Music Theater Festival in Philadelphia announced that Larson had been chosen to receive a relatively new award they'd begun presenting annually to a young songwriter in Stephen Sondheim's name, the Stephen Sondheim Award.

Larson very proudly traveled down to Philadelphia to receive his prize in the name of his idol. Since *Superbia*, Larson had been sending virtually everything that he wrote to Sondheim for comment and approval. In each instance, he'd always received some words of encouragement and often detailed advice.

"It was right around that time or perhaps a little later," noted Weitzman, "that I got a call from a playwright named Billy Aronson, who'd had a few readings at Playwrights Horizons. I knew he was a Yale graduate and I knew he was funny. Billy said to me that he wanted to do a musical based on *La Bohème* and was looking for a collaborator. This clicked with me immediately. Great idea, I thought. 'Where do you want to set it?' I asked. 'The Upper West Side,' Billy said. Alright, I thought, you know, maybe that's not ultimately it, but, okay.

"I gave him a couple of names. 'Call Jonathan Larson first,' I said. And he did."

Larson took to Aronson's notion immediately. Together, they wrote three songs, one about opening a restaurant in Santa Fe, one love duet, "I Should Tell You," and one song about paying the rent, which Larson had suggested should be the musical's title.

"They did a demo and gave it to me and I thought it was great," said Weitzman. "Absolutely great. About two months later, though, there was this growing rift between Jonathan and Billy because their lifestyles were so different. Billy was married with kids. Jonathan was living the Bohemian life. Clearly they were at odds. Though Jonathan's lifestyle, I thought, sure gave him the edge in terms of writing a musical based on *La Bohème*.

"That was the end of that, so far as I knew. They decided to split apart. Then, about a year later, this would have been 1991, Jonathan called me and said, 'I can't get *Rent* out of my head.'"

Weitzman suggested that Larson call Aronson.

"Call him and say, 'I really want to work on this and I don't think we're right together, can we make an arrangement so I can continue to work on this project,' recalled Weitzman. And Jonathan said, 'Is that all I have to do?' And I said, 'Yes, of course that's all you have to do.' So he did, and they made an arrangement, albeit a loose one, and Jonathan started to write *Rent* himself.

"I felt sad, to be perfectly honest," admitted Weitzman, "because I wished he had a collaborator. It was one of those moments — in fact, maybe it was the only time, as I think about it — where I let go of a piece I thought had potential. I can't say I didn't have a pang, though, wondering: God, is this going to be successful?"

Larson gave *Rent* everything he had for the next four years. He wrote it and rewrote it. He played it in public, he played it in private, he played new songs he'd just completed for friends on their answering machines. All of the earnestness in his soul and the ambition in his gut were poured wholesale into *Rent*.

The show would not just be a musical, it would be an opera, and not just an opera but a rock opera, "a *Hair* for the '90s," set in New York's East Village, and not just a *Hair* for the '90s but a testament to the plague of AIDS. This last element had recently penetrated Larson's sense of the show, inspiring him to return to it in the fall of 1991 after he'd learned, within a matter of two months, that three more friends now had the disease. Their illnesses and, ultimately, their deaths would haunt Larson and, increasingly, give *Rent* an even stronger under-current of fleeting mortality.

In the summer of 1992, Larson was riding his bicycle along East

Fourth Street, between the Bowery and Second Avenue in the East Village, when he passed a theater called New York Theatre Workshop, just across the street from La Mama. In its thirteen-year existence, New York Theatre Workshop had a history of taking chances and making those chances more than occasionally pay off.

Larson knew this. From the street, it was also clear that New York Theatre Workshop was in the middle of some major renovations. Larson climbed off his bike and stuck his head inside. The new performance space was going to be vast, larger than some Broadway proscenium stages. Larson was impressed. The next day he cycled back and dropped off a tape and a script of *Rent*.

"I have this vision of him on his bike, like a newspaper boy," mused Ira Weitzman, "flinging his script at Off-Broadway theaters and the New York Theatre Workshop being the only one that picked it up. Which was terrific for both of them."

New York Theatre Workshop sponsored Larson's first staged reading of *Rent* in June 1993. The reading revealed a musical that was a mess. A mess with some really great songs.

"There was a lot of passionate discussion after that first reading about what should come next and how soon," recalled James Nicola, New York Theatre Workshop's artistic director. "Most musicals are collaborative and the creators also have social time together. In Jonathan's case there was none of that. He'd been sitting in a room by himself for a long while and he was really anxious to get out of there. The last thing he wanted to hear was that he had to go back into his little garret and write some more in solitude."

Larson had submitted *Rent* to the Richard Rodgers competition in 1993, without success. The rules stated no show could be re-submitted. But Larson contacted Stephen Sondheim, who headed the Rodgers panel, pleading to be made an exception. Sondheim agreed. In January 1994, *Rent* won the Richard Rodgers Studio Production

Award, a $45,000 grant that would help finance a full workshop at New York Theatre Workshop.

To direct this workshop, Nicola brought in a director named Michael Greif, soon to be appointed artistic head of San Diego's La Jolla Playhouse. Greif listened to a tape of *Rent* on his Walkman while flying in from California to meet Larson in New York in January of 1994. "What impressed me," he remembered, "was its youth and enthusiasm, and that it was a musical about contemporary life. Jon was writing about some people I felt I knew, that I sort of loved, or had loved in my life." [16]

Nicola wanted a director who was both tough-minded and cool-headed, an antidote, he felt, to Larson's impassioned optimism, which had led Larson, in *Rent*, to render AIDS, homelessness, and drug addiction with a wide-eyed, if endearing, naïvete.

"*Rent* was very fragile material at that time," Nicola recalled. "It was so easy for it to become sentimental or hokey. I felt Michael had the right sort of dryness and sharpness to balance Jonathan's writing."

Greif and Nicola battled Larson over nearly every word. Larson fumed and pouted, argued and, in the end, rewrote. According to Greif, by the time they were done, nearly half of the show as it had existed in the 1993 workshop, was gone,[17] though a good number of *Rent*'s finest songs were already present in 1993, including, "Light My Candle," "Will I," and the indelible, "Seasons of Love."

"*Rent* was in fact missing the very elements I wished it would have had, particularly in the storytelling," reflected Ira Weitzman. "However the melodies were incredible. When I heard 'Seasons of Love,' I thought: Who could write a song like this in the theater nowadays? It's a heart wrenching contemporary ballad. Unfortunately, it didn't make a whole musical. And I was arrogant enough to think that Jonathan Larson would not succeed with *Rent*. I really wanted to work on his next piece. *That one*, I thought, would be the one."

Running from October 29 through November 6, *Rent*'s first extended workshop proved, in many ways, a triumph. Word seemed to have gotten around about this rock opera. A younger, downtown audience predominated. And nightly, many of them stood and cheered. A pair of 30-something, aspiring theatrical producers— Jeffry Seller and Kevin McCollum—saw the show once, then returned with a Wall Street investor named Allan Gordon a few nights later. Impressed, the trio decided to offer Larson and NYTW seed money, "no strings attached," as confirmation of their interest in *Rent* as it evolved. "We took out our checkbooks," said McCollum. "We didn't have a lot of money. But we believed in Jonathan."

Yet, Greif and Nicola were troubled. *Rent*'s tangled narrative remained as confusing in many ways as the show's score was inspiring. A dramaturg was hired and Larson again went back to work, still alone, but now with some professional company. The goal seemed within reach.

"I went to my board after the workshop and said, we want to produce this," said Nicola. "You may not believe it, I said, but what you saw at that workshop was exactly what we wanted to see which is—what works, what doesn't. If we do *Rent* here, it's going to be the largest thing we've ever done by far, at least double the budget of the biggest play we've ever produced. I remember I said to them, of anything that we have ever done at NYTW, if our work goes well, and if everything falls into place, this is the play that has the most potential for wide audience appeal. So, we might want to try and figure out how to find that money without involving commercial producers.

"I was not convincing enough," Nicola concluded. "What I said was too qualified. And I could hear it. But I didn't feel that I could really say this is going to be a hit. I couldn't do that."

In the end, Seller, McCollum and Gordon put up a total of nearly $125,000, supplementing $125,000 from NYTW for a production of

Rent to open in January. In exchange, the trio obtained the rights of first refusal for a commercial production after *Rent*'s NYTW run.

In the fall of 1995, Larson quit his job at the Moondance Diner. "For the first time in my life," he told friends tearfully, "I feel like I'm really working in the theater."

A painstaking search for a cast of fresh young voices and faces commenced, leading finally to the hiring of fifteen relative unknowns, including a few who'd appeared in the 1994 workshop. A five-piece onstage band would play Larson's 35-song score.

Rewrites continued throughout the six-week rehearsal period, which began in mid-December. To the last moment, these enforced rewrites provoked grave questions. Would Larson satisfy his producers and his director? Was Larson himself satisfied with *them*?

"Jonathan called me very early on about Michael Greif," recalled Stephen Sondheim. "He was terribly upset, in fact he was just about in tears. He felt that Greif was not committed to *Rent* in the right spirit and was not contributing anywhere near what Jonathan wanted from a director for his show. Jonathan actually asked me, in my capacity as a former-president of the Dramatists Guild, what the proper procedure was to get Greif fired from *Rent*. I told him he should wait until after this production at New York Theatre Workshop was up and running and then he could disengage Greif if the show moved; like *Hair*, which was directed by Gerry Freedman downtown and Tom O'Horgan uptown. I thought it was important that Jonathan see things through so that his show did open. Of course, Jonathan never lived to see that opening, so Greif never was, in fact, fired from *Rent*."

In the end, Larson neared the finish line with *Rent* altered in three fundamental ways. The show's underlying empathy, its gentle but overwhelming sense of tolerance, of celebration and love in the face of death, had become more pronounced than ever. The chaotic plot, while clarified here and there, remained in some ways more unwieldy than ever. And Larson had miraculously managed to improve an already superlative score, penning the songs "Take Me or Leave Me" and "What You Own" more or less at the last minute, while nailing down what would become Larson's own tragically self-defining number in *Rent*, "One Song Glory," salvaging it from the bones of an existing tune he'd once called "Right Brain."

"F.Y.I.," wrote Larson anxiously in Christmas cards to friends near the end of 1995. "RENT runs at N.Y. Theatre Wkshop. Jan. 25– March 3. Seating is limited. To order tix: 212-460-5475."

What happened next was almost indescribably unfair.

Three nights before *Rent*'s final dress rehearsal, Larson complained of terrible chest pains while watching an act two run-through. He was taken by ambulance to Cabrini Medical Center where emergency room doctors diagnosed food poisoning, pumped his stomach, and sent him home.

Larson suffered in bed for the next two days before asking a friend around 11 PM Tuesday night to take him to another emergency room. At St. Vincent's Hospital the diagnosis this time was a viral infection. Again he was sent home.

The night of *Rent*'s final dress, January 24, Larson still had chest pains, back pain, and a low-grade fever. He nevertheless grabbed a cab to the theater and watched his musical unfold before a passionately enthusiastic invited audience. The *New York Times* Arts & Leisure section had noted that *Rent*'s opening coincided with the 100th anniversary of Puccini's original *La Bohème* premiere; a coincidence Larson himself had not noticed. A writer had been dispatched. In the wake of *Rent*'s last rehearsal, Larson sat, weary but triumphant, for his first *New York Times* interview. He then returned home past midnight, threw a tea kettle on the burner of his kitchen stove, and suffered a massive rupture along his aorta, perhaps as long as 20 inches. The cause? An aortic aneurysm, a congenital weakening in Larson's arterial wall. His roommate found him dead on the kitchen floor about 3:30 PM, the burned tea kettle still on the fire.

Rent opened at New York Theatre Workshop on February 13, 1996. Any ingenuousness that might once have clung to Larson's impossibly hopeful paean to life despite the pall of imminent death had been swept away. Everything about *Rent*, from its harried story-line to its heartfelt music, suddenly seemed unbearably of a piece.

The show ended its run downtown on March 31 as a phenomenon. Film stars, pop stars, Wall Street tycoons, and street kids had besieged the New York Theatre Workshop for tickets. David Geffen had signed up the show's original cast album for his record label. ("It's funny," noted Sondheim. "I sent Geffen some of Jonathan's songs from *Rent* before Jonathan died and he turned them down.") Martin Scorsese had joined in a bidding war for the film rights. *Rent* re-opened on Broadway at the Nederlander Theater on April 29, dominating the Tony Awards that year after winning the Pulitzer Prize.

Larson had always believed he would transform not just the Broadway musical but musical theater itself. Always working within the tradition, he injected it with music—from rock and roll to gospel, and even hints of rap—that propelled the form into the 1990s. Larson had believed in two things: himself and the power of the American musical. His faith, in the end, was rewarded.

CHAPTER 13

HOW GLORY GOES

Only heaven knows how Glory goes,
What each of us was meant to be.
In the starlight, that is what we are.
I can see so far...

—Floyd Collins

What sort of a musical theater season did *Rent* all but eclipse in 1995–1996? In fact, an unusually fertile one that had begun, eerily enough, with a new musical score by Jonathan Larson. *J. P. Morgan Saves the Nation* was a goofy, sprawling, self-consciously off-the-wall rendering of the life of Wall Street's most lionized financier. Written for the avant garde En Garde Arts theater company, whose specialty was so-called "site-specific theater," the piece, with lyrics by Jeffrey M. Jones, was performed for about a month or so throughout June and July 1995 at the junction of Broad and Wall Streets out in front of the Federal Building, just opposite the New York Stock Exchange.

J. P. Morgan Saves the Nation was full of prancing, chanting, dance-challenged Lower Eastside chorines and pointless downtown theatrical obscurantism. Larson's music, however, was, in retrospect, heartbreakingly impressive. Departing from the rock and roll fusion that had impelled him to write *Rent*, Larson revealed just how capable a musical theater composer he was in an array of musical modes, from pure vaudeville to pastiche classical and back again. Of course, Larson's achievement was barely noticed. *Rent*'s break-through was still some seven months away.

Chronicle of a Death Foretold was a venturesome musical theater experiment adapted from the Gabriel García Márquez novella and masterminded by director-choreographer Graciela Daniele for Lincoln Center Theater.

"That was such an amazing experience," remarked Ira Weitzman, "taking the written word and translating it into an innovative movement piece that still managed to tell the story in the style of Márquez. The fact that it took place in Latin America and had an all-Latino cast, many of whom were appearing on Broadway either for the first time or for the first time as characters other than maids or thugs, that was meaningful too. Luis Perez, virtually the best dancer in New York at the time, had a mustache and a goatee and I said to him, 'Luis, I think Graci wants you to shave.' And he said, 'But, if I shave this, I'll never get any work on TV. They only hire me if I look like a Latin bad guy.'

"Among the things I most loved about *Chronicle*," added Weitzman, "were the letters we got from kids in high school, written on loose-leaf paper, that said, 'I never saw my culture on the stage before. Thank you for that. Your music was so much like what I hear at home that I just wanted to get up and dance.' *Chronicle* was pure musical theater. It wasn't esoteric, it wasn't 'Meredith Monk interprets *Chronicle*.' It was just theater, music, and dance."

With a basic score by Bob Telson and a book by Jim Lewis and Michael John LaChiusa, *Chronicle of a Death Foretold*, which opened on Broadway in June at the Plymouth Theater, was almost entirely danced, generating erotic heat if not especially riveting narrative tension. The show was exquisite to look at, though, and resulted in a significant, poetic departure from Broadway's norm.

Bed and Sofa at the Vineyard Theater in February by Polly Pen functioned at an even further poetic remove from any norm. Working in collaboration with bookwriter Laurence Klavan, Pen created a "silent movie opera" by adapting an actual silent film, Abram Room's 1927 classic about three Russians sharing one tiny apartment and one bed.

The show had a fabulous miniaturized set by G.W. Mercier, amusing miniaturized direction by Andre Ernotte and a score that, even by Pen's standards, was monumentally miniature.

Victor/Victoria was the cynical opposite of these three authentically experimental musicals, a non-revival revival-variant that recycled for Broadway the 1982 Blake Edwards/Henry Mancini/Leslie Bricusse film musical with its original star, the wondrous Julie Andrews, reprising her leading role. Where the film had been droll and witty, though, the Broadway version was leaden and obvious. After opening in October at the Marquis, it survived entirely on the strength of Ms. Andrews' sorely put upon presence.

Big was just bad. It was another blaringly obvious stage adaptation of a recent film hit, one that had not been a musical originally and barely became one now, despite the efforts of some very talented pros: composer David Shire, lyricist Richard Maltby, Jr., and book-writer John Weidman. *Big* opened in April at the Shubert Theater and, without the benefit of a Julie Andrews–caliber star, closed six months later. Interestingly, neither show — the season's two biggest in terms of budget and scale — were nominated for Tony Awards.

In any other season *Bring in 'da Noise, Bring in 'da Funk* would have been *the* defining event. Launched by George C. Wolfe via a pro-tracted workshop at the New York Shakespeare Festival, where Wolfe had taken over as producer and artistic director in 1993, *Noise/Funk* was a "tap/rap" musical that blew into Broadway's Ambassador Theater in April of 1996 after absolutely dazzling Shakespeare Festival audiences for 85 performances downtown.

Noise/Funk did have a book of sorts by the spoken-word poet Reg E. Gaines. This book traced the history of oppression against African Americans but rendered it as the evolution of a beat and the expression of that beat in motion. To describe *Noise/Funk*, though, was to deprive it of nearly everything that gave it brilliance — its spontaneity, its unpredictable structure, its soul, its seething rhythms and, most significantly, its furious, electrifying performances. Wolfe took a few young tap dancers, including the finest hoofer of his generation, the then-21-year-old Savion Glover, and managed to turn them loose and frame their artistry simultaneously.

Noise/Funk brought the essence of the street into a Broadway theater with far more authenticity than *Rent* did. Its funk/hip-hop musical score by Daryl Waters, Zane Mark, and Ann Duquesnay was far more contemporary than *Rent's*. Its performers were as young, as gifted and largely as unknown as *Rent's*. And its politics were far more incendiary.

Yet, *Noise/Funk* lacked *Rent's* melodic richness and its empathetic heart, to some extent, and it certainly lacked anything as explosive from a P.R. point of view as Jonathan Larson's death. The show got deserved rave reviews, particularly for the visionary choreography and dancing of Glover, who seemed to be inventing a new style of tap dancing, a new method of theatrical dancing, and virtually a new mode of confessional expression on the spot. Wolfe's scintillating direction also triumphed over Michael Greif's at the Tonys. But *Noise/Funk* never did entirely escape the shadow of that other rave up new musical. Together, though, the two certainly turned Broadway upside down and inside out, trailblazing a fresh new direction not for the future but for the here and now.

"I love going into a rehearsal room and not knowing what the hell is going on," said Wolfe, "then making myself available as a director to whatever that action might be. If you're forced to know things too soon in the theater you end up coming up with stale truths. And an audience can feel if you're recycling the truth. About half the numbers in *Noise/Funk* I literally dreamed when we were in workshop. I'd come in and say, 'Alright, I had a dream about this.' And then Savion would take that and begin to shape it and visualize it. *Noise/Funk* told its story in a completely new way. And that's what I'm interested in with musicals. You just can't compare the spirit and reach of *Noise/Funk* and *Rent* with anything else out there. Nothing else was in the same league."

Actually there was one more musical of spirit and scope that year, one that ended up absolutely buried by *Rent* and *Noise/Funk*'s success. This musical also surfaced Off-Broadway at Playwrights Horizons. It opened in March 1996, just a month after *Rent* did, receiving some respectable reviews. It closed three weeks later.

Floyd Collins was a very odd piece of work, a musical that depicted the heartbreaking hopes, dreams, and death of a dirt poor Ozark hillbilly trapped in a cave in Kentucky in 1925. Its story was a true story. It's stirringly original, string dominated score[18] was written by a 31-year-old composer/lyricist named Adam Guettel. The piece was Guettel's first full-length musical produced in New York. Yet, in its deceptive, off-hand sophistication, in its overpowering musical imagination, *Floyd Collins* was perhaps a more important musical step for musical theater than even *Rent*.

Who was Adam Guettel? A child of musical theater royalty, no less. He was the son of Mary Rodgers — composer of the 1960 Broadway hit, *Once Upon a Mattress* — and the grandson of Richard Rodgers. This bloodline was both a blessing and a curse for Guettel, who seemed slightly paralyzed by its implications.

"For years, I thought I'd be a failure if I didn't manage to have a show on Broadway before I was 30, as my grandfather and my mother both did," he confessed. "Now that I'm past 30 and haven't, I can breathe again. I realize it's okay."

Guettel had written a first musical more or less when he was eight. "Then I was blocked for six years," he insisted, only half-kidding. "I started again when I was fourteen. I also started taking jazz piano. I was singing professionally as a boy soprano soloist at the Met and New York City Opera. But I didn't really find a window into writing until jazz piano gave me a kind of little toolbox, a quaint set of chords, little building blocks, to start writing with."

Guettel began to experiment with those building blocks. He also became a jazz bass player, "for about ten days," he laughed, "gigs and clubs and things. But I didn't have enough to say on the bass. I also didn't want my entire life to be about *um-dum-dum-dum*. I just wanted more."

Guettel, at fifteen, had played some of his music for Stephen Sondheim, one of his mother's oldest friends. "He gave me some very helpful comments, although I, in my sort of coddled state, felt he was being discouraging when in fact I was just being talked to in a professional way. He was incredibly generous with his time and with his mind and he gave me some really helpful comments. I was used to hearing, 'Oh, my God, that's brilliant. Wow! I can't believe you're only fifteen and writing that,' from my mother and my adoring, supportive friends. So, to me, it was a shock to my system when Sondheim said, 'Okay, this is a mess. But this is how you can fix it.' I appreciate it now. That's what I want in a critic, especially one of his stature. I wish I had appreciated it at the time."

Guettel's fifteenth year also was the year of his grandfather's death.

"I wouldn't say that I grew up with his music markedly more in my life than the average kid of my generation, but he was a very important part of me. I saw a lot of his revivals at Jones Beach Theater and I think I saw some at Lincoln Center when I was very young. I also saw some of his last shows on Broadway; *Two by Two, Rex, I Remember Mama*. He wasn't well at all by then; by the time I was really cognizant of him, he was becoming kind of foggy. I think when he no longer was able to write, that was sort of the end for him."

Guettel attended Yale College, where his Concerto for Jazz Quartet and Orchestra won the Yale Concerto Competition. A one-act musical that he wrote and orchestrated at nineteen based on a Dr.

Seuss story languished after Guettel lost the rights. He graduated in 1987. A full-length operatic version of Dickens' *A Christmas Carol* followed in 1989, written for Hartford's Trinity Repertory Theater in collaboration with the director and playwright Tina Landau.

In 1990, the year after Jonathan Larson received it, Guettel was given the American Music Theatre Festival's Sondheim Award. The following year, the Festival commissioned Guettel and Landau to write something new.

"Tina and I both had a bunch of ideas. One, she had found in a Reader's Digest *Life in the Twenties* book, this tiny, one paragraph blurb about a guy who'd gotten trapped in a cave down in Kentucky and the sort of media carnival that ensued. There was even a little picture of him, under the headline 'Deathwatch Carnival.' Floyd Collins.

"'Well, that's the one,' I said, when Tina mentioned it. 'That sounds like fun.'

"His world just seemed magical to me," Guettel explained. "Floyd's world invited me in as a composer and allowed me to set up camp in there, to define the piece through music. The musical language that I came up with for Floyd underground felt very freeing for me. It didn't come out of the music above-ground, it was Floyd's separate magical universe—though the two were somewhat related. The whole echo device, which was one of the very first things I thought up, just had sort of a celestial feeling to me. Then, I also had to do that thing above-ground most composers do to set a piece in some time and place. I had to take in what was actually going on in Kentucky in the 1920s, what music was being made—'hill music,' as it turned out, Appalachian music—and run it through my own function machine to come up with music that didn't ape it but rather harkened to it.

"I loved all that research," added Guettel. "It was really fun. It took me months, though, to put the first note on paper, probably three or four months, because the tone was really hard to find."

In late 1991, Guettel sang the first 25 minutes of *Floyd Collins* to Tina Landau, little of which, he claims, actually survived as part of the final score. Eight months later there was a workshop of the first act. A year later, *Floyd Collins* debuted in Philadelphia and a year after that Playwrights Horizons premiered it in New York.

"I couldn't believe how long it took," moaned Guettel. "My whole wunderkind thing seemed to just be melting before my eyes; I wanted so desperately to be this wunderkind because my grandfather had been, Stephen Sondheim had been, even my mother had a show on Broadway before she hit 30. It all weighed on me. God, what a relief it is not to have to worry about that anymore."

Floyd Collins truly sounded like no other musical had before, though Guettel's gifts as a composer did parallel those of his grandfather. He had a vivid capacity for dramatizing character through melody. He knew with a terrific immediacy what elements of a story could be enhanced by music. His lustrous and original use of harmony was positively enrapturing. Guettel also had been listening a great deal to the music of his own generation and aspects of pop, jazz, and even rock and roll permeated his invented "hill" sound.

But then there was that Rodgers family gene. In Richard Rodgers' music, beyond the beautiful melodies, there is an overwhelming quality of yearning, of reaching for transcendence that is impossible to put into words (though Oscar Hammerstein certainly tried). This quality was present with an entirely different and distinct voice in Guettel's music. Practically, it registered in Guettel's note sequences, constructed often in seemingly limitless ascending patterns that never seemed to resolve when and where a listener anticipated. Yet, Guettel's unexpected choices, the resolutions he arrived at, always felt far more satisfying than anything a listener *had* expected.

"I can't say that I studied my grandfather's work in any academic way," Guettel insisted, "or in any systematic way, or even in a chaotic way. Osmotic, maybe. The permeable membrane. The more I try to do this work, the more respect I have for him, though. The time and place of his shows and how they synchronized with where America was at that time, all that stuff is almost secondary to me. The basic dramatic techniques and the surefire instincts that he had about where a number should go, how a scene builds toward a number — he was just very, very, very good at it. Acquiring those skills, just the little I learned on *Floyd*, was mind-blowing to me. The difference that the subtlest things can make in affecting an audience. The great satisfaction that comes with making a change based on a hunch, after having watched the audience, and having it pay off; people enjoying things more, getting something more clearly."

To hear Guettel describe his joy in the minutiae of musical theater craft, one would think he was as devout about the art form as his grandfather had been. On this point, though, he demurred.

"Musical theater in the abstract I'm sort of in love with," he conceded. "I have an uneasy fascination with it and it's really satisfying when it works out. I'm in love with the idea of writing for live human beings who are singing their emotions and moving a story forward through music. But that's so theoretical. Musicals are also a completely marginalized, scoffed at, sort of contemptible field that gets no respect. And they shouldn't have any, for the most part — I don't think musicals have gotten an unfairly old-fashioned reputation. They are old-fashioned in most cases. Plus, they are a very difficult thing to do well, and they're very seldom done well.

"My generation, though, is stuck with the task of trying to reverse that old-fashioned perception. It's not what I want to be spending my energy on; I just want to try to tell my stories in music. But that's the nature of the beast."

Guettel paused and smiled just a little guiltily.

"I'm also in a slightly different situation than a lot of my working colleagues, in that I can do this at my own pace and choose only the projects that I really identify with, because I have the means to. That's probably the greatest legacy my grandfather left me, in practical terms. For me, the value really is in trying to create the most original, moving work that I can, however long it takes. Which isn't to say those aren't the ideals of a lot of people but I just don't have to make the compromises that some people have to make just to get something on. Which can sometimes be very self-defeating. I bet if I were a little poorer I'd probably write faster."

In this sense, of course, Guettel was the antithesis of his willfully poverty-stricken bohemian peer, Jonathan Larson. The two nevertheless shared a similarly righteous aesthetic integrity which, for Larson was enhanced by being poor, and for Guettel was enabled by the cushion of inherited wealth.

"I was friends with Jonathan," said Guettel. "We both had kind of similar ideals. I don't know about goals, but we both wanted to make a statement. I never felt any kind of competitive edge. We were very supportive of each other's incoming, long and hard–fought, first shows. We were kind of on the same schedule and we knew it. It was exciting. We even helped each other with casting. We'd both been working on these things a long time. I'd actually spoken to Billy Aronson too back in 1989 about his *La Bohème* thing. I knew then that it wasn't for me and I still feel I'd never have been able to do the job Jonathan did with it.

"I really thought that his score just bloomed in its last incarnation," Guettel marveled. "It just went to a whole other level of dramatic usefulness and memorable-ness. His overall creation of *Rent* as a piece is like this indestructible vessel for high-energy emotional performances. And that's really one way of defining a good musical theater score: Giving your performers an opportunity to do that and inspiring them to do that. A lot of fantastic scores don't. They aren't that open. *Rent* is just this wide open—fill-me-with-whatever-you-have-every-night—kind of thing. I completely admire it for that. That's not my natural state as a writer. I am an emotional writer but my natural inclination does not create those kind of opportunities. I have too many specifications sometimes, I can be a little persnickety and bossy and over-technical. One of the great things about Jonathan's work was its generosity to the performers. He gave them what they needed and didn't give them more than they needed. It's an art unto itself. But," Guettel added, "I'm learning."

CHAPTER 14

THIS IS THE MOMENT

This is the moment,
This is the time,
When the momentum
And the moment are in rhyme!

—Jekyll & Hyde

Cameron Mackintosh admitted that he was disappointed. Back in 1992 he had generously assigned a fraction of the enormous profits from his many musicals to set up a foundation for the development of new musical theater in America. The money, close to $2 million, had wound up divided among three non-profit New York theaters: Playwrights Horizons, Lincoln Center Theater, and the Manhattan Theater Club, to be spent over a period of five years, a period that, in 1997, was drawing to a close.

"What I had hoped," said Mackintosh, "was that the American theater industry would join in. Sadly, it hasn't happened. There is a great thirst, I think, to re-establish the American musical tradition. This was to kick start things. It's a shame that other people haven't come forward.

"In a nutshell, I get 200–300 musicals sent to me a year," Mackintosh went on, "and most of them, I'm afraid, are pretty awful. Every year I get at least a dozen Cyranos. I got fifteen Hunchbacks last year—'Quasis,' I call them. A particular favorite of mine, which came from the United States, was an ingenious but ghastly combination of *Wuthering Heights* and *Jane Eyre* called *Jane Heights*. I also received a musical about the Krupp family that really made *Springtime for Hitler* seem like *Marat/Sade*.

"I read them all, though," insisted Mackintosh. "I don't get through all of them, with some you just know in two songs exactly what it's going to be like. Occasionally, though, you find someone that is talented. Unfortunately even when they're talented they often can either write a good tune only or a good lyric only or an interesting idea for a show but very rarely do you find all the parts sort of coming together. What I look for first is a story that grabs my attention but also an author's interpretation that is original and has a theatrical vitality."

Mackintosh denied that his era of big musicals was over on Broadway.

"It's simply not true," he said.

So, would Mackintosh be signing over another $2 million for five more years now that the first two million had been spent and the first five years had expired?

"No," Mackintosh replied. "I'm not in a position to at the moment. I'm not saying that down the line I won't. But no. Not now."

In 1997, the average new musical commission to a composer (and/or lyricist) from a non-profit theater was between $15,000 and $20,000. This was hardly enough to carry anyone through the protracted, multi-year development cycle of a new work. The average production budget for a non-profit musical was perhaps $100,000, enough to pay for an orchestra of three to six musicians, at the most.

"You always have to whittle down the number of musicians you can use in a show," acknowledged Michael John LaChiusa. "It's just back-breaking and it does impose limits on what your music can sound like. When you hear how wonderfully orchestrated a Rodgers and Hammerstein score is, it imprints those melodies on your brain. When you don't have that luxury, it constricts the aural experience for an audience. That's one big reason they can't whistle your tunes. They can't hear them properly."

At each non-profit theater in New York where the development of musicals was actively being pursued in 1997—basically, at Playwrights Horizons, Manhattan Theater Club, the New York Shakespeare Festival, and the Vineyard Theater[19]—there now existed what one might call a designated Ira Weitzman, an administrator in charge of ferreting out musical theater talent. These administrators were, respectively, Weitzman, plus Wiley Hausam at the New York Shakespeare Festival, Douglas Aibel at Vineyard Theater, and Lee Johnson at Manhattan Theater Club.

From July 1996 to May 1997, the Manhattan Theater Club had sponsored eleven workshop readings of new musicals and nine "presentations," in which writers auditioned their new work. During that same period, Lincoln Center Theater, the Shakespeare Festival, Vineyard and Playwrights had each staged between three to five new musical workshops.

"Writing for workshops, though, is writing for workshops," pointed out the Public's Wiley Hausam. "You get no training in working before an audience, in sitting at the back of a house and listening to an audience respond and then ruthlessly adjusting from there. Plus, you get infected by—call it experimental aesthetic, if you want to—this thing now pervading the non-profit institutional world that theater is not meant to be entertaining, it's mean to be self-referential. Nobody will pay to come and see that in a musical. From *Oklahoma!* through *West Side Story* the best musicals were built on the premise that you had to satisfy the customer first and then you could rise to the level of art."

"Many shows have suffered from today's developmental process," agreed the Vineyard's Douglas Aibel. "They've actually been diminished by too many workshops, too many artistic directors, directors, dramaturgs, pulling them apart, tearing and tugging away at the writer's vision. It's almost like an endless washer/dryer cycle. The old generation had their developmental process in Boston or Philadelphia doing out-of-town previews where a tough commercial producer was cracking the whip and dollars were riding on every decision and as a result these writers gained an incredible objectivity about their work. Quick judgements and cool-headedness. I wonder if you can only learn that with money on the line."

Clearly, the successes of *Rent* and *Bring in 'da Noise, Bring in 'da Funk*, as well as the existence of Adam Guettel's *Floyd Collins*, reflected pretty positively on the not-for-profit musical theater process. Despite all arguments to the contrary, something seemed to be going right. None of these three musicals had been created "with money on the line," but rather through the workshop process, at least initially. Yet, the practical reality enunciated by Hausam and Aibel was hardly refuted by these successes either. In the end, all three shows had finally coalesced onstage in the theater, before paying audiences.

It would have been too much to expect that the revolutionary excitement generated by these three musicals would immediately be reflected on Broadway. And it wasn't. The 1996–1997 season, though impressively active, with at least four new book musicals, ended up disappointing by any standard, but particularly in light of the hopes generated by *Rent*, *Noise/Funk*, and *Floyd Collins*.

All four of the season's new musicals opened within days of each other during the last week of April. Broadway producers had so little faith in the attention spans of their own industry members that they'd taken to bunching their big musical premiers at the last possible moment before the season's May 1 Tony Awards eligibility deadline, figuring that the last musical seen might very well be the only musical remembered.

Titanic opened first at the Lunt-Fontanne Theater, boasting a really big set, a really big cast, and a really big, bulky score by the composer and lyricist Maury Yeston. What *Titanic* lacked was any depth at all. Its bigness was solely from stem to stern; nothing in this musical's infamous sinking tale ventured below the surface. Yeston's score iterated a handful of anthemic musical phrases and then reiterated them again, and again, and again, couched in big, fat, enriching orchestrations by Jonathan Tunick and turgid choral arrangements for *Titanic's* many strong voices. The show was dead from the deck down. It also was an irresistible target for cheap puns. Of course, it ultimately won the Tony Award for Best Musical of the season.

Steel Pier came next at the Richard Rodgers Theater. Set during a Depression-era dance marathon, the show's book crossbred two stale genres: the who's-left-standing-at-the-end contest tale and the back-from-the-dead ghost romance. The poor, weighted-down result proved a major blunder for all concerned, especially the usually reliable songwriting team of Kander and Ebb and the choreographer Susan Stroman. It closed fairly quickly.

The Life, at the Ethel Barrymore Theater, was a flawed attempt at recapturing the supposedly halcyon days of 42nd Street before the city's recent, increasingly successful, clean-up of the hookers, junkies and assorted lowlifes who'd claimed the neighborhood for themselves in the late 1960s. As ever, composer Cy Coleman supplied some terrific melodies but the crude, profane, and terminally un-hip lyrics contributed by Ira Gasman undermined Coleman's effort. *The Life* was garishly ugly in ways that only a Broadway musical shooting for street relevance and missing badly, could be.

Jekyll & Hyde, the last of Broadway's April musicals that year, was in its way the most insignificant and yet the most disturbing. A calculating exercise in soul-less Andrew Lloyd Webber style, the show marked the full-time arrival on Broadway of an American-born Andrew Lloyd Webber clone named Frank Wildhorn.

Born in Harlem, raised in the Bronx, Queens, and then Florida, Wildhorn had made his fortune in Los Angeles writing hits for everyone from Whitney Houston to Kenny Rogers. A self-taught musician, he'd placed over 200 of his songs on the pop charts, yet still harbored Broadway ambitions.

"I guess I'm part of a generation influenced very much by the music of the '70s and '80s, because we are all products of our own generation," the 38-year-old Wildhorn explained. "Though I have always been a fan and a student of musicals, I was very disillusioned by the American musicals of the 1970s and '80s. They just didn't speak to me. The kind of melodic and harmonic musical vocabulary that I'm interested in exploring, I just didn't hear. In fact, if you take the European shows away from the '70s and '80s, there wasn't much there at all. My influences from an American point of view are much more Leonard Bernstein, Gershwin, and the guys who were pop-song writers. I get called a pop-song writer when I do theater, but I don't apologize for that whatsoever because the fact of the matter is, if those guys were alive and writing today, they'd be trying to write hits, not music for fifteen people in Greenwich Village. They'd be trying to write for as many millions of people as, well, I am. I feel very strongly that if the future of American musicals is going to be a healthy one, it has got to combine the vocabulary of popular music of today with theater music, because we want our own generation to understand and come to the theater and become theater fans. To do that, I think you have to speak to them a little bit. I do that."

In theory, Wildhorn's music would seem to have been just what the Broadway musical needed, infusing the sounds of the moment, the sounds of Top 40 radio, circa 1997, into the Broadway musical mainstream. In reality, though, Wildhorn's music was crushingly banal, comprised almost entirely of treacle and bombast, with very little nuance between. Just like the sounds of Top 40 radio, perhaps. But insufferably so.

In fact, like Lloyd Webber, Wildhorn was firstly a very astute businessman.

"I won't dare do a musical unless there's an album out first," Wildhorn maintained. "It is so hard, whether you're Andrew Lloyd Webber or Frank Wildhorn, it takes so long and you spill so much blood and guts trying to get a new musical on that, if I'm going to do it, I want to make sure I have the support of the music industry to get the score that I've written out into the world. I feel very strongly about that."

Wildhorn had started working on *Jekyll & Hyde* in 1979 while still a student at U.S.C. The musical's first reading had come under the august auspices of John Houseman, when Houseman was creative director of U.S.C.'s theater department, though Wildhorn actually had not been a theater major but a history major.

Jekyll & Hyde (with a new book and lyrics by Leslie Bricusse) received its first professional production in 1990 at the Alley Theater in Houston, after a concept album of the musical had already been released. From 1995 to 1997, the show toured America, traipsing through the regional theater wilderness, bringing to the masses its musical message of reassuringly familiar pop bombast and a schoolbook title easily confused with *The Phantom of the Opera*.

"*Jekyll & Hyde* took a different route than any musical has ever taken in America," insisted Wildhorn, with characteristic understatement. "It's the only American musical to have two albums out before it hit Broadway [the second, a two-CD recording, had been released just prior to the show's first national tour in 1995]. It's certainly the only musical to have as many hits around the world sung by as many people. And this was all before opening night on Broadway. It's the only American show to have a full national tour before opening on Broadway as well. And that's with no Tony Awards and no stars. It's kind of a grass roots kind of thing. But during the tough times for the show, the fact that these two albums were out there selling hundreds and hundreds of thousands and spreading the music all around the world kept the show alive."

One New York drama critic described *Jekyll & Hyde*'s score as music to skate to.[20] Others were even less kind.[21] The show, however, at first managed to survive at the Plymouth Theater largely on the strength of return ticket buyers (self-described "Jekkies") who'd seen *Jekyll & Hyde* on tour and now wanted to see it again on Broadway.[22] By adopting film and pop music marketing techniques already pioneered on Broadway by Lloyd Webber and Cameron Mackintosh—releasing all-star compilation and even original cast albums well in advance of a new musical's opening, conceiving new musicals with an eye to pop demographics—a slick pop-song purveyor like Frank Wildhorn had forged a direct link to America's pop music consumer. Thus, when Wildhorn said, "I just want a show that can be commercial, that can sell records, that can create stars, that crosses over, and all that kind of stuff," one was compelled to listen. Warily.

CHAPTER 15

PURE AND BLAMELESS

Oh, with lips like those
I'd look almost shameless
Oh, but add the nose.
Now I'm pure and blameless.

— *Violet*

"Who would choose this field?" asked Ira Weitzman one afternoon in a restaurant some few blocks from his former office at Lincoln Center, "given what you have to go through."

Weitzman had recently been informed by Lincoln Center Theater that his services as a full-time employee no longer were required. Hereafter, he was told, he'd be working on a part-time, per project basis.

"Still," Weitzman insisted, "I remain...well, maybe not optimistic, just not pessimistic. I continue to fall in love with writers and their work. And there will always be more writers than corporations. Won't there?"

What had happened? André Bishop, Weitzman's long-time employer, said little. Clearly, though, none of Weitzman's projects, from *My Favorite Year* through *Hello Again* to *Chronicle of a Death Foretold* had made Lincoln Center Theater any money. And, in the increasingly corporate, bottom-line oriented universe of musical theater in New York in the 1990s, even for a so-called not-for-profit theater, this fact mattered.

"I couldn't fool myself that Lincoln Center Theater was simply Playwrights Horizons uptown," Bishop would only say. "It can't be. Which doesn't mean we don't have workshops and readings here, and all that. But it is a much more public venue."

"I'm at a crossroads," said Weitzman. "The work that I like to do is not inherently commercial and that leaves me wondering where my place is in musical theater now. I tend to gravitate toward shows that have something to say politically, in the sense of the politics of *Falsettos*—social politics—or that have an emotional intimacy. Or both. I tend to be moved by pieces that are fundamentally humane."

Weitzman was now very much the long-running invisible man of recent musical theater history. Always in the shadows, he had rarely received specific, billed credit for his Playwrights Horizons work. Until his arrival at Lincoln Center Theater with the title, Director of Musical Theater, Ira Weitzman had practically been title-less.[23]

Even Weitzman found it difficult—though not impossible—to quantify what it was that he did.

"I created a method of doing something that hadn't really been done in the non-profit theater," he said. "Sometimes I feel like a man out of time. Though I can't say that I would want to go back in time either, the shows way back when were pretty shallow. But there were these producers who were hands on and creative; all these impresarios, Sam Harris, George Cochran—people I idolize, who were really for the artists. They also were great businessmen but that was when it only cost a fraction of what it does today and everything recouped in three months."

Weitzman was not a producer, not officially, at least. Many in the industry minimized the importance of his contributions to the musicals he'd worked on. And yet, through his nurturing of new talent, Weitzman had clearly helped shape the evolution of musical theater over the previous two decades.

Was this a good thing? Under Weitzman's watch, musicals had grown more intimate, more personal, and in that sense, often more self-indulgent. Was the cause of musical theater really advanced by terminally sensitive musicals? Clearly, in commercial terms, the answer was a resounding no. But in terms of art, the answer was a far more conflicted perhaps.

In the wake of his disengagement from Lincoln Center Theater, Weitzman had recently returned to Playwrights Horizons, where he'd been warmly welcomed—also on a part-time basis.

Of course, he brought a new musical with him: *Violet*, by the 36-year-old composer Jeanine Tesori and the 35-year-old lyricist Brian Crawley. *Violet* opened at Playwrights in March 1997. The story of a facially scarred teenaged girl down South in the '60s who sets off on a bus journey in search of a televangelist she believes has the power to heal her, *Violet* was a quintessential Weitzman project. It was small in scale—cunningly directed by Susan Schulman. It was big at heart, with some terrific performances, especially by Lauren Ward as Violet and Michael McElroy and Michael Park as the two young soldiers who vie for her. It was, at times genuinely moving, with soulful '60s-period-derived tunes from Tesori and nifty, well-integrated lyrics from Crawley.

Tesori, a rare female composer in this overwhelmingly male-dominated medium, had studied music in her Port Washington, Long Island home until she was fourteen, ultimately pursuing a pre-med major at Barnard College for two years before giving that up to return to music for good. After conducting the orchestra for an Off-Broadway musical called *City Suite*, when she was nineteen, Tesori had gone on to receive many Broadway conducting and vocal-arranging jobs, including supplying the dance music for *The Secret Garden* (where she'd worked with Schulman) and conducting the original Broadway production of *Tommy*. All along, though, Tesori had dreamed about writing a musical herself.

"I saw a Showtime movie, this student film called *Violet*," she recalled. "I found out it had been based on a short story, *The Ugliest Pilgrim*, by Doris Betts, which I read and loved. That book then went into my drawer. When I was doing *Tommy*, though, it just struck me one day that it was time."

Tesori joined the BMI musical theater workshop.

"BMI was a wonderful stepping stone for me just by giving me a deadline, which I absolutely need and I think a lot of artists do. It's very difficult to write in limbo. I met a wonderful group there, including Brian Crawley.

"Brian was very new to musicals and I'd been around them by that point for a long time, so we decided we'd talk about five or six classic musicals—their structure, what made them work, just the two of us. I chose *West Side Story*, *My Fair Lady*, *Gypsy*, *Sunday in the Park*, and *Carousel*. They're all just beautifully structured, really well-written. I think that all of those teams were ruthless about making their shows work."

Tesori then took *The Ugliest Pilgrim* out of her desk drawer. "It was a thorny route, getting the rights," she said. "As soon as we got an agreement, though, I left the city for about seven or eight months, rented a house, put a grand piano in it and just did nothing but write the show, read, and plan trips down South for research. Brian and I worked mostly by fax and phone. As soon as we had six songs done we submitted them to the Eugene O'Neill Music Theater Conference and, well, we got the top honor, which is you get two weeks near O'Neill's old home on the water in Connecticut working with actors, everything free.

"We didn't set out to write a Broadway show or even an Off-

Broadway show, we just wanted to write something that could be done in regional theaters. I still believe that if you tell a story and you tell it well, people will come. It's the only thing that interests me about writing for theater. It's the only thing that interests me about seeing theater."

"How did I pick *Violet*?" asked Ira Weitzman. "I knew Jeanine, I had tried to hire her a great many times as a musical director, and finally one day she said to me, 'I'm taking six months off to write,' and I said, 'To write what?' and she said—she was just like me in this, it would have been my answer too—'I can't tell you yet. What if it isn't good?'

"After the O'Neill Conference, Jeanine and Brian did a little reading on Theater Row. At that point *Violet* was one-act long with three-quarters of that first act written. I had a scheduling conflict and couldn't make their reading. My assistant at the time, Chris Burney, went, came back, and said, 'Check it out, it's your kind of show.' I was on the phone faster than a speeding bullet. 'Jeanine, I'm sorry I couldn't make your reading but Chris said it was wonderful. Do you have a script and a tape yet?' 'We're making the tape today,' she said.

"When they sent it over, I listened to the first song and I didn't even listen to anything else. I called them up and said, 'What do you need? I'll give it to you.'"

Violet had a four-day workshop at Lincoln Center Theater in March 1995 and another longer one in August.

"We were ready at that point," said Tesori. "It's always amazing to me what you learn when you first see your work onstage in a workshop with staging and everything. Things that you believed to be right and precise and true somehow don't work and you not only see that but you also see why. I don't like doing more than one workshop, though. After that the returns truly diminish."

Tesori, Crawley, and Weitzman waited until April 1996 for a

commitment from Lincoln Center Theater to formally schedule *Violet*. Lincoln Center Theater had a one-year option on the piece. But when Lincoln Center Theater failed to schedule *Violet*, relations between the theater and Weitzman began to sour. It was agreed that Lincoln Center Theater would relinquish its option on *Violet* and let Weitzman take it with him.

Though no one cared to acknowledge it, there was an expectation that *Violet* would transfer to an Off-Broadway or even a Broadway house once it opened. The necessary reviews, especially the review from the *New York Times*,[24] were not, however, "money reviews." *Violet* was not a boffo musical. Its pleasures were more subtle and thoughtful. Many critics missed them altogether.

Violet also was hardly flawless. The choice to leave Violet's scarred face a matter of metaphor rather than an onstage visual reality may have deprived the show of its central drama. What was this pretty, pretty young girl so worried about, audiences couldn't help but wonder? One tended to lose sight of the show's fundamental premise.

Still, *Violet* was an extremely well-realized, original, yet accessible piece of work. It deserved to be treated better.

"I'm not actually disappointed, strangely enough," Tesori admitted. "When I started, I thought I should write because I felt like I had something to say. My expectations were nil, this simply was something that I had to do. I needed to. And I did. Now, I can do it again. There'll be more."

CHAPTER 16

HAKUNA MATATA

Hakuna Matata!
Ain't no passing craze.
— *The Lion King*

Garth Drabinsky could have been a character created by Disney. There was something cartoonish about his grandiosity, a Cruella De Vil, Dalmatian-coat preposterousness about his purported criminal wickedness. Stricken by polio at age three, the 46-year-old Drabinsky even walked with a villainous limp. Plus, he was a Canadian. Nothing about the man suggested that he should truly be taken seriously.

Yet, as just about everyone on Broadway saw it in 1997, Garth Drabinsky was the industry's new "two ton gorilla" (according to one producer too intimidated to speak for attribution). With impressive speed and seemingly bottomless resources, Drabinsky had, in just four years, powered his Toronto-based Livent Entertainment Corporation into the forefront of Broadway musical theater production, voraciously snapping up potential properties for musical adaptation and hiring some of the best and brightest theatrical talent around to do his bidding. He'd acquired two landmark 42nd Street theaters, recombining them into one cavernous home base for Livent musicals: the Ford Center for the Performing Arts. Yes, this was the first Broadway theater to have its naming rights sold, to a car company, no less.

Ragtime was Livent's first original new musical to hit Broadway when it opened at the Ford Center in December 1997, following two lavish

Livent revivals—of *Show Boat* and *Candide*, respectively. The production path pursued by *Ragtime*, as willfully laid out by Drabinsky, was an unorthodox one that now would serve as a blueprint for all future Livent project development, Drabinsky proclaimed. This included many controversial innovations, including the use of market-testing focus groups to fine-tune *Ragtime*'s script, and the sponsoring of a contest to select the show's composer and lyricist. Ten songwriting teams had been invited to submit four songs each, head to head, before Lynn Ahrens and Stephen Flaherty captured the commission.

Many in the non-profit world considered this selection process absurd or worse, an abdication of judgment and taste. That Ahrens and Flaherty were non-profit alumni who had here made good, rendered the whole business either modestly encouraging or even more ominous, depending on one's point of view.

"I don't think a competition is productive," reflected Stephen Sondheim. "But, then again, how else was a Garth Drabinsky going to hear the work of new, young composers? A competition was kind of the way I got the job on my first musical, *Saturday Night*; it just wasn't a competition on tape, it was an in-person audition. I got the script and Lemuel Ayers, the producer, and Julie Epstein, one of the book writers, told me to write three songs on spec, so I picked three spots and wrote three songs. Did anyone else submit other than me? I know they approached Frank Loesser but he turned them down. On the other hand, everybody auditioned for *Gypsy*; Carolyn Leigh and Cy Coleman, Betty [Comden] and Adolph [Green]. Carolyn and Cy submitted a song called 'Be a Performer,' which eventually ended up in another of their shows, *Little Me*. It's not so much that competitions in and of themselves are wrong-headed. It just depends on whose head you're talking about."

"The corporate structure of my company is set up on a film studio model," Drabinsky himself explained, in characteristic corporate-speak. "The object is to be an integrated structure that not only owns the theaters but has the complete capacity to develop new material from inception. Out of that pressure-free environment I think the best work comes. Since I came out of the film world, I learned a lot of bad things and a few good things. One of the good things was that they were way ahead of theater in terms of utilizing analysis and research. People don't lie, you get 150 of them together, there's a consensus usually and that's great. I love consensus."

"There has been an abdication of creativity and responsibility by our producers," observed Jujamcyn's Rocco Landesman, who'd recently rocked Broadway's insular inner circle by entering into a landmark agreement with the industry's leading national tour packager, Pace Theatrical Group. This new combination, Landesman promised, would also be modeled along the lines of an old Hollywood film studio. That the words "film studio" now underlay the operations of three of Broadway's most powerful theater producers: Livent, Pace-Jujamcyn, and of course, Disney, was more than a little scary. Still, as Landesman saw it, "By going largely with writing team–originated ideas, rather than initiating our own projects, as film studios once did, we've seen millions just get burned. I believe we may be looking at an era's end here. The producers have gotta get a grip."

Corporate fiscal responsibility was the catchphrase on Broadway in 1997 and the soon-to-be-indicted Garth Drabinsky was that catchphrase's poster boy. Disney-esque? Dalí-esque would be more accurate. Yet, Broadway producers and creative types alike all prostrated themselves before Drabinsky and his siren song.

Drabinsky had first become a force in the entertainment business in Canada in 1979 when he'd gained control of Cineplex, a movie house owner with eighteen screens. Merging Cineplex with the Odeon corporation in 1984, Drabinsky had created North America's second-largest movie theater chain, only to be forced out of Cineplex Odeon in 1989 by his own shareholders after engaging in some "very aggressive accounting methods." [25] Drabinsky then set up Livent with business partner Myron Gottlieb. Though the company only managed to hang on to one Toronto theater, the Pantages, in settling Drabinsky's Cineplex Odeon account, it also secured for that theater the exclusive exhibiting rights to one show, Lloyd Webber's *Phantom of the Opera*, for its Toronto run. Parlaying *Phantom*'s massive Toronto success, Drabinsky took Livent public in 1993. Shortly thereafter, he hit New York and Broadway.

"When we develop musicals," Drabinsky said, "there are a number of parameters that I live by. One, because we're a public company and we have an infrastructure and we have financing and we have a lot more than one show being developed at a time, I don't rush any show into production. I don't want to be sitting in New York in a 1,500- or 2,000-seat theater trying to fix a show, which is insane. What I want to do is to give a creative constituency enough time to luxuriate if you will, in examining and re-examining, evaluating and re-evaluating the material. How does one do that? First of all they need to submit it to me as the first interface in that process and I want to have the time to rigorously scrutinize, criticize, and evaluate it myself. After we've gone through that process, then I want to bring together a group of actors and let them read the work. During the reading of the work, we use the preparation for the reading as another form of workshop to further cultivate and change the work even before the reading process is over. There may then be much more structural work to be done, a second reading may happen and then other layers of the creative team will be in place by that time, so you'll have a lighting designer and you'll have a choreographer and you'll have your sound people and your scenic design and you'll have costumes and they all can look together at the work as a team, standing back. Then I've historically given people *time* to workshop a show. It's not a one- or two-week situation with actors and music stands in front of them, but it's really a rehearsal hall, with minimum props and minimum lighting, a couple of pianos, and a lot of great actors. Put it on its feet, I say. We let our imaginations rule but beyond that I want to see whether or not there's a fluid transition from scene to scene happening, whether there's coherence, whether there's immediate emotional connection with the characters. If all that is happening, then I know I'm on my way to solving the problem.

"That's the environment that I've attempted to create," concluded Drabinsky, "so that the best people in the theater have an opportunity to work in comfortable circumstances, and not necessarily in New York, often in Toronto, where it's cheaper and it's Canadian dollars being spent rather than much, much more expensive American dollars. That's been the theory from the beginning."

Of course, this sounded just great to Broadway's creative community.

"Garth is one of the few, if not the only producer now, who is also a great promoter," said Graciela Daniele, who worked for Drabinsky as *Ragtime*'s choreographer. "Garth plans things extremely well and allows the authors and the cast to have time. The collaborative effort that I'm used to having, especially with Ira Weitzman, say—is the same as working for Garth, with one big difference, of course: economics. When we do a show for a non-profit, there's not much money, so we have to be extremely frugal, work rather fast, and constantly think about the budget. In *Ragtime* we did numerous readings and workshops, and then we did a production in Toronto and one in L.A. before coming to New York. It's like it used to be in the old times when I was a performer, the out-of-town experience, which was so helpful because the more you work at something, you improve."

Ragtime was an enormous $10 million machine of a musical. Its sets were massive, its cast was too. Daniele's choreography along with the direction of Frank Galatti seemed to keep both in constant motion. *Ragtime*'s narrative, taken from E. L. Doctorow's sprawling best-selling novel, encompassed an unusual number of plots and had at least five central characters.

"I like musicals that have numbers of characters in them," explained Drabinsky, "not one story but three or four stories that overlap, because that gives you reason to depart and thus keep people absorbed. There needs to be a reason for singing; not to stop the show and say, okay, let's sing, but to project the story and keep it moving, keep it ahead of the audience. *That* is another problem."

Ragtime's onstage impact was that of a huge, gleaming Mack truck efficiently rolling over its audience. The adjective that best summed the show up was: well-tooled. Ahrens and Flaherty's score and Daniele's choreography lent the proceedings a measure of humanity, as did many of the principal performances, Brian Stokes Mitchell's and Audra McDonald's, in particular. Still, the overwhelming impression was that of a new corporate product efficiently assembled by a team of professionals.

Many who'd seen *Ragtime* in one of its earlier incarnations testified that this calcification had occurred through the very process that Drabinsky had designed. *Ragtime* had been hammered at until it was almost all polished surface. Sometimes, apparently, the luxury of too much time creating a musical was as debilitating as the burden of too little.

There was one other vital lesson that Drabinsky's *Ragtime* production helped illustrate, by omission. This lesson, extraordinarily enough, was delivered that same season by the big, bad Walt Disney Company—Broadway's other "evil" corporate presence in 1997—with its visually stunning production of *The Lion King*.

Disney's lesson was a simple one. Despite the company's reputation for micro-management (a reputation that certainly rivaled Garth Drabinsky's); despite the fact that Disney's previous cartoon-to-Broadway musical transfer, *Beauty and the Beast*, had been a by-the-numbers, theme park–quality adaptation; despite the fact that *The Lion King* was Disney's most valuable cartoon property, the most successful cartoon feature ever made, actually—despite all of this—Disney chose to back a director with an independent vision for *The Lion King*, rather than impose its own vision on some director. What Disney had somehow figured out, which Drabinsky never did, was a fundamental secret to making any successful musical: Entrust it to one true artist's vision and let it ride.

In *Lion King's* case, that artist was Julie Taymor, a veteran *avant garde*, non-profit theater iconoclast who combined an astonishingly original design sensibility with a wide-ranging, multi-cultural mastery of traditional theatrical arts and crafts, including and especially puppetry.

Taymor's aesthetic could well be described as the antithesis of Disney's. Her creations were always fiercely individual music-theater works that never condescended, never pandered to the lowest common denominator, and never compromised. From the earliest work of her career in the 1970s, through recent pieces created with her longtime partner, the gifted composer Elliot Goldenthal — shows like *The Green Bird*, a *commedia dell'arte* puppet extravaganza, and *Juan Darién*, a ritualistic riff on Mexican death art — Taymor had continually blended inspired puppetry with an extraordinarily unfettered theatrical imagination.

Disney first approached Taymor in 1995 about taking on *The Lion King*. Her response was reticent, to say the least. Once she said yes, though, she completely re-imagined *The Lion King* for the stage, imposing upon it her unique theatrical aesthetic in a manner that proved perfectly organic. It opened in November 1997 at the New Amsterdam Theater — the newly-restored 42nd Street former-home of Ziegfeld's *Follies* — that Disney had refurbished at enormous expense. *The Lion King* was an instantaneous smash hit, a whirl of intricately crafted puppets and glorious African-inspired design elements, the likes of which no one on Broadway had ever before seen.

And yet, what *The Lion King* was not, from a strictly musical point of view, was an original musical. The movie version had been salted with five original songs by Elton John and Tim Rice, three of which had become immediate song favorites for children, the anthemic

"Circle of Life," the farcical "Hakuna Matata," and the romantic pop ballad "Can You Feel the Love Tonight." The film also had won an Academy Award for its soundtrack, by veteran soundtrack composer Hans Zimmer, a symphonic Hollywood exercise ornamented with rampant Africanisms.

Bringing *The Lion King* to the stage had meant bolstering this slender score with enough new songs to justify calling the results a musical. How this augmentation was accomplished—where the music came from and why—represented a benchmark in the displacing of Broadway musical theater tradition by movie-style Disney corporate culture.

The notion that a Broadway musical was generally the work of a single composer and/or lyric writer was a cherished convention in modern musical theater. *The Lion King*, however, did not abide by it. Though Elton John and Tim Rice were billed as the show's lead composer and lyricist, they did not, in fact, write the new Broadway score alone. Rather, program credits revealed a score composed by committee, with no fewer than seven composers and lyricists cited, including Taymor herself, plus a crew of film-industry music professionals, all of them veterans of *The Lion King* movie.

Musical theater scores generally consisted of original songs written to a script's specification, supplemented perhaps by an occasional "trunk song" culled by the composer from previous work. *The Lion King* also proved atypical in this regard. John and Rice were only reenlisted to compose three new tunes for the Broadway *Lion King*. John said he was at first perplexed by his limited role.

"They told me: 'We want three new songs—these are the situations.' They didn't ask me for any more than three. Which I wondered about at first. But I think they were looking to mix in more authentically African music, to accentuate the African; a very clever move on their part. In fact, some of the African things work better than some of my things."

Taymor confirmed that her prime musical concern in re-making *Lion King* was to make the movie's authentic, subsidiary African music more prominent. To accomplish this goal she was aided by a cache of pre-existing, Disney-owned music.

"When I was first offered this job," she said, "along with a CD of the soundtrack, I was given an album called *Rhythm of the Pridelands: Music Inspired by Disney's The Lion King*. I was told that anything I could figure out to use on it was a plus. I had really been thrilled by the sound of the South African chorus in the movie and the sound behind that chorus was a musician named Lebo Morake (Lebo M.). *Rhythm of the Pridelands* had more of Lebo's music. A lot more. And that really excited me."

A performer since the age of nine, Soweto native Lebo M. had been a product of South Africa's nightclub scene before attending the Duke Ellington School of Music in Washington, D.C. and then working in Hollywood.

"When Disney approached me to write the soundtrack," Hans Zimmer said, "I knew exactly who I wanted to work with. I just about had to send out search parties into the African bush to find Lebo. He *is* the movie."

Lebo M.'s *Lion King* film contribution had consisted of background music co-written with Zimmer along with vocal arranging in his own African idiom. The glorious Zulu cries that opened the movie so thrillingly were also shouted out by Lebo M. himself.

Recorded primarily at Zimmer's studio, *Rhythm of the Pridelands* had been conceived as an opportunity for the film's team of supporting musical contributors to capitalize on the movie's vast success. The disc contained eleven songs, most of them sung by Lebo M. and co-written with another composer/lyricist who'd played a significant role in the movie, Mark Mancina, a composer of blockbuster film soundtracks, including *Speed, Twister* and *Con Air*, and a Grammy winner as co-arranger and producer of *The Lion King*'s soundtrack album. For Broadway, Mancina was again tapped as something of a ghostwriter.

"I was hired to put *The Lion King* musical together with Julie," Mancina said. "My responsibility was the entire score, whether that meant adapting new songs, re-writing songs, writing new songs, writing new score, adapting old score. My only other collaborators were Julie and Lebo. Everybody else whose name is up there was only involved in that they may have written a melody or something that ended up being adapted to the theater from the film. But they were not directly involved in the creation of our show. Tim Rice attended a meeting once in a while and a few performances. Otherwise they were not there."

Elton John acknowledged that he never actually saw a performance of *The Lion King* on Broadway until opening night. "I intended to," he said. "But unfortunately there were deaths and funerals to attend and I just didn't feel like traveling."

As Mancina explained it, "Elton submitted demo tapes. The form was then completely left up to me — how many choruses, what keys, modulations. For Elton it was: 'Here's the melody, here's the lyric, good luck.'"

Taymor confirmed this. "Mark and I did an enormous amount of work with Elton's songs to make them fit with the scenes and the characters. And Mark wrote some other score stuff based on Hans Zimmer's music in the movie. Most of the rest came from songs on *Rhythm of the Pridelands* that I loved. 'Lea Hallala,' by Lebo and Hans Zimmer, became Nala's song 'Shadowlands,' with a new lyric by Mark and Lebo. 'Lala,' by Lebo, Zimmer, and his partner Jay Rifkin, one of the *Rhythm* CD's producers, became 'Endless Night,' which I wrote a new lyric for because it was just easier than telling a new lyricist what I wanted. 'The Lioness Hunt' and 'Grasslands Chant' are all Lebo's, written right from the choreography. And 'He

Lives in You' was a song idea Mark had with Lebo for the movie that was never used. The minute I heard it, though, I knew it was on a level with 'Circle of Life;' that it was our other major theme song."

"Lebo and I had never worked in any kind of theater and Julie loved that," maintained Mancina. "She loved our inexperience because it kind of made it limitless for us. I really felt that 30 to 40 percent of what we did would get cut out of the show, that Disney would come along and say, 'Well this is too long, this is too African, kids won't get this.' But in fact they left everything exactly the way we wrote it."

"Nothing was thrown out," Taymor marveled. "Everything worked. It's not like I think every single song is my favorite thing in the world, but I do think they all have their place."

That the music worked at all was a further tribute to the strength of Taymor's vision and the omniverousness of her aesthetic. For the *Lion King* score seemed ultimately to have been composed by Julie Taymor using multiple composers as her instruments.

"People expect this to be an Elton John musical," said Taymor. "And that's really not the case, nor do we pretend that it is. I'd like this to be seen as an exciting, positive collaboration rather than, 'Oh, there were so many composers.' What I love about all the music is that the South African sound and the orchestrations pull all of the pieces together so that it's not one eclectic mess. *Lion King*'s power is that it is a true bridge between Western pop, South African pop, and South African traditional music."

Elton John, for one, seemed persuaded. "You have to work by committee," he said. "It's part of the process, I guess. I mean, who am I to argue?"

Could a truly unified score emerge when a musical's official composer never laid eyes on his production until opening night? Could a dramatically coherent musical be created by proxy?

With the advent of *The Lion King* the answer to that question for all practical purposes was, yes.

But this didn't make it a good thing.

CHAPTER 17

SATURN RETURNS

Take me up to a higher altitude.
Take me all the way!
— *Saturn Returns*

The 1997–1998 musical theater season on Broadway was as busy and as varied as any in at least 20 years. Partly, this was indeed the result of economics — not the much-touted economics of corporate responsibility but the diametrical opposite, in fact: Wall Street was on a roll and there was investment money out there for Broadway to burn. As a result, beside the two corporate behemoth musicals, *Ragtime* and *The Lion King*, which dominated and all but blotted out the rest, there were four more significant new productions on Broadway in 1997–1998; four that, in scale, quality and subject matter really ran the gamut.

The first, *Side Show*, opened at the Richard Rodgers Theater in October. The true story of a pair of Siamese twins who'd been minor Depression-era celebrities, *Side Show* had a robust, nearly sung-through, score by Henry Krieger and Bill Russell, and nice performances by Emily Skinner and Alice Ripley as the twins. Watching these two fall in love with different men, while vowing to each other that, "I Will Never Leave You," was certainly one of musical theater history's weirder moments. *Side Show* was an eccentric original, as far removed from corporate conformity as one could get. Some loved it, some hated it. Indifference was not an option.

Next, by a matter of days, came *Triumph of Love* at the Royale Theater, a musical adaptation of the 18th-century farce by Marivaux.

Producer Margo Lion, backed by Jujamcyn, placed a very noble bet for her $3.5 million venture on an unknown 30-year-old composer named Jeffrey Stock. To a great extent, the bet paid off. The Yale-educated Stock, though not earth-shakingly original, contributed a Sondheim-inflected score that complemented elegantly Marivaux's tale of romantic conquests in the face of age and gender-bending misunderstandings. One song, the sensuous and conflicted "Serenity," stood out, with lovely lyrics by Susan Birkenhead, as sung to perfection by Betty Buckley.

Yet, *Triumph of Love* was severely weakened by the broad, comic-book tone imparted to it by its director, Michael Mayer. The charm of its individual parts did not cohere. Critics were stinting in their praise, audiences largely unmoved.

Margo Lion saw it another way. "Modest-sized musicals in small Broadway houses are an indulgence today," she reflected. "For something this unknown you need the *New York Times* behind you and/or a massive marketing budget. At least one or the other."

Triumph of Love had neither.[26] It faded away quickly, in *Lion King*'s wake.

The third major Broadway musical that year was Frank Wildhorn's *The Scarlet Pimpernel*. Yet another concept album by-product, the show, which opened in November at the Minskoff, offered music interchangeable with Wildhorn's score for *Jekyll & Hyde*. No attempt seemingly had been made to convey character or dramatic situation beyond the generic application of the Wildhorn ballad style and the Wildhorn anthem style. Savaged by critics,[27] the musical refused to die, distinguishing itself solely by remaining open despite half-sold houses.[28]

The season's final musical, Paul Simon's *The Capeman*, which opened at the Marquis Theater in January 1998, also was the season's greatest disappointment, even with all the negative press that had anticipated it. On paper, Simon had seemed such an ideal choice for the hazardous crossover from pop music to Broadway. His gorgeously crafted pop songs had always been filled with drama and character. As a Broadway newcomer, he seemed a natural.

But Simon, a notoriously controlling perfectionist, could not accommodate himself to the collaborative exigencies of musical theater. The evolution of his musical quickly had become front-page news as one creative team member after another was jettisoned or jumped ship.[29]

Capeman's book—written by Simon with the Noble Prize–winning poet Derek Walcott—told the story of Salvador Agron, a sixteen-year-old Puerto Rican street gang member who, in 1959, murdered two teenagers in a New York playground while wearing a long, red-lined, black cape, gaining for himself the tabloid nickname, "The Capeman." The show would have been a tough sell under any circumstances. Simon's difficulties working with established musical theater professionals only exacerbated an already fraught project.

Capeman onstage was an often muted, oddly withdrawn affair, as if Simon's own reticence communicated itself almost physically to the production. Yet, Simon's score was charismatic and intriguing, filled with a haunting 1950s doo-wop romanticism, infused with raw Latin rhythm. The music, however, made little effort to engage or advance the dramatic narrative. By the second act, what should have been cathartic had grown stolid and tedious.

Some critics struggled to distinguish the show's legitimate strengths from its many liabilities.[30] Others did not.[31] All too soon *The Capeman* was history.

Off-Broadway, *Hedwig and the Angry Inch* brought a welcome touch of the kinky and bizarre to musical theater's universe, along with a decidedly untraditional score entirely composed of heavy-metal/glam-rock pastiche. When it re-opened for a commercial run at the

Jane Street Theater in February 1998 following a couple of brief showcases over the previous two seasons, younger, downtown audiences especially flocked to it.

A one-man performance piece, essentially, by its author and star, the actor John Cameron Mitchell, *Hedwig* related the hilariously troubled life-story of an East-Berlin rock singer, his botched sex change operation, and life on the road in America.

Accompanying Mitchell onstage was a band, Cheater, led by the show's swashbuckling 32-year-old composer and lyricist, Stephen Trask.

"Rock and roll is so theatrical," insisted Trask. "So much character is developed in rock and roll."

A product of the Connecticut bar band circuit and Wesleyan University, Trask had met Mitchell in 1990 while flying back from California, after both had changed seats to escape the in-flight movie. Four years later, they'd begun writing *Hedwig*, a show, as Trask put it, "about a rock star looking back over his life and searching for his other half."

Trask conceded he had little patience for musical theater. "I'm interested in all forms of American music," he said, "except Rodgers and Hammerstein. I don't like the sacrifices you have to make to write a musical. I mean, why put a bad song into a show just to have it in the show? The form never moved me."

Trask also admitted he'd had little actual theatergoing experience. "The only theater I've ever seen has been whatever shows John has been in. Still," he concluded, "I want to continue working on a mix of theater, rock band, film and dance, like *Hedwig*, except with people paying attention to *me*."

In March, Adam Guettel finally returned with *Saturn Returns*, his song cycle follow-up to *Floyd Collins*, at the New York Shakespeare Festival.

"Half of the material was based on these classical Greek myths that I'd been interested in for a long time," Guettel explained, " stuff that I'd written privately over the years. The other half came from this 19th-century hymnal that I happened upon, this book of texts without music that sort of spoke to me in a bookstore, even though I'm Jewish. So I bought it and just started writing music. The original title for the piece actually was *Myths and Hymns*."[32]

Saturn Returns had sensational songs, instantly recognizable as the work of Adam Guettel, whose voice now was arguably the most distinctive in musical theater. The melodies roiled with such sweet, awful desires and hopes, always reaching, it seemed, for satisfactions not just out-of-reach but out of place and time. There was wit too, and even slapstick humor, both in the intricate tunes and in the frequently ingenious lyrics.

What the show lacked was a performance tone onstage that tied up all this marvelous music into the theatrical occasion it deserved. Director Tina Landau seemed torn between the impulse to simply allow the songs to speak for themselves and an urge to apply cabaret performance values that were strictly from Vegas. There was also unavoidable frustration in sitting and listening to so much spectacularly original theater music absent a story to drive it.

"My general taste is totally counter to this sort of thing," Guettel conceded. "I hate wishy-washy pieces about the world and faith, I like stories. But I found myself drawn to this material."

When was Adam Guettel going to give the world another new musical?

Adam Guettel could not say.

Perhaps the most inspiring development of the wildly eventful 1997–1998 musical theater season was not an onstage event at all but rather the release of a debut solo album, *Way Back to Paradise*, by the three-time Tony Award–winning Broadway singer and actress Audra McDonald.

Way Back to Paradise functioned as an introduction not merely to McDonald's extravagant vocal gifts but also as a primer, an orientation guide, to the work of the four most promising young composers in musical theater: Guettel, LaChiusa, Ricky Ian Gordon, and Jason Robert Brown, plus one talented newcomer, Jenny Giering. Their songs were the sum of McDonald's debut; fourteen songs in all.

Sequenced as a suite, these songs illuminated the many facets of both McDonald and her composers' expressive range. There was the innocence and joy of Gordon's "Dream Variations," written for *Only Heaven*, a Langston Hughes song cycle; the transporting ecstasies of sorrow in Guettel's "Come to Jesus," which had been part of *Saturn Returns*; the desperate devotion of Brown's "You Don't Know This Man," from a forthcoming new musical by Brown called *Parade*; and the exhilarating, unflinching fury of LaChiusa's title song, composed for an operatic adaptation of *Medea* that McDonald soon would be tackling onstage.

Debut solo albums selflessly shared with others certainly were not the rule in the music-theater business. McDonald, however, did not seem to understand this.

"When it's music that fills my soul there's just no fear," she insisted.

Born in Berlin, Germany, McDonald's musical destiny seemed, in retrospect, so genetically predetermined that, McDonald liked to say, if she hadn't sung well, "I probably would have been sent back." Her father, a career military man, had been a music major in college. Her mother, an educator, and both of her grandmothers, were pianists who sang. Raised in Fresno, California, where six of her aunts toured as a gospel troupe, McDonald's initial musical apprenticeship had been served at a local dinner theater beginning at the age of eight, where she'd fallen in love with the Broadway musical. A later headlong dive into opera at the Juilliard School proved devastating. "It just wasn't me," McDonald said. "I had danced around the room singing to Barbra Streisand. That's what I wanted to do."

Granted a "mental sabbatical," as she described it, from Juilliard, McDonald had landed a part almost immediately in a touring company of *The Secret Garden*. Slipping back into town to hurriedly audition for Lincoln Center Theater's then-impending production of *Carousel*, McDonald performed spectacularly, only to faint mid-song on the stage of the Mitzi E. Newhouse Theater. ("In my mind, I was done, but I heard people running and these cries: 'Pick her up!'") She got the job anyway and wound up winning a Tony Award as Carrie Pipperidge. For her next audition—Terrence McNally's *Master Class*—McDonald cancelled in panic a half-hour before the call. Again she got the job and again won a Tony. Her third Tony Award, for *Ragtime*, had come without any notable audition disasters.

As Ethel Merman had Gershwin, Porter, and Berlin, Audra McDonald now had Brown, Giering, Gordon, Guettel, and LaChiusa; which was a nice thought. Asked what she hoped people would take away from her record, McDonald answered fiercely: "A desire to know these composers better." Reminded that *Way Back to Paradise* was in fact *her* record, she giggled, then sobered quickly, "I'm nowhere near finished with these boys," McDonald insisted. "And the girl."

CHAPTER 18

ELABORATE LIVES

We all live such elaborate lives.

— *Elaborate Lives: The Legend of Aida*

The face of the Walt Disney Company on Broadway had many masks in 1998. Some were daring and innovative like those of *The Lion King*, others were theme park–safe yet intimidating; both beauty and beast. All were nearly impenetrable. Behind these masks, though, stood two real characters—a matched pair of Disney executives who together constituted the company's unvarnished Broadway face.

Peter Schneider was president and Thomas Schumacher vice president, respectively, of both Walt Disney Theatrical Productions and Disney's feature animation division out in Hollywood. Unknown and mostly unseen in New York save for a triumphant, nationally televised dash to the stage of Radio City Music Hall in June to jointly claim *The Lion King*'s Tony Award for Best Musical, they were, in 1998, Broadway's most powerful concealed weapons.

"Hi. We're the Disney guys."

At 9:30 on a Monday morning in August, 1998, Schneider and Schumacher stood at the head of a long table in a large New York rehearsal studio at 890 Broadway facing 60-some-odd Disney employees, all of them nervously contemplating their first day on a new job. *Elaborate Lives: The Legend of Aida*, Disney's follow-up musical to *The Lion King*, was about to begin rehearsals for an October 7 premiere out of town at the Alliance Theater in Atlanta.

159

The Alliance was a well-regarded regional theater with a mostly white subscription audience and an aggressive, nationally renowned artistic director named Kenny Leon, who was black.

Beaming mischievously, Schneider and Schumacher worked the crowd of administrators, cast and crew; just a couple of wisenheimers who happened to be paying the bills.

Schumacher: "We're very informal."

Schneider: "Yeah, we just don't like to talk."

Schumacher: "We don't?"

From the sidelines, Leon watched with a detached smile. "I love watching those guys work," he muttered.

But what exactly was the Alliance Theater's role in all this? Would it have any influence at all on this huge Disney production in its midst?

Leon's smile widened. "Absolutely none," he said. "But we're feeding at the top of the food chain."

Elaborate Lives had no masks. A rock and roll retelling of opera's *Aida* story, it did have a multi-racial cast of twenty-eight relative unknowns, á la *Rent*, including a *Rent* alumna, Sherie Scott, as the pharaoh's daughter Amneris, and Heather Headley—Broadway's original Nala in *The Lion King*—as Aida, the Nubian slave whom Radames, Amneris' betrothed, loves and ultimately martyrs himself alongside. The show also would have a pioneering laser-powered set that disdained conventional cables and pulleys in favor of theme-park technology devised by Disney's legendary Imagineering unit; the central element—a vast, protean pyramid that deployed dizzyingly before finally entombing Radames and Aida forever.

Elaborate Lives represented a reuniting of many of the disparate talents who'd helped Disney conquer Broadway over the last five years, including Elton John and Tim Rice, *The Lion King*'s for-the-record composers; Linda Woolverton, *Beauty and the Beast*'s primary scenarist; and Rob Jess Roth, that show's Broadway director. *Elaborate Lives* also had no animated ancestor. It would be the first Disney musical conceived from scratch.

"The fact that *Elaborate Lives* wasn't a movie first has its advantages," insisted Disney president Michael Eisner, the man Schneider and Schumacher mordantly referred to as "Dad." "Yes, we had a six-year tryout, as it were, with *Beauty and the Beast* and *The Lion King* because they were movies. We then took *Beauty and the Beast* to a regional theater in Houston to develop it as a musical. We took *Lion King* to a theater in Minnesota. And now we're going to a smaller, less expensive venue in Atlanta with *Elaborate Lives* because this is, by design, a smaller, less expensive show. Dealing with a treasure like *Lion King* we had more to lose by screwing up than with something like *Elaborate Lives* which, if we screw up, nobody will remember."

In a little over five years, the Walt Disney Company had become Broadway's most powerful and successful producer of musicals by tapping its reserve of pre-sold animated feature films and remaking them for the stage. Menken and Ashman's *Beauty and the Beast*, the company's initial cartoon/theater transfer, was still running on Broadway and had thus far spawned companies in eleven cities worldwide. *King David*, the nominal second production, actually had no animated antecedent either. A ponderous, cantata-scale Bible pageant by Menken and the lyricist Tim Rice, rather than a full-fledged musical, it had re-opened the Disney-renovated New Amsterdam Theater on 42nd Street in 1997 for a limited run before giving way to *The Lion King*, the cornerstone of Disney's newfound Broadway supremacy.

"*Beauty and the Beast* and *King David* were not done by Peter and Tom," Eisner explained. "We just sort of did them out of corporate. When theater became a more strategic direction for the company, though, we had to make a more formal arrangement. I grew up in New York, I personally loved the theater and I personally knew enough about it to know that we should stay away from it.

"*The Lion King*, however, enhanced our brand," Eisner continued. "It made us relevant. We've been okay around the world, but in the intellectual community in New York we surprised them with *Lion King*. All of which was not pre-planned. We got lucky. But Peter and Tom made that happen. In fact, I would not have gone into Times Square if I didn't have them on board. We are not in the real-estate business and I would not have gone into New York real estate particularly, if I wasn't convinced that we could compete creatively on a level that was essential in New York. I was confident because of them."

If Schneider and Schumacher were known for anything on Broadway right now it was for their audacious hiring choice of Julie Taymor to oversee *Lion King*'s stage transformation. Yet, in *Elaborate Lives*, Disney was returning creatively to the company fold, dispensing with outsiders like Taymor and employing instead a team largely drawn from the Disney world of animation and theme parks.

Wasn't this something of a step backward?

"No," Schneider answered tersely, as he and Schumacher resumed their seats, their welcoming chores before cast and crew completed. "It's not."

"*Elaborate Lives* actually came first," Schneider eventually elaborated, now standing before another long table in a somewhat smaller room across the hall, where ad agency prototypes of prospective *Elaborate Lives* logos had been laid out for consideration. "At the same time four years ago that we started considering *The Lion King* for Broadway, Elton and Tim mentioned wanting to do another project that was not animated. We had this children's book we'd bought for animation, *Aida Story* by the opera diva Leontyne Price, that we came to think might be better as a stage musical."

Schumacher nodded. "The story didn't seem quite suitable for animation; a little serious," he explained. "But there was a time there when we wondered which show was actually going to open the New Amsterdam Theater."

The team of Schneider and Schumacher were an extraordinarily well-oiled tandem. Both men spoke fast, though Schneider spoke just a bit faster. Both were approximately the same height, maybe five-foot-ten, though Schneider was wiry, where Schumacher was less so. In sneakers, jeans and a Gap pullover, Schneider projected youthful friskiness, though he was clearly the elder, at 47. Schumacher, 40, was contrastingly studious yet styling in designer eyeglass frames, Italian loafers and a couture linen suit. Like the animated characters in the movies they produced, the two men wisecracked endlessly. As in those same animated films, though, the craft, intelligence and sheer labor underlying the façade was clearly prodigious.

"Spectacular, actually," observed Michael Ovitz, the Hollywood power broker and, at this time, a new Broadway shadow power in his own right. Earlier in the month, Ovitz, after buying a large stake in Garth Drabinsky's increasingly financially straitened Livent organization, had ousted Drabinsky altogether, charging him with doctoring his company's books.[33] The prospect of Ovitz and Disney now going head-to-head on Broadway rather than just in Hollywood was both titillating and a bit disorienting. Did Ovitz hope to restructure Livent along the lines of Schneider and Schumacher's Disney Theatrical operation?

"I should be so lucky," Ovitz replied. His humiliatingly attenuated (however well-compensated) stint at Disney a few years before, as Eisner's stymied second-in-command, clearly had left Ovitz with, among other things, a lasting appreciation for Schneider and Schumacher's symbiotic talents.

"They have great give and take. People say they practically finish each other's sentences, but in fact they don't finish each other's sentences, they respect each other's sentences. I imagine they've probably had a ton of disagreements but you'd never know it. They're simply one of the best marriages I've ever seen."

Eisner put it even more pertinently. "From *Little Mermaid* to *Mulan*, and now *The Lion King* on Broadway, Peter and Tom have made every creative decision while letting me come in and play with them on occasion. They choose the ideas, they hire the casts, they assign directors, artists. They are the orchestra leaders."

Though Schneider and Schumacher's professional interplay often verged on the virtuosic, Schneider seemed to strike the major chords in business affairs while deferring to Schumacher on aesthetic matters. The division of responsibility, however, remained fluid. "People always ask us who does what?" Schumacher laughed. "We both know our primary domain yet we both expect the other to cover both sides."

At a production meeting following *Elaborate Lives'* first full rehearsal runthrough later that day, it was Schumacher who set the agenda, grilling the collaborators, with Schneider chiming in from across the table.

"It's a score of ballads," Schumacher began somewhat ruefully, turning to the show's musical director in lieu of composer Elton John, who was again absent in the line of duty, having chosen to remain in England. "And I don't see any way out other than heaving stuff over the side. We've had this problem before," Schumacher added, staring sardonically at Schneider. Their eyes met. "*Pocahontas*," both muttered simultaneously, naming one of their recent animated films. "'If I Never Knew You,'" added Schumacher. "An exquisite Alan Menken ballad. But audiences didn't want to hear it." He paused. "We took it out."

Schneider seemed genuinely crestfallen at the thought. "I'm still not sure we did the right thing."

Schumacher gazed proprietarily at his boss, who was due momentarily to catch a plane back to Los Angeles. "Peter," he asked, "did you eat?"

Nobody had my job before me," said Schneider a week later, back home in Burbank, in the bosom of the Disney Animation building that he'd basically built, a cavernous corporate hive of over two thousand animators and writers, computer technicians, and number-crunchers all laboring in the service of Disney cartoon magic beneath the giant, spangled, pointy sorcerer's hat that crowned the place. Schneider's day had been consumed with meetings — animation, story board, executive board, budgetary — an avalanche of narrative, visual, and fiscal details. Animated films were almost incomprehensibly complex undertakings. Yet, between them, Schneider and Schumacher appeared to have a grasp, if not a stranglehold, on each aspect of the process. In the nine or so different animated features currently percolating at various levels of development around Disney, no story thread, no drawing, no computer manipulated frame, no celebrity composer's tune or orchestral cue seems to escape their attention and nothing was final until they said so.

From its humble beginnings in 1923 under Walt Disney and his brother Roy, the Disney company had of course enjoyed a run of unprecedented success as the industry innovator in feature animation, riding Snow White, Pinocchio, and Bambi, to say nothing of Mickey Mouse, to the summit of American popular culture. In the wake of Walt Disney's death, though, in 1966, the vaunted animation division had fallen from pre-eminence.

"Animation was not a business fifteen years ago," Schneider explained, sprawled on his office sofa. "The company went through this cataclysmic change when Michael Eisner, Jeffrey Katzenberg, and Roy Disney's son, Roy, Jr., took it over in 1984. Their vision was to restore live-action movies and thereby revive the company. But

Roy, as mastermind of the takeover, along with Frank Wells and Stanley Gold, when asked by Eisner and Katzenberg what he wanted, said: 'Give me animation.'

"There were 190 people here making a movie every three or four years," Schneider went on. "On a flight to Tokyo for one of the first board meetings, Jeffrey turned to Roy and said, 'Roy, you need to go hire yourself *your* Jeffrey Katzenberg.' Jeffrey was very frustrated. Roy's a very clever, wonderful, special human being who embodies the soul of what I think Disney is. But Roy was not a manager. 'Michael has me,' Jeffrey said. 'You need someone who can run your business for you.'

"So Roy turned to Bob Fitzpatrick, head of the California Institute of the Arts at the time, who'd just run the L.A. Olympic Arts Festival here, where I'd met him and worked for him. At the time I was unemployed. I'd just gotten married, had a kid, was living back in New York. Roy went to Bob and asked, 'Do you know anyone who knows about animation, film, and can do this and that?' And Bob said, 'I know somebody who doesn't know anything about film, anything about animation, but does this and that really well.'

"I interviewed with Roy, I interviewed with Michael and then Jeffrey. I was 34. And they hired me. Why? Because it fundamentally made no difference who they hired. They didn't care. Roy cared. But in retrospect, Jeffrey and Michael couldn't have cared less. Animation? Who cares. It wasn't making any money. As a matter of fact it was losing money. You couldn't close it down — animation was Disney. Though they were threatening to. The only reason they didn't was because of Roy. I got lucky because they weren't that picky."

Born in Scotland, raised in the United States, Schneider had graduated from Purdue University in 1971 with a degree in theater and aspirations to be a director. Five days after arriving in New York, he

went to work Off-Broadway at the WPA Theater "pounding sets," as
he put it. Schneider lingered in the city for five years, then headed
for Chicago to run the St. Nicholas Theater, an ambitious new
enterprise undertaken by four talented theatrical unknowns: actor/
directors Stephen Schachter, Patti Cox, Bill Macy, and the playwright David Mamet. "I myself was not doing a lot of directing,"
Schneider admitted, "so I went and interviewed for the job. They
didn't know any better and so they hired me. I had four very fabulous years building that theater up into something quite special. And
then it fell apart and I left."

Schneider went to London with the musical *One Mo' Time*, spending
two years there working for the show's producers, the Apollo Group.
He then came back to interview for the Olympic Arts Festival job.

"A year off in New York was supposed to follow the festival," said
Schneider, "because that's what my wife, Hope, wanted. But we had
this baby, and no money, so I took a job on the WPA Theater's Alan
Menken–Howard Ashman musical, *Little Shop of Horrors*, before
Disney hired me in 1985."

The trajectory of Schneider's rise at Disney actually was plotted on
a theatrical plane. "I took all the things I'd learned from producing,
directing, managing theater," said Schneider, "and applied it, but
now with a whole lot of money."

Schneider began to bring in people from outside Disney, many of
them theater people. One was Howard Ashman, the lyricist and
librettist whose work on *Little Shop of Horrors* had impressed both
Schneider and Jeffrey Katzenberg. Ashman brought along his composer partner Alan Menken. "While Disney still had a lot of talent,"
Schneider said, "it was all flat—no one would make a decision—a
legacy of no one wanting to do anything that Walt wouldn't do. I
brought in people with opinions and passion. Also I got lucky. The
video cassette was invented."

In a span of five years, from 1986 through 1990, six new animated features were released under Schneider's supervision, including, *Who Framed Roger Rabbit?* a joint project with Steven Spielberg and Robert Zemeckis, and *The Little Mermaid*, a full-fledged Ashman and Menken musical. All of the movies did appreciably well. The latter two, though, grossed astonishing sums.

Schneider smiled. "And suddenly everyone realized, 'Oh my God. There's money to be made in this business.'"

Born in San Francisco, Thomas Schumacher was the grandson of a former silent film studio head, the son of a political lobbyist, a graduate of UCLA, and a worshipful lover of the theater. In 1983, at the age of 26, he found himself sharing his tiny office at Los Angeles' Mark Taper Forum with some guy who'd been brought over from London to coordinate the theater component of the Olympic Arts Festival. "That was Peter," Schumacher recalled, sitting now in his richly decorated Disney Animation building office. "I was the only person who'd have lunch with him. Everyone else was kind of bothered that an outsider had been brought in."

When Schneider and his future wife were promoted to run not just the theatrical component but the entire Olympic Festival itself, Schumacher was invited by Schneider to come work for them as a line producer. "I have never in my life gotten a job that I applied for, except working at a department store once," Schumacher disingenuously maintained. "Every other job I've ever had has been because someone asked me to do it."

As a byproduct of the Olympic Festival's overwhelming success, Schumacher became the co-founder and associate director of the Los Angeles Festival of Arts in 1987. The English language premiere of Peter Brook's *Mahabharata*, the American premiere of Cirque du Soleil, performances by Ingmar Bergman's theater company and a vast John Cage retrospective were just a few of that festival's many eye-popping cultural achievements, undertaken under Schumacher's co-auspices. It was then that Schneider began pestering his old office mate to, "Come to Disney."

"I thought, I could never fit in there," Schumacher remembered. "I was about to turn 30. I had all the pre-conceived notions about Disney. I didn't feel like a Disney person, even though I'd worked extensively in children's theater — studied it, directed it, toured as a professional puppeteer one summer. My plan always had been to run a small regional theater somewhere. Plus, the money Peter offered was actually a little less than I was already making. Why did I finally come? Peter. It seemed like a great adventure."

Schumacher quickly progressed from producing his first animated feature, *Rescuers Down Under*, to shepherding the films *Nightmare Before Christmas* and a project first known as *King of the Beasts* but soon called *The Lion King* into production. Schneider and Katzenberg began pressuring Schumacher to give up his individual producing duties and become executive vice president of development for the entire animation division. Finally, he did, launching projects that soon included *Pocahontas*, *Toy Story*, and *The Hunchback of Notre Dame*. It was right around this time, 1991, that the film *Beauty and the Beast* was released and effusively received by many critics as a musical that bettered anything Broadway could offer. This started Disney president, Michael Eisner, thinking something that even Walt Disney himself had never conceived: perhaps Disney should be on Broadway.

Schneider and Schumacher tried to dissuade him.

"I was very hesitant," said Schneider. "I didn't think the company had the expertise. It was also hard for me because I thought *Beauty and the Beast* was a perfect movie. Plus, I wasn't in charge. I have a very hard time being involved in projects when I'm not in charge. So Michael Eisner, Jeffrey Katzenberg, Bob Mctyre [Disney Theatrical's then-senior vice president] and Rob Roth brought *Beauty and the Beast* to Broadway while we just watched."

Neither Schneider or Schumacher would offer an assessment of *Beauty and the Beast*, on the record, beyond stating that it was, "unfairly dismissed" by Broadway critics in 1994. That same year their animation division released *The Lion King*. When it inevitably came under consideration as Disney's next Broadway venture, Eisner asked Schneider to help out. "But I said, 'Michael, either keep the whole theater business—which is fine," Schneider recalled. "Or give it to me and Tom. And Michael said, 'Okay, it's yours.'"

"Peter and I knew that *Lion King* would have to be different," Schumacher went on. "Not just different. Push-the-envelope unique. Astonishing. And we got lucky. We caught Julie Taymor at the exact right moment in her career."

It was, Schumacher, in fact, who first proposed Taymor as a potential candidate for *The Lion King*.

"I met her on the telephone in 1987 when I was in charge of programming as associate director of the Los Angeles Arts Festival. I phoned Julie about a production of hers called *Liberty's Taken* that I'd heard quite a lot about, after she'd staged it for two weeks outdoors in Massachusetts in 1985. Though we couldn't get it together to do the piece in Los Angeles, I then began following her career. When Michael Eisner insisted a 'brilliant idea' was needed for *Lion King*, I found myself thinking: Julie Taymor."

To many (including Taymor herself), she was a shocking choice, a self-described "non-profit baby," whose adventurous, cross-cultural stage concoctions had often challenged even institutional theaters' threshold for experimentation.

"There was trepidation on both sides when Peter and Tom first approached me," Taymor remembered. "They worried that I was too far out and I worried that they were Disney. But once we really started to get into it, once I came up with ideas and a direction that they could back and present to Michael Eisner, there was incredible support. And tremendous understanding. Real understanding. Because they really know theater. More so than most any New York producer."

Side by side, in a shadowy back row of the Alliance Theater, Schumacher and Schneider hunker down behind their respective laptops, catching up with their multi-tentacled enterprises. It is Wednesday September 17, and *Elaborate Lives'* first official preview is a few hours away.

Already this week, the two have attended a reading in New York of *The Hunchback of Notre Dame*, another animated adaptation, slated for a 1999 premiere in Berlin. They have hosted a media-besieged Democratic National Committee benefit performance of *The Lion King* attended by both President Clinton and Vice President Gore, winding up in a photograph with the pair on the front page of the *New York Times*; a source of guilty delight for the two of them. Finally, they have joined Michael Eisner and Elton John in Atlanta for a first look at *Elaborate Lives*.

On this day, they have endured endless tech rehearsals, sorted through Eisner's notes, passed on their own suggestions to all concerned, obsessed over their pyramid set's sporadic malfunctioning, rejected every in-performance publicity photograph (out of more than five hundred) shot for the show's media campaign by a very famous (and expensive) former *Rolling Stone* photographer, and approved prospective trailers for upcoming Disney Animation releases. They have e-mailed the Coast, Orlando, Paris, New York. And it isn't quite three o'clock yet, Atlanta time.

"I do sometimes worry," Eisner conceded. "Their main responsibility is animation. That's 90 percent of their job. That is the more important place for them to spend their time. I reluctantly assigned them to do the theatrical work because I had no choice. But I prefer them creating product for two thousand theaters, not one."

Gnawing on a protein bar, Schneider slips ever lower in his seat—the signature Schneider slouch, a progressive descent into Posturepedic oblivion. Schumacher pulls a fresh bottle of spring water from his shoulder bag. "This is the essential difference between making movies and making theater," he announces dryly. "With movies they bring you water. With theater, you bring your own."

Schneider's head is nearly lower than seat level. The box office has just alerted him to an uninvited presence in the audience tonight, a theater columnist from one of the New York dailies, who surreptitiously, if somewhat ineptly, has purchased a ticket with his personal credit card.

"There's too much interest in what we're doing," Schneider muttered. "Go away! Leave us alone! On *Lion King* nobody cared. We had to beg people to come."

"Fundamentally, a lot of this company now swings on animation," Schneider had remarked the week before. "So how do you get to the next step? There's much more competition. Good is not good enough, you have to attempt to break boundaries every time, astound people. That's what we did with *Lion King*. Disney has the resources, power, and creative expertise to—sometimes, not always—push the art form to places people don't expect. And when we do that we win big."

But was making a cartoon movie musical really the same as creating one for the stage? Could the same formula apply? Should the same formula apply?

"They keep saying that animation is just like doing musical theater,"

Julie Taymor had observed doubtfully. "I don't quite get that. It's not been my experience."

"I actually think a big part of their brilliance is the fact that they operate so well in two diametrically opposed processes," Michael Ovitz had insisted, "the live theater and animated film. You couldn't find two more different processes."

Schneider would have none of it. "The process of development of an animated or stage musical is fundamentally the same," he insisted. "It's about nurturing artists, giving them the space to work, demanding the best from them, asking the right questions; working with people who are bright enough to realize they don't have all the answers.

"What bugs me the most," he added now, rising, "is that people try and reduce Disney to a corporation. They don't understand that the people who do the products—their fundamental taste and what they think is good—make the product."

His eyes and Schumacher's lock. "So when people say Disney does bad things…"

Schumacher smiled wryly. "Or, Disney does good things." he added.

"It's not Disney, the company," concluded Peter Schneider, heading for the door. "It's the individuals who are doing it. It's not 'them,'" he called over his shoulder, "It's us!"

CHAPTER 19

YOU DON'T KNOW THIS MAN

You don't know this man.
You don't know a thing.

—*Parade*

In November of 1998, 28-year-old composer/lyricist Jason Robert Brown found himself in extraordinarily rarefied circumstances. His first full-scale musical, *Parade*, written in collaboration with a Pulitzer Prize–winning bookwriter, Alfred Uhry, and directed by a multi-Tony-Award-winning legend, Harold Prince, was about to open at the biggest non-profit institutional theater in the country, Lincoln Center Theater, in a co-production with *Parade's* initiator and original developer, the once-mighty Livent organization.

"That's a lot of faith," acknowledged Brown, with an understandable hint of apprehension.

Parade was no Disney musical. Its story was the true story of Leo Frank, a Jew in the deep South at the turn-of-the-century, falsely accused of murder and ultimately lynched. For Brown, whose music tilted strongly toward the accessible, the anti-commerciality of this ugly story still suited him fine. "I'm trying to express something very individual and specific," he maintained. "Disney has a very different aim. Maybe I'd be willing to do something for Disney. On paper. But when it gets down to: 'You've gotta write more major chords and give them a song they can hum,'—well, I think I'd bridle at that."

Born in Ossining, raised in Rockland County, Brown had completed two years of composition studies at the Eastman School of Music. His meteoric rise was, he readily acknowledged, largely attributable to Prince's daughter, Daisy, who'd first heard Brown in a Manhattan piano bar and wound up persuading her father that this young unknown could and should compose his next big musical, after Stephen Sondheim passed on the project.

"I called Daisy and I said, 'Daisy, your dad just asked me to write his next musical,'" Brown recalled, "and Daisy said, 'I know, isn't that great?' and I said, 'No, I'm petrified.'"

Brown's first produced musical, *Songs for a New World*, had been a revue put together at the WPA Theater just three years before.

"Before that, I don't know that I ever actually finished anything," Brown admitted. "*Songs for a New World* was like the best of everything that I'd ever started and couldn't deal with getting through to the end of. In the first draft I'd say 80 percent of the thing was songs I'd written for other shows. By the time it actually got on stage that was down to maybe 40 percent."

"Daisy Prince heard me sing some of this stuff as a piano bar customer and said to me, 'Oh, that sounds great,'" Brown went on. "A couple of months later I asked her if she would direct my show. At the same time I was playing for this cabaret group called The Tonics that Stephen Sondheim and Hal's wife, Judy Prince, had taken a shine to. So I was now constantly around Hal, I just seemed to be circling him like a vulture. Hal got Livent to pay for a kind of first reading for *Songs for a New World*, they were having this summer festival up in Toronto and they paid for us to come up."

"Jason Robert Brown has never even composed a chamber musical per se," said Garth Drabinsky at the time. "It's Hal's choice to go with Jason for *Parade*. At first I didn't support the decision, I didn't think it was an intelligent idea. The reality is you just don't know who necessarily is best suited for work.

"I love music of the late '50s and '60s when people were talking about feelings in a big way," Drabinsky added. "Nobody talks about feelings any more, just a lot of pretty ugly music. I feel the music of shows and composers, and I think I can discern who is too complex and twisted, and at the same time those who use the twist and the complexity from time to time to excite, energize and bring you deeper, as opposed to turning you off. That's a fine line."

Unlike, many of his peers, Brown had not always been persuaded that theater music was his future. "I was going to be Billy Joel," he said, "I was going to be Elton John, I was going to play the piano and scream. The stuff I was writing just eventually ended up evolving into more theatrical things, which was only half intentional. I always planned, I probably still plan, to be a rock star one day. And yet I've ended up writing this big musical."

For Brown, writing *Parade* had not been easy.

"I thought the idea behind it was great. I struggled because I wished I was older, I wished I was Southern; I worked extra hard to make sure this didn't sound like a 28-year-old liberal from New York writing this Southern lynching story. That was my biggest fear, the perception of me as a young composer who'd never written anything. I didn't want to be presumptuous or pretentious. I spent a lot of time working with country styles, listening to archival recordings of Southern bluegrass—which is not necessarily endemic to Georgia—but I was looking for a sound that I could filter through myself. I would start playing some old song on my piano and then I wouldn't turn the page, I'd just keep playing what I thought came next, what I thought it should be. Musically, the hardest thing was: I'm still a very contemporary writer. The challenge was to not…you know, get funky. I've spent my whole life listening to Stevie Wonder. I'm ready to write that but I just can't right now."

Since the release of Audra McDonald's *Way Back to Paradise* CD earlier in the year, Brown had found himself bracketed with McDonald's other favorite young composers. "My aesthetic and Michael John's aesthetic and Adam's aesthetic are very different from what is generally thought of as the Broadway musical," Brown insisted. "I'm not sure that, with the exception of this project, I'd even know how to write a Broadway musical. I'm just going to keep on writing and, you know, maybe it'll come out a hit, maybe it'll be a pop song—whatever's going to come out. Writing for the pop charts, there's so much competition. I've never been willing to be a small fish in a big pond. The luxury of writing for musical theater is it's a very specialized gig, it's a real trick, a very specialized game. Now I have some expertise. I would love to continue learning about it."

For all the talk about its difficult subject matter, *Parade* proved disappointingly pedestrian, both politically and dramatically. Onstage at the Vivian Beaumont, crowds muttered and swarmed, shuttled around by director Prince as fluidly as ever. But little was said or sung that cut very deep. Leo Frank's plight was diagrammed rather than dramatized. Frank could have been any generically put-upon musical theater hero, and an especially uncharismatic one at that; so inward he seemed almost a cipher. Frank's Jewishness and the anti-Semitism it engendered floated by like so many musical notes on a bar staff, notes that were read but were barely struck.

Brown's score was proficient but almost completely undifferentiated. As in so many big musicals of the past two decades, march-time predominated. The only true moment of emotional engagement and heartfelt characterization turned up late in the second act with "All the Wasted Time," a stirring love song sung by Frank and his wife, Lucille.

Yet, Brown's debut remained an auspicious one. Rich melodic phrases repeatedly struck the ear, only to fall away undeveloped. That disconnect certainly seemed a matter of experience. It also may well have been a function, in part, of the Livent factor. Removed from Garth Drabinsky's smothering artistic embrace (though, admittedly, Drabinsky had recently been removed himself), Brown would someday perhaps write something with more of the distinctive songwriting personality that *Songs for a New World* and Brown himself suggested that he possessed.

Parade was one of three new musicals Lincoln Center Theater had announced it would produce over the next two years; a "celebration of new musicals," on into the new millennium. The last would be *Marie Christine*, Michael John LaChiusa's operatic treatment of *Medea* written for Audra McDonald. The first, *A New Brain*, had, in fact, opened in August at the Mitzi Newhouse Theater, bringing *Falsettos'* composer William Finn back to the stage after a prolonged absence due to illness, an illness that Finn, in characteristic fashion, had chosen to musicalize. Finn's return was most welcome but *A New Brain* exhibited much of the self-indulgence and compositional carelessness of Finn at his most infuriating, with little of the inspiration and innovativeness of Finn at his best. The show had closed just after its initial subscription run.

Lincoln Center Theater's sudden shift back toward musical theater had brought Ira Weitzman unexpectedly back uptown (though still on a freelance basis) to help shepherd this millennial trio of new musicals.

"I was beginning to feel, oh, my God—we've just got to get back to doing new musicals," André Bishop tried to explain. "And then suddenly it became a celebration—let's end the 20th century doing these three new musicals."

"The trick is paying for them," noted Weitzman. "Even a theater with the resources of Lincoln Center is hard-pressed to pay for three in a row. The fact that Livent paid partly for *Parade* at Lincoln Center, because it had developed it, represents a growing trend, I'm afraid. The issue is 'enhancement money'—commercial producers paying institutional theaters to help them develop their shows. Until recently, a non-profit theater would just put a show out there and some commercial producer would pick it up. That was called producing. Now that has changed. Projects are now being initiated by the 'enhancers'—the commercial producers—and delivered over to the non-profit theaters."

"Non-profit theaters who want to do musicals today must rely on enhancement money," André Bishop insisted, but Weitzman would only concede the point cautiously. "You can look at corporate enhancement money with a harsh eye and say, this isn't what a non-profit theater should do," he observed. "Or you can say that for-profit organizations, like Livent and even Disney, are simply adopting the developmental ways of the non-profits. If a show is good, I don't see anything wrong with that. The whole world is becoming one giant corporation and certainly the theater is undergoing a gigantic corporate takeover. Does that fact influence the end product? Of course it does."

Weitzman paused. "I just hope the shows I work on are not."

George Wolfe, for one, found it all "astoundingly dangerous. The corporate thought process defining the artistic journey results in mediocrity becoming the standard," he maintained. "When an American musical really works it is somehow the individual soaring. No corporate structure can duplicate that."

Countering bad reviews with corporate marketing was what Frank Wildhorn's musicals had most excelled at over the previous two years.[34] Critics had not been kind to Wildhorn's *Jekyll & Hyde* in 1997. They were downright hostile to his *Scarlet Pimpernel* in 1998.[35] Neither had even remotely broken even at the box office, yet both continued to run, *Pimpernel* in a recently re-tooled, cheaper, scaled-down, and heavily promoted, revised production.[36]

Marketing accounted for much of this, agreed Rocco Landesman. But was that really the whole story?

Landesman smiled. "Peter Schneider said to me the other day—we were trying to figure out *Jekyll & Hyde*—and he said: 'Big singing.'

And I thought, 'Yeah, big singing!' Wildhorn's musicals come down and just blast it at you. There's no other explanation for *Jekyll & Hyde.*"

This realization had not prevented Landesman from producing Wildhorn's newest opus, *The Civil War*, which opened at Jujamcyn's St. James Theater in April 1999. "It was a show that we could try out of town, play some Pace tour markets, play Broadway—one of our own houses—and then be guaranteed a long road tour," explained Landesman, just a touch sheepishly. "It was perfect."

Not quite. Again the critics savaged Wildhorn.[37] And the Civil War, as it turned out, was not nearly so marketable a musical topic for tourists or even hardcore Wildhorn-ites. In a Tony Award competition between Broadway's only original new musicals that year—*Parade* (which had already closed) and *The Civil War*—Wildhorn lost out to young Jason Robert Brown for Best Musical Score. *The Civil War* and *Parade* both lost out for Best Musical to *Fosse*, a compilation of the deceased choreographer's best dance bits. Shortly thereafter, *The Civil War* closed.

So what had changed on Broadway one year since the dawn of Disney's *Lion King*?

"The business climate," insisted Landesman. "All sorts of new sources for capital."

"The working climate," maintained Graciela Daniele. "The triumphant acceptance of Julie Taymor as a director and a woman."

"I don't think it's clear yet," said André Bishop.

"Not all that much has changed in my lifetime," noted Harold Prince. "Musical theater is about creating things. And hoping people want to see what you put out there. Honestly. That hasn't changed at all."

For George Wolfe, the operative word was: "Vigilance. This year has been about the corporation, the corporate thought process," he agreed. "But no corporate structure can duplicate an artist's impulses. The minute the structures start to believe they are the source, well, it's over. But," he said, "we'll see."

CHAPTER 20

DREAM TRUE

Dream beyond time and place,
Dream of grace,
Dream of me and you,
Dream true.

—*Dream True:*
My Life with Vernon Dexter

Jason Robert Brown was an overnight sensation in 1998. 48-year-old lyricist Patrick Cook and his 37-year-old composer partner Frederick Freyer were anything but. Unlike Brown, the two had paid years of non-profit dues. And unlike Michael John LaChiusa or Adam Guettel, Cook and Freyer wrote show tunes that were not revolutionary.

In February, their *Captains Courageous* finally opened at the Manhattan Theater Club after a ten-year odyssey that illustrated what a new musical by a relatively unknown team had to endure to reach a New York audience.

Cook and Freyer had first met at the BMI Workshop in 1984; Freyer was just out of Harvard, where he'd written some musicals, Cook had been an actor for some time. He'd also been a composer but, as Cook put it, "Rick's better, so I teamed up with him. I was always writing as an actor. Finally, I made a life choice: Am I pretending I'm writing or am I really writing? That's when I joined BMI."

Cook and Freyer's *Captains Courageous, the Musical*—adapted, of course, from the classic Rudyard Kipling novel and 1937 Hollywood film—was birthed at a BMI Workshop in 1988. It was next presented at the O'Neill Music Theater Conference in 1990, at Ford's Theater in Washington in 1992, at Connecticut's Goodspeed Opera House-at-Chester in 1994 and, finally, in a series of Manhattan Theater Club readings and workshops from 1996 through 1997.

"The process," Cook maintained, "served us well. We just had time to work, without an enormous amount of pressure. We had one director at the O'Neill Center and then Graciela Daniele directed our first production at Ford's Theater. It was great to work with different directors, getting the input of some very smart people."

"If you had asked me when I was graduating from college whether I would have wanted my career to proceed at this more methodical pace, I probably would have said no," Freyer admitted, "I want to go right to Broadway right now. But the truth is we were very new at this back then.

"We missed the generation where you could come right out of college and have a Broadway producer commission you to write a show," Freyer continued. "Instead, we've been studying musicals, not really formally but semi-formally through BMI, and also just on our own. We know a lot about the history and a lot about what the conventions are. There was a time when many people just wanted to throw it all out and start with something completely fresh. I think now there's more of a sense to build upon what was done before."

"There's a particular kind of magic that is hard to find today," added Cook, "that launching moment in a musical from dialogue into song. I just love seeing musicals that go from scene into a song but so many shows are through-composed these days, you have very few dialogue scenes. I think that's where the wonder of it is. I just start crying. It's a lost art form."

Freyer agreed. "Musicals are the one form in which you can tell a story and also really dig down and move people. That's what I hope we do in this show. That's what we want to do. That's the only reason why we do what we do."

Captains Courageous received a handsome production from the Manhattan Theater Club. The intention to move the show, perhaps to Broadway, once its limited subscription run had ended was, if not clear, then implicit. But after all the years of non-profit development, *Captains Courageous* did not survive more than a few weeks before paying New York audiences. Its musical numbers, though well-constructed, did not manage to move ticket buyers and critics sufficiently.[38] Its intentions were noble. But intentions simply were not enough.

Theater critics had not been very kind to new musicals since *Rent*, though it could be said that new musicals had not been especially kind to critics, either. You'd hardly know this, though, to judge by the quantities of original cast album releases that continued to flood record stores and Internet music sites in 1999. Since *Rent*, dozens and dozens of new musicals had come and gone, on Broadway and off, mostly to lackluster reviews. Nearly all of them were still available on CD.

How had these shows come to be recorded? Certainly their sales on CDs to a niche audience of enthusiasts — those truly interested in new musicals (probably about five thousand hardy souls nationwide) — hardly justified the cost of recording them.

Some in the music industry maintained that recording new shows was really a long-term bet — that the same creative team signed at a loss might one day produce a hit. But that was quite a gamble. Major labels, like Sony Records, had on occasion been known to jump on a potential Broadway blockbuster, as they had with *Side Show* in 1997. Atlantic had turned its musical theater division over to the composer Frank Wildhorn as a virtual fiefdom. But *Side Show* had faded, while Wildhorn's allure seemed largely manufactured.

In fact, a significant majority of all recent cast albums had been produced by just three people operating at three very different record companies: Billy Rosenfield, senior vice president for shows and soundtracks at RCA Victor; Bruce Kimmel, the man in charge of musical theater at a largely film soundtrack–focused Los Angeles record label named Varese Sarabande; and, to a lesser but no less influential extent, Robert Hurwitz, the president of Nonesuch Records.

More people would hear the recordings that these three underwrote than ever actually attended the shows themselves. In this sense, these executives had performed more than just a service. They were the indirect guardians of musical theater's history, if not its future.

At 45, Rosenfield was the man behind many of the more important cast recordings of the decade, from big-budget extravaganzas like *Ragtime* to cutting-edge works like *Bring in 'da Noise, Bring in 'da Funk* and even Stephen Sondheim and John Weidman's *Assassins*.

Rosenfield's reasons for recording a particular show often came down to one word, he said. "Relationships. We know that to get the smashes down the road, there have to be relationships established with promising composers early on."

One young composer Rosenfield had embarked on a relationship with early on was Jason Robert Brown; Rosenfield had recorded Brown's *Songs of a New World* in 1997. The messy financial problems of the Livent organization almost had sunk that relationship, however, soon after *Parade* opened the following year. With Livent disappearing into a morass of red ink, Lincoln Center Theater found itself left holding Garth Drabinsky's $5 million musical in the face of very mixed reviews. As a result, according to Rosenfield, *Parade* nearly lost its informal agreement with RCA for a cast album.

Jason Robert Brown remained livid about the whole thing.

"Livent dropped out shortly after our reviews came out," said Brown.

"They announced they would not spend another dime on *Parade*. RCA had an agreement to record all of Livent's shows. But when Livent pulled out of *Parade*, RCA higher-ups said they were pulling out, too. I had to go to Billy and ask him: "What if we pay for this record and you just distribute it? Would that get it recorded?' Billy said yes."

According to André Bishop, Lincoln Center Theater "was determined to make the album, even though, God knows, we could ill afford to do it. We canvassed everyone for money, including our board members."

Brown, too, enlisted everyone he could think of. "In the end," Brown said, "RCA put in $25,000, Lincoln Center put in a chunk, the producer Scott Rudin put in some, and the Gilman Gonzalez-Falla Foundation, which has helped support a lot of musical theater composers over the years, put in $60,000 or $70,000. Even Roy Furman, Ovitz's new number two guy at Livent, gave us a little money. Somehow, we pulled it together."

Nonesuch Record's Robert Hurwitz also used the word "relationships" to explain his commitment to Audra McDonald and Adam Guettel. Though better known for recording the classical and world music eclectics who dominated the Nonesuch catalogue, Hurwitz's label had in the last three years, released McDonald's *Way Back to Paradise* as well as Guettel's *Floyd Collins* and *Saturn Returns* (under its original title, *Myths and Hymns*).

"In every area in which we record, I look to establish long-term relationships with artists whose talent is so big the world eventually is going to come around," Hurwitz explained. "It would be very risky for me to work with Adam and Audra if I was just going to work on one record. Fortunately, for the price of a medium-sized Broadway musical, I can work with them both for the next ten years."

Out on the West Coast, Kimmel, though a devout fan of the brassier Broadway musicals of the 1950s and '60s, had carved out his own corner of cast album turf recording smaller musicals produced mostly Off-Broadway, including Polly Pen's *Bed and Sofa* in 1996.

"If I love something and believe it's going to have a life, then I do it," Kimmel explained. "We've done the occasional Broadway show, like the last revival of *The King and I*. They can run as much as $250,000 to record. Off-Broadway musicals cost us in the early teens and up. They sell anywhere from 4,000 copies. Still, most break even. And for the littlest musicals, having a CD really helps generate stock and amateur productions."

The 34-year-old composer/lyricist Andrew Lippa, had been absolutely tickled to have his first produced show, *jon & jen*, recorded by Kimmel in 1995. "The recording stamped legitimacy on the whole thing," Lippa recalled. "It made me feel like a writer.

"Did I make any money from the record?" added Lippa, rhetorically. "Oh, no. If not for Bruce, though, a lot of us wouldn't have records. Bruce works very quickly and very cheaply but he does them. We did ours in one day. And it's out there. You can get it on Amazon.com."

Ricky Ian Gordon was the fourth composer featured on Audra McDonald's *Way Back to Paradise* CD. Unlike Cook and Freyer, Gordon already enjoyed fairly substantial success, a success that had largely come, unlike LaChiusa's, Guettel's and Brown's, away from musical theater. Gordon, 41, was best known as a composer of individual art songs and song cycles that had become staples in the repertoire of divas from Teresa Stratas to Renée Fleming. A commissioned opera, *The Tibetan Book of the Dead*, had been presented by the Houston Grand Opera in 1996. His music, a shimmering admixture of Debussy, Ravel, and Britten crossed with Bernstein, Blitzstein, and Sondheim, was both adventurous and easy to like, packing a visceral emotional punch all the more impressive for its compositional rigor. In 1999, Gordon stood alone on his own patch of creative musical terrain.

Raised on the south shore of Long Island, Gordon had entered Carnegie Mellon University as a pianist but emerged a composer. "I started writing music all the time," he said. "I mean, a song a day. Ferverous, scary discipline. By the time I came to New York, I had this...well, body of work."

In 1991, Adam Guettel invited Gordon to perform at his loft in a joint recital benefiting the Gay Men's Health Crisis. Two weeks later Guettel's mother, Mary Rodgers, invited Gordon to her apartment for an impromptu encore. By the end of that evening, Gordon had a publishing contract with the Rodgers and Hammerstein organization.

His new musical for the Vineyard Theater, *Dream True: My Life with Vernon Dexter* opened in April of 1999, a diaphanous memory play about sexual identity and transcendence, written in collaboration with the director (and, for this project, lyricist) Tina Landau. Though Gordon's music for *Dream True* was lush, lyrical, intricate, haunting and, at times thrilling, the dramatic side of *Dream True* often dragged interminably. Gordon's first real foray into the world of musical theater in New York ended up a frustrating experience. Still, it confirmed that there would be more to come from this very original voice.

"I used to be afraid of everyone in the theater," Gordon conceded. "I just found it all frightening—it's a world of virulent opinions. And now I love it. I love the community of artists. Recently, Adam asked me what I felt we were trying to do in the musical theater. I had never put it into words before. We're trying to create musicals where people can be as complex spiritually, intellectually, and emotionally as they are in their lives. A theater where, when someone opens their mouth to sing, they simply don't leave anything behind."

CHAPTER 21

WILD PARTY

I think we're due to have a wild party.
The time is right to toss a huge she-bang.
— *The Wild Party*

The final musical theater season of the 20th century should have belonged to Michael John LaChiusa. In December 1999 *Marie Christine*, his operatic Creole *Medea* written for Audra McDonald, opened at Lincoln Center's Vivian Beaumont Theater, to be followed in April 2000 at the Virginia Theater by *The Wild Party*, LaChiusa's and librettist/director George C. Wolfe's take on Joseph Moncure March's 1929 verse epic of Roaring Twenties hedonism. Co-produced on Broadway by Wolfe's Joseph Papp Public Theater in tandem with some very weighty commercial producers, *Wild Party* was a $5 million musical that boasted a high-profile cast headed by Mandy Patinkin, Eartha Kitt, and the movie actress Toni Collette.

Two major original new musicals in one Broadway season was an enormous achievement at any time (even for Rodgers and Hart, who did it fairly often) but particularly at this time. It could, and should, have been acknowledged that LaChiusa (and by inference, his songwriting generation) had at last arrived on Broadway. But few critics felt disposed to say so.

Why?

To be fair, both *Marie Christine* and *The Wild Party* were musicals

191

about some very unsympathetic folks—a mother made mythic for having killed her children, in the former; a loathsome, abusive vaudeville clown, his tart of a lover and their sycophantic circle of acquaintances, in the latter. Clearly, LaChiusa had decided that to step up in class from one-act canvases, easily approachable full-length musicals would not do. The seriousness of his ambitions would have to be stated in direct proportion to the unappetizing sum of his subjects—the *Sweeney Todd* challenge, essentially.

"It's been exciting to play around," LaChiusa acknowledged. "I like tradition very much but I get tired of it. An audience does want to see their Nellie Forbush fall in love, fall out of love, fall back in love; they like that and they expect it when they go to a musical—even 20- or 30-year-olds. It's a challenge to challenge that."

For *Marie Christine*, LaChiusa had produced a pan-operatic gumbo of a score, full of fierce African drumming, loose-limbed New Orleans jazz inflections and an astringent, at times atonal, melodic palette. Though McDonald gave a tour de force performance that many critics judged to be the production's only redeeming feature, it was fascinating how felicitously her vocal and dramatic brilliance blended with the show's many under-appreciated charms: the roguish vocal allure of Anthony Crivello as Marie Christine's husband; the blistering intensity of Vivian Reed as her mother; the bawdy soulfulness of Mary Testa as a tart-tongued bar owner; exquisite orchestra settings by arranger Jonathan Tunick; and strong choreography by Graciela Daniele.

Yes, there were flaws. Daniele's physical staging seemed bound by an excess of aimless circling. LaChiusa appeared to duck the show's climactic murderous moment by not supplying Marie Christine with a final song to frame her children's death. Ultimately, as a challenger to *Sweeney Todd*, *Marie Christine* inevitably fell short. Still, the only question left unanswered after the curtain came down was, what could *Marie Christine*'s crime as a musical have been that so many saw fit to convict it out of hand?[39]

Response to *The Wild Party* seemed even less justified.[40] This score was sexy and, at times, quite memorable. LaChiusa audaciously chose to recreate and reinvent period songs of the 1920s with a contemporary bite. To a great extent he succeeded.

Under George Wolfe's direction *The Wild Party* cooked. Obviously, the characters were a creepy crew and again one might question the wisdom of making them sing at all. But LaChiusa and Wolfe pulled it off, abetted by a frighteningly intense performance from Patinkin, predictably lusty work from Kitt and an unexpectedly luminous turn from Collette.

"Once you're into creating something," insisted LaChiusa in the end, "no critic's going to get in the way of that. They said some pretty stupid things about *Floyd Collins* and *Violet* too. There's still nothing that beats the joy of doing a musical. There's a shot of adrenaline when the curtain goes up that's never going to go away. I think writing musicals is the only thing to do; the hippest, hottest thing. I think everybody should be writing them. In another five years everyone's going to be."

The critical vituperation that often greeted LaChiusa's achievements in 1999–2000 reflected a disturbing backlash against a young composer who dared to confound critical expectations. An encouraging ear and eye were desperately needed to decipher the promise of these new works, to applaud the actual achievements while acknowledging the degree of failure. Instead, a climate of fear and loathing had come to engulf the already shaky realm of new work, particularly new work that dared to be adventurous.

For years, many had bemoaned the bleakness of musical theater's future, particularly on Broadway, because there were no young writers on the way up. Now that a few talented risk-takers had arrived, it seemed increasingly clear that the bleakness of Broadway's future was more a function of the community's own stagnant aesthetics. Audiences, and critics, too, apparently did not want new musicals by new voices. They wanted new musicals by new voices who sounded like old ones.

Not that this was a particular surprise. What else after all had the reign of Andrew Lloyd Weber been about? Still, LaChiusa's rough, century-ending season confirmed one's grimmest suspicions.

You would have thought that a single *Wild Party* musical would have been enough for any theatrical year. The world of musical theater, however, was a funny place. Somehow, another *Wild Party* actually had preceded LaChiusa's by a matter of months.

Produced by the Manhattan Theater Club, this $1 million version had been written by Andrew Lippa. In the who-was-there-first sweepstakes, Lippa stated that he'd found a copy of *The Wild Party* four years earlier in a bookstore and had brought his idea for the show to Lee Johnson, director of musical theater at the Manhattan Theater Club, who'd encouraged him to proceed, giving the first act a reading in August of 1996 and the completed show another reading in November of 1997. A full workshop had followed in April and May of 1999, yielding Manhattan Theater Club's production of Lippa's *Wild Party* in February 2000 with help (i.e., enhancement money) supplied by Lippa's childhood friend, Jeffrey Seller, along with his partner Kevin McCollum, two of the original producers of *Rent*.

For the record, LaChiusa maintained he'd read *The Wild Party* at the suggestion of someone a few years earlier as well, placing the book on his shelf of possible future projects. When the New York Shakespeare Festival offered him a residency in 1998 and the idea of a musical about show business was discussed, LaChiusa said he'd suddenly recalled *The Wild Party*. An initial reading had ensued at the Public Theater in the Spring of 1998. A cast that included Vanessa Williams, Patinkin, and Kitt was then assembled for a successful private workshop of the show in February of 1999. Almost immediately the Shakespeare Festival decided to produce their *Wild Party* and, moreover, to do so directly on Broadway, though negotiations over both casting and a theater had dragged on torturously.

Didn't the Shakespeare Festival realize that the Manhattan Theater Club was already engaged in a *Wild Party* of its own?

"I never consider another theater's schedule when creating my own," insisted George Wolfe. "There's plenty of room for everybody's *Wild Party.*"

Didn't the Manhattan Theater Club realize they would be bucking a star-filled, Broadway-scale *Wild Party* from the Shakespeare Festival when they decided to press on with their version?

"We don't view doing our work as bucking anything," insisted Lynne Meadow, artistic director of the Manhattan Theater Club. "I think it's interesting that two artists quite independent of each other were attracted by the same story."

As LaChiusa viewed it: "The poem is so hot and sexy, it's no wonder everyone wants to set it to music."

Lippa was a bit less sanguine. "I can't lie that it doesn't affect me. But you can either roll over and play dead or you can fight to the death. No, I didn't think of it as a war. Still, once it was actually happening, I just felt, bring em' on."

Raised in suburban Detroit, Lippa said that growing up he'd been most strongly influenced by Andrew Lloyd Weber's *Jesus Christ Superstar* and *Evita*. After getting a degree in voice at the University of Michigan and trying to be an opera singer, he'd studied with composer William Bolcom, who'd encouraged Lippa to pursue his own writing. Very slowly and sporadically Lippa had begun to write musicals. His *jon & jen*, a kind of pop opera for two characters, was produced Off-Broadway at the Lambs' Theater in 1995. He'd also contributed a couple of new songs to the existing score of *You're A Good Man, Charlie Brown* for its short-lived revival in early 1999.

Lippa had been working regularly as a Broadway musical director and as a pianist when he first picked up *The Wild Party*. "I decided," he said, "I would make it my *Cats*."

His *Wild Party* illustrated how differently two young writers could approach the same material. Both scores were situated unmistakably within the musical theater tradition, but with purposeful twists. Where LaChiusa had composed period songs with updated lyric content, Lippa had opted for much more transparently contemporary power ballads and trendy pop grooves that traversed everything from R&B to Latin to swing. The up-to-the-minute eclecticism of his score tended to pull the spotlight away from the show itself and keep it focused instead on the composer and his gifts, gifts that were clearly plentiful.

"I'd rather be Mark Wahlberg than Stephen Sondheim," Lippa conceded, laughing. "I'd rather be adored for what I look like than what I think."

This tongue in cheek, throwaway observation actually cut to the heart of the matter where new musical theater composers were concerned at the close of the 20th century. You could aspire to be Stephen Sondheim—admired, largely from afar, innovative but also, at least for a general audience, intimidating. Or you could be Mark Wahlberg—cute, buff, and accessible. Somehow, the middle ground between these two poles had been ceded to the Lloyd Webbers and Wildhorns. Whether it could be regained by the next generation of writers remained an open question for the new century.

Kat and the Kings had kicked off that century early on Broadway, opening the 1999–2000 season at the Cort Theater in August 1999. The nostalgic story of an apartheid-era Capetown, South Africa, neighborhood in the late 1950s, and the exceptional mixed-race doo-wop harmony group that had come out of it, *Kat and the Kings* possessed a strong cast, nifty music by Taliep Petersen, and a juvenile book and lyrics that simply could not be overcome.

Saturday Night Fever, the musical, opened at the Minskoff Theater in October 1999, a cheesy gambit whose ham-fistedness as a stage adaptation made the previous season's *Footloose* (yet another film-to-stage fiasco) appear profound by comparison.

The Disney Company's *Aida* at last arrived on Broadway in March 2000 at the Palace Theater, following a nearly two-year odyssey of top-to-bottom rewrites and revamping. *Elaborate Lives* had been a disaster down in Atlanta. Little had worked as expected, or at least hoped for—not the cartoonish script, not the theme park–style direction, not the Imagineer's fabulously expensive pyramid set, not even the awkward, non sequitur title, taken from one of Tim Rice's lyrics. To their credit, "the Disney guys"—Schneider and Schumacher—had grasped this quickly and had rightly decided to begin anew at who knows what expense.

Bob Falls, the artistic director of Chicago's Goodman Theatre, was brought in to stage an entirely new musical retitled *Aida*, rewritten by Falls himself and the playwright David Henry Hwang, with new sets and costumes by Bob Crowley, the widely admired British set designer. All that remained from Atlanta was the Elton John–Tim Rice score, along with that production's two original female leads.

The score worked far better than musical theater purists might have expected. John's music was fairly well-integrated with *Aida*'s script; clearly the pop star had set aside some time in his busy schedule this go-round to attend a rehearsal or two. Rice's lyrics were characteristically glib, sloppily rhymed and carelessly scanned, but catchy.

Aida onstage was pure kitsch, intentionally punctured by anachronisms that allowed for a runway fashion show, vogueing, and Ninja fighters in Pharaonic Egypt. The results were crude and frequently tasteless. But the show was fun for tourists, teens, and Elton John fans. Which was all that Disney could have asked for.

The most successful musical theater producer of the 1999–2000 season was, in the end, Playwrights Horizons, which turned out not one but two very diverse, original musical hits. Even Playwrights, though, was no longer developing musicals on its own.

"We would never have been able to do two musicals in one season if there weren't commercial producers attached," admitted the theater's artistic director, Tim Sanford.

James Joyce's The Dead had arrived first, in October, an adaptation of the James Joyce novella by playwright Richard Nelson, with music by the Irish composer Shaun Davie. The show, essentially, had come to Playwrights via the Broadway producers Gregory Mosher and Arielle Tepper, who'd been seeking an Off-Broadway partner for their latest commercial venture.

"*The Dead* cost about $600,000," acknowledged Sanford, "which Playwrights split with Arielle and Greg 50/50. But it was right up our alley, the kind of musical we've been after lately, musicals out of the musical theater mold, musicals that are not about show music."

The Dead proved to be that rare thing, an understated musical. Its charms were hushed and modest, its songs so integral they barely intruded on the action at all but rather seemed to emerge without overt effort, only to gain increasing, unexpected power.

Playwrights' second musical of the season was a fancifully titled new work by a first time composer/lyricist/librettist named Kirsten Childs. *The Bubbly Black Girl Sheds Her Chameleon Skin* was truly something new, both musically and in its subject matter. Musically, it re-shaped the sha-la-la of '60s girl group refrains and Motown riffs into dramatically cogent theater songs for the stage. No previous musical had really touched that sound before except to pay homage to it, as *Dreamgirls* had. *The Bubbly Black Girl* also managed to turn this light-hearted music into an extraordinarily probing instrument for exploring the boundaries of race.

The show's novice author actually was a theater veteran in her mid-40s, a former Broadway dancer and actress from an African American family in Los Angeles, who'd come to New York after college intent on studying modern dance only to win a part in a touring company of Bob Fosse's original production of *Chicago*.

"If you were black," recalled Childs, "you couldn't get a job in the musical theater in those days unless you had your hand on your hip and were wagging your sassy head or had a big gospel voice. I guess that's why I finally started to write a musical myself. I wanted to prove that black show folks could do something besides wag their heads.

"I found that I was good at writing lyrics," continued Childs, with a lingering note of surprise. "From Motown to Laura Nyro, the thing I'd always loved were the words and what they could make you feel. In 1989 I entered NYU's graduate writing program in musical theater as a lyricist and book writer exclusively. But because my father loved harmony groups when I was growing up, I started buying a cappella music tapes in all kinds of languages and singing along with them; I'd take a line and sing it into a tape recorder and then I'd take another tape and sing another line while the first tape was playing—just to hear what it sounded like. And one day I realized I could do the same thing making up my own melodies.

"I decided I was going to write what I felt in my heart as a black woman. About how you're always supposed to uphold this image; how some people hide behind being surly and other people hide behind being bubbly and I was just tired of it. I knew some of it was taboo and I figured I was probably going to be kicked out of certain communities for revealing this stuff. But it had been preying on my mind since I was a child and I'm an adult now so I figured, what have I got to be afraid of? I started to write it as a fairy tale about this little black girl who had these issues. And then I just sat back and waited for everybody to beat me up. But people of all colors—not just black people—they've been laughing and crying, and telling me that they see themselves up there. Which surprised me as much as anyone."

One of the people who approached Childs was Ira Weitzman. "I was blown away when I first heard the show the previous summer up at the Eugene O'Neill Conference," remembered Weitzman. "It was quirky. It was funny. And in taking on the racial stereotypes of the last 30 years, it was absolutely shameless. I immediately phoned Tim Sanford at Playwrights and said: 'This is for us.'"

There was, however, already fierce competition for the show. The Manhattan Theater Club, the New York Shakespeare Festival and the Vineyard Theater too all wanted *The Bubbly Black Girl*, as did Wind Dancer Productions, a cash-rich production company formed by three television executives, Matt Williams, David McFadzean and Carmen Finestra, who between them had created and/or produced *The Cosby Show, Home Improvement*, and *Roseanne*. Unsurprisingly, Wind Dancer won the rights with a lot of cash. It was then pragmatically decided, however, that the musical still should be developed at Playwrights Horizons.

"I do wish," conceded Tim Sanford, "that the commercial theater community and everybody with an interest in musical theater would just give Playwrights a subsidy to develop new musicals with no strings attached. But they don't do that anymore."

The Bubbly Black Girl should have gone to Broadway. The show received warm reviews and its backing was already in place in the form of Wind Dancer, who'd presumably bet early on *Bubbly* with just that intention—to move it. Yet, somehow, through a combination of inexperience and, possibly, last-minute trepidation over *The Bubbly Black Girl's* political incorrectness, the ball was dropped. Not even an original cast recording emerged to preserve the show for posterity.

The Dead, on the other hand, did make it to Broadway, re-opening in January 2000 at the Belasco Theater. *The Dead* even garnered a Tony nomination for best musical that year, only to lose out to *Contact*, a piece produced by Lincoln Center Theater comprised entirely of dance vignettes choreographed by Susan Stroman to pre-recorded classical, pop, and jazz standards. In other words, a new musical with a pre-recorded score and no live singing at all. A new nadir for new musicals, if you cared to look at it that way.

A Chorus Line. Donna McKechnie and Michael Bennett backstage (circa 1975). Photograph courtesy Photofest.

Top: Playwrights Horizons, in the beginning (1977). Photograph courtesy Playwrights Horizons.

Bottom: William Finn (1981). Photograph © Jack Mitchell, courtesy Playwrights Horizons.

Opposite: *March of the Falsettos.* Michael Rupert, Alison Fraser, James Kushner, Chip Zien, Stephen Bogardus (1981). Photograph © Susan Cook, courtesy Playwrights Horizons.

Opposite, top: Andrew Lloyd Webber (circa 1990s). Photograph courtesy Photofest.

Opposite, bottom: Michael Crawford and Sarah Brightman in *Phantom of the Opera* (1988). Photograph courtesy Photofest.

This page: Harold Prince and Stephen Sondheim in rehearsal for *Merrily We Roll Along* (1981). Photograph courtesy Mary Bryant.

OPPOSITE: Audra McDonald (circa 1990s). Photograph courtesy Photofest.

TOP: The composer-lyricist Michael John LaChiusa (at the piano) with Ira Weitzman in a Playwrights Horizons rehearsal space (1997). Photograph © Suzanne DeChillo/*The New York Times.*

BOTTOM: Stephen Flaherty and Lynn Ahrens outside Playwrights Horizons during the run of *Lucky Stiff* (1988). Photograph © Gerry Goodstein, courtesy Lynn Ahrens.

THIS PAGE: *Sunday in the Park with George*. Mandy Patinkin as George Seurat. Bernadette Peters as Dot (1984). Photographs by Don Perdue, courtesy Photofest.

OPPOSITE: Stephen Sondheim, Bernadette Peters and James Lapine on the set during rehearsals for *Into the Woods* (1987). Photograph courtesy Photofest.

THIS PAGE: *Rent* (1996). Photograph by Joan Ma[...]
Carol Rosegg, courtesy Phot[...]

OPPOSITE: Jonathan Larson in front of New [...]
Theatre Workshop box office during *Rent*'s [...]
workshop (1994). Photograph © Allan La[...]

This page: Adam Guettel (1997). Photograph
John Halpern, courtesy Photo

Opposite: *Floyd Collins.* Martin Moran as Sk
Miller, Christopher Innvar as Floyd (199
Photograph © Joan Marcus, cour
Playwrights Horiz

Opposite, top: George C. Wolfe and Savion Glover rehearse *Bring in 'da Noise, Bring in 'da Funk* (1995). Photograph © Michal Daniel.

Opposite, bottom: *Bring in 'da Noise, Bring in 'da Funk* at the The Public Theater (1995). (Foreground/left to right:) Savion Glover, Vincent Bingham, Jimmy Tate, Baakari Wilder. (Background/left to right:) Raymond King and Jared "J.R." Crawford. Photograph © Michal Daniel.

This page, top: Peter Schneider and Thomas Schumacher with their Tony Award for *The Lion King* (1998). Photograph © Anita & Steve Shevett.

This page, bottom: *The Lion King.* "Circle of Life." Tsidii Le Loka (1997). Photograph © Joan Marcus.

Top: "Little Old Ladyland" from the orig
Broadway production of *The Prod*
Photograph © Paul Ko

Bottom: Nathan Lane as Max Bialystock
Matthew Broderick as Leo Bloom in "Finale" f
the original Broadway production of *The Prod*
Photograph © Paul Ko

CHAPTER 22

WHAT SINGS

Sylvia Herscher could have looked at it that way. In fact, all by herself, Sylvia Herscher and her long life in the theater put *Contact* to shame.

"Who am I? I wasn't unique," she insisted. "Lots of people did what I did. It's just that I was lucky. Timing. In real estate it's location, in the theater it's timing. A confluence of everything coming together and a lot of luck. That's all."

Most Tony Awards are self-explanatory. Best Musical: *Contact.* Nothing could be clearer. Then there are the honorary Tonys handed out for something called "Excellence in Theater." In 2000, the actress Eileen Heckart got one, along with the then-seven-year-old in-concert musical revival series, *Encores!*[41] A third honorary Tony went to Sylvia Herscher.

Who?

The facts were as follows. After a fifty-year theatrical life spanning several careers — as a general manager, a producer, a music publisher, an agent — Sylvia Herscher, age 86, was retired. She'd been the composer Jule Styne's "right hand" for many years; the composer Jerry Herman's self-avowed "mentor" for even longer. In her own words, she'd been "a theatrical matchmaker;" in Herman's words, "the woman who arranged things," the living embodiment of his greatest leading lady, Dolly Levi herself.

"I brought Sylvia every one of my new scores first," Herman readily acknowledged. "I clung to her—for her ears and her instincts. You can't go to school for that. Sylvia, more than anyone I've ever known, represented an entire world that has disappeared."

Always she functioned in the offstage shadows. The threads of her professional existence were spun with incredible finesse. Unraveling their intricate weave revealed something quite marvelous—one of the best kept secrets, in a sense, of Broadway's increasingly mythic past, a past that *Contact*, with its pre-recorded, pre-fabricated score, practically negated.

Herscher's work with Styne, for example, had included assisting on his celebrated 1952 revival of *Pal Joey*, which had meant sitting as a referee between the show's book writer John O'Hara and its composer Richard Rodgers, who would not speak to each other. She was the associate producer for Styne's 1955 hit comedy production *Will Success Spoil Rock Hunter?* and his general manager for the musicals *Hazel Flagg*; *Mr. Wonderful*; *Say, Darling*; and, of course, *Gypsy*, among others.

"Jule was a madman," Herscher recalled, "the most wonderful madman; writing with one hand, producing with the other. I learned more up there in that little office of Jule's over the Hellinger Theater. I learned what makes a song work. What makes a scene work."

Did she always want to be in the theater?

The question brought a crooked smile. "I wanted to be an actress."

Born Sylvia Kossovsky in New York City to Eastern European immigrant parents of modest means, Herscher studied piano from the age of five and, as she remembered, spent her life at Carnegie Hall. "For me, it was serious music and theater, concerts and Eva LaGalliene's Civic Rep. Not musical theater. Not at first."

She graduated from college in 1934, married in 1935 and worked a variety of jobs, including summers in the borscht belt serving up theater at Rosenblatt's Hotel in Glen Wild, New York. "That's when I started doing musicals," she said. "Though I made the guests listen to Eugene O'Neill, too, on Sunday nights—all his one-acters. They actually began to like it after a while.

"I didn't decide I couldn't be an actress," she went on, "it was decided for me, if you know what I mean. Then I had a family—two children. My husband Seymour worked in the Bulova watch company, he was Artie Bulova's assistant. When they were looking for somebody to do publicity and P.R., Seymour interviewed a guy named Alexander Cohen—in 1942, I think—and Alex was hired. Then Alex began to produce. Seymour eventually left Bulova and joined Alex in 1959. They were together until Seymour died six years ago."

It was Cohen who truly gave Herscher her start. "My parents believed that every woman should have a career. Once my kids were born, I wanted to work again. Alex first gave me a job doing publicity for a *King Lear* he was producing with Louis Calhern in 1950. Then he and Jule Styne were going to do a show called *Make a Wish* and Jule needed a secretary. Jule used to say he got stuck with a secretary who could neither type nor take dictation. Which was true. If you were a working woman in those days you could be, maybe, a doctor—but the sciences came not trippingly into my head, you see. Or you could teach—and I knew I could never teach. Or you could become a secretary. The way not to be a secretary was to not learn how to type. And so I never did. Within a few years I was Jule's general manager.

"Jule and Alex had one thing in common," Herscher announced, as if realizing the fact herself for the first time. "They were never afraid to fail. They dusted themselves off and started all over again. So different from today. Everything today is by committee. Jule thought *Pal Joey* should go on, *Pal Joey* went on. We went to a factoring company, and Jule put up all of his ASCAP royalties as collateral to get the balance of the money he needed to open that show. If he believed in something, he got it on. Alex was the same way. Courage of your convictions — go out and do."

In 1960 Herscher went out and joined William Morris. "Jule stopped producing," she explained simply. "The agency thought I might represent performers, but it became very clear early on that my strengths really were with writers. There were producers who were interested in adapting a book, I would meet with them and find the right playwright. Composers looking for a project to musicalize, lyricists looking for a composer; whenever there was a situation that needed a little something, they would throw me in there. That's how I met Jerry Herman. For whatever reason, there was a problem with who should direct his first show, *Milk and Honey*. I got involved and everything worked out very nicely. Jerry and I met. And we realized that we were truly soul mates. I don't think a week goes by still that we don't speak."

After five years, she moved on to Edwin H. Morris, one of Broadway's leading music publishers. "Buddy Morris wanted to become a producer, which is why I signed on. But it became very apparent that if you're publishing eight or ten top composers and lyric writers, you can't choose to produce A and not B.

"Still, it was a joy. So much talent: Harold Arlen. Charles Strouse and Lee Adams. Jerry Herman. At Morris a composer got support — financial and emotional. You made a commitment to what you heard.

"It wasn't always art," Herscher added. "In 1965 I saw this little show, *Man of La Mancha*, up at the Goodspeed Opera House in Connecticut. And I didn't particularly like it. But I knew it was going to make money. I said to Buddy, let's get *Man of La Mancha*.

Not for art, it isn't art, but for money. And he said no." She shrugged. "After that he never said no to me again.

"*Grease* was not a great show. I picked it up after hearing a runthrough downtown in the East Village. I went and I had a good time. I thought, this is gonna work. I arranged for the entire office to go to the last preview. And nobody would talk to me after that. They all hated it with a passion. Of course," she added, "they sure got over that.

"Ed Kleban," Herscher suddenly recalled. "Ed left his job — he'd been working in record producing — and came to meet with me. 'I have a show I've written,' he said, 'music and lyrics.' *Gallery*, it was called. I arranged for Michael Bennett to hear this score. Michael wound up very impressed with the lyrics. He asked Ed if he would mind coming downtown to see some of the workshops he'd started with dancers and to meet this composer named Marvin. And out of that came *A Chorus Line*. Which we published."

Herscher sighed. "Soon after that Buddy sold the company to his lawyer John Eastman. You know, you end with *A Chorus Line*, it's time to get out. I went to work as head of the theater department at G. Schirmer. By the late '70s I saw things were really changing. In 1982, I retired."

Which isn't to say that she stopped. "I've just made a new musical," Herscher practically crowed. "It's called *Haunted*, based on an old Victorian novel. I put the writers together, they'd never met each other. Things are rippling and rumbling. And I blackmail, I use every weapon in the book. How long do you think I have to live, I tell the producers? Let's get moving.

"This is the difference between theater then and theater now," she went on. "It's boring after a while to talk about. But you could have so many new things going then because there were people who were ready to take the chance. Now, unless you can show somebody the bottom line, forget it. Money—the importance of money—has had a profound effect on everything we do, so why not the theater too? Of course, Jule and Alex all expected to make money. But they also recognized that failure was possible too. And they went on their own gut. It was a passion. And that's not what we have now. Now we have calculation."

She grew silent, a trim, tiny woman with astonishingly alert eyes magnified by great enveloping spectacles. "I don't like to talk about it," Herscher said, "because I really start to cry." She actually did begin to cry for just a moment. "I was involved in so many. Sometimes your heart broke, but if this didn't work the next did. Now, what they consider great…and I don't even know who *they* is. I just don't understand. I try to remember a musical that left me feeling something. I can't."

Her eyes brightened. "I listened to Audra McDonald's first album—listened to it very carefully, to all the new writers. And obviously they aren't writing for me. But, if I could only work with some of those kids. Because this is the talent of the age. I get so upset! Working is hard now for everyone, but they have to understand that it's working with the specific people that make sense—that's what's important. And it's so hard to find the projects that sing.

"That's where I can help," insisted Sylvia Herscher. "I know what sings. Still."

CHAPTER 23

A SHOWBIZ MAUSOLEUM

It's like a putz museum,
A showbiz mausoleum.

— *The Full Monty*

The Producers arrived on Broadway in April 2001 and gleefully marched the Broadway musical resolutely backward in time. The shtick, the girls (both young and old), the tunes, the governing taste, all were determinedly old-school and audiences loved it. So did critics. As the screenwriter and entertainment industry pundit, William Goldman, put it in *Variety*: "Come back to the theater. All is forgiven." [42]

It happened practically without warning. No one at first seemed to take very seriously whispers that 75-year-old Mel Brooks had reworked his legendary cinematic paean to bad taste and Broadway musicals into a new stage musical with words and music ("Springtime for Hitler" included) by none other than Mel Brooks. And then, inexorably, audience enthusiasm during the show's out-of-town tryout in Chicago began to build momentum. By the time *The Producers* reached New York, ticket buyers and critics alike seemed to be panting in anticipation.

Yes, out-of-town tryout. Even *The Producers*' development route was a throwback.

"Mel insisted," recalled *The Producers*' director and choreographer, Susan Stroman. "He doesn't come from this world but he knew how important it was to go out of town because of the comedy. Just the tilt of an actor's head can get a bigger laugh and an actor needs to find that in front of an audience. Producers balk because going out of town automatically costs you, like, a million and a half that you know you're going to lose. But then, we made money in Chicago."

"Nobody expected that," added *The Producers'* set designer, Robin Wagner. "Nobody really understood what a following Mel has."

"*The Producers* is my love letter to the Broadway I loved that no longer really exists," Brooks acknowledged, "from *High Button Shoes*, to *Guys and Dolls*, and *Forum*. Musical comedy. There hasn't been a down and dirty musical comedy in forever. Nobody even uses the word anymore. I lived for that. It's in my blood. I couldn't wait to go out of town and find out what stinks and fix it up. I have too much respect for Broadway to fool around; Rodgers and Hart and the Gershwins and Cole himself and Irving himself..."

And Andrew Lloyd Webber?

"And Andrew Lloyd Webber," Brooks allowed, "who doesn't write many funny songs."

It would have been gratifying to believe that *The Producers'* liberating presence on Broadway was somehow related to the removal from the scene of *Cats* and *Miss Saigon*, those seemingly immovable monuments to British musical theater know-how, which had both finally closed just prior to *The Producers'* arrival.[43]

But, of course, that wasn't really true.

"Certainly, it was the close of a chapter," conceded Ira Weitzman. "But I don't think that it was cause and effect. Though something definitely seemed to have been freed up."

Disney's Peter Schneider felt he knew precisely what that was. "Theaters," he said. "The most important thing when developing new work is knowing you've got the right theater to take your work into. We waited three years with *Lion King* looking for just the right venue before the New Amsterdam finally made that show possible. So, yes, you might say that the liberation of the Broadway and Winter Garden theaters could trickle down to encourage new work. But," Schneider added, "I doubt it."

"I would love to have seen *Cats* go on forever," admitted Gerald Schoenfeld, longtime landlord and co-producer for both *Cats* and *Miss Saigon* as chairman of the Shubert organization. "*Cats*," maintained Schoenfeld, "was one of the saviors of the American musical theater. It produced a golden age."

To contribute to a golden age (good or otherwise) a musical (good or otherwise) has to employ the appropriate creative team. Even *The Producers'* maladroit impresario, Max Bialystock, understood this. For Bialystock, onstage at the St. James Theater, the failure of his "surefire flop," *Springtime for Hitler*, was absolutely dependent on securing the services of a director named Roger De Bris. For Mel Brooks, the successful transformation of his 1968 film classic into a Tony Award–winning hit Broadway musical required one similarly bald-faced collaborative overture.

"Two and a half years ago my husband Mike Ockrent and I got a call saying Mel Brooks wanted to meet us," Susan Stroman recalled. "'Sure,' we said, 'maybe next Thursday.' No, we were told, he wants to meet you right now. About an hour later I opened our front door and there stood Mel Brooks. He didn't say hello. He just launched full voice into the song, 'That Face,' which now opens our second act, marching down my long New York hallway and jumping up on top of my living room sofa to finish the tune.

"'Hello,' he finally said, 'I'm Mel Brooks,' before going on to sing a few other songs he'd written for the show. Only then did he stop to announce: 'I want to make a musical out of *The Producers*. And you're the people I want to help me.'"

Certainly what literally made *The Producers* a musical (at an estimated cost of $10.5 million) were the sixteen new songs Brooks wound up composing to supplement the three he'd originally created for the movie. What helped make *The Producers* a smash musical, though, were a host of ingenious *coups de théâtre* that Brooks and Stroman went on to devise for many of those songs in collaboration with set designer Wagner, costume designer William Ivey Long, and Brooks' book-writing partner, Thomas Meehan. Yes, the movie was a mother lode of brilliant comedic source material. And yes, *The Producers'* acting company, led by Nathan Lane and Matthew Broderick, were a very funny bunch. To truly understand the almost incomprehensible critical and commercial frenzy that the show generated, though, one had to look to the production's seemingly breezy creative details. The real answers resided there, in the blithe marvels that these well-matched collaborators had wrought.

"To begin with, everyone had to be on the same page," insisted Stroman. "And for that you had to immerse yourself in the world of Mel."

The nascent production had received a terrible initial body blow in December of 1999 with the death from leukemia of the 53-year-old Ockrent, best known for his Tony-nominated staging of the musicals *Me and My Girl* and *Crazy for You*. "We lost Mike," Stroman recalled, "and about two months later Mel came to me and asked me to continue. Of course, it was painful. But the best remedy for grief is laughter. And, needless to say, Mel makes me laugh. Not only while working. He's also very funny to eat with."

Wagner had worked with Stroman on *Crazy for You*. "I brought Robin in for the first read-through of Mel's barely finished script," said Stroman. "Robin is the master of the backstage musical. And *The Producers* is all about the theater."

"Everyone in the room just *kvelled* all the way through," remembered

Wagner. "It just landed. You don't hear material like that without six weeks of rehearsal. That script seemed so complete. Mel and Tom had already worked out all the problems of designing this show; how to get actors from one place to another. Every transition was a natural transition."

Stroman nodded. "*The Producers* has all the elements of a traditional musical comedy but in fact it's directed and designed with a very contemporary eye. An audience today has far more cinematic expectations; they need the plot pushed forward at all times. And that even applies during set transitions. Nobody wants to sit through a blackout anymore. I insisted no set change be more than seven seconds long. I didn't want an audience to wait more than seven seconds."

But what about the show's now infamous breakout bits? What about the file cabinets, the pigeons, the little old ladies with walkers, and the storm troopers? In terms of creative gestation, who made what happen where?

"First Mel had to let go of some of the screenplay," answered Stroman. "Initially he was a little reticent. For example, we gave Leo Bloom a secret desire to be a Broadway producer—which isn't in the movie. Mel came to like that. The challenge of Bloom's first song, 'I Wanna Be a Producer,' then became the fact that it was this grim Dickensian scene—all these accountants, everybody at the same desk with the same picture of the boss behind them—but we had to make the girls Bloom fantasized about appear in it magically. That's when I asked Robin about file cabinets and he said, sure, we could have file cabinets. 'Good,' I said, 'what if the girls come out of the file cabinets?' So Robin built file cabinets that were big enough to contain my six-foot-three-inch showgirls."

"They have no room in there," Wagner laughed. "The cabinet mustn't look big enough to hold a person, so you don't see it coming, particularly when Bloom first pulls out a drawer and produces his hat and his stick. Two seconds later the cat's out of the bag; or, rather, the girls are — six of them."

The movie, of course, had no magic file cabinets. It did, however, have pigeons. Real ones, kept in a rooftop coop by the Nazi playwright Franz Liebkind. The musical turned these "doity disgusting boids" (as Liebkind's building "concierge" in the movie described them) into terribly cute puppets.

"The pigeon puppets were my idea," Stroman said. "After *Lion King* everybody was so obsessed with putting puppets into shows, I thought, what if we had puppets that were actually funny. What if we found somebody who could build pigeon puppets to sing backup vocals behind Liebkind?"

As Wagner remembered it: "We were going to have hand puppets originally sticking through a black drop. But then I found this guy in Brooklyn who makes really big puppets — he also wound up working on our Nazi marionettes in the 'Springtime for Hitler' number."

"At first, his pigeons were as big as giant turkeys," Stroman laughed. "But he shrunk them down, made sure their wings could move. And behind those pigeons now are four of my showgirls."

Wagner grinned. "Four other pigeons."

"They sing and they move the puppets," continued Stroman. "Which makes the pigeons very human. Because the girls react to whatever Liebkind does."

Beyond pigeons, the movie also had plenty of little old ladies. None of them, however, wielded their walkers as dance partners.

"The genesis for our old lady with walker kick line," said Stroman, "was a speech Mel had in the movie for Max Bialystock that began: 'I'm about to launch myself into Little Old Ladyland.' 'Oh, yeah?' Robin and I thought, 'Well, how about a little old lady theme park?'"

Wagner took it from there. "The set started as a Valentine card, in my mind, filled with little old lady lace. One of my great theater memories was Boris Aronson's original design for the Sondheim musical, *Follies*—this fantastic abstract set, in the middle of which appeared this perfect little valentine for the section called 'Loveland.' I meant mine as an homage to *Follies*, though it seems to have come to be regarded as a parody. That was not my intention. But you just can't leave people like Stroman around with toys like that. It just blew up from there because Mel, being who he is, develops everything and Stro's the same way, she'll take an idea out about ten levels and then end it with a capper.

"First came the old lady Rockettes with walkers. Soon we were dragging trampolines into rehearsals just to see what we could do with them. That was the signal for me that all bets were off. I said to Stro, 'You've been using a lot of swings uptown in *Contact*, why don't we try a few down here?' Finally Mel said, 'Well, as long as the old ladies are swinging, can't we lose one? What if one doesn't come back?'"

"You can't be afraid to try anything," said Stroman. "It's all about taking chances. What you suggest might not be right at that moment, but it could spark something in someone's imagination to take it further."

"The mirror we use for the overhead Busby Berkeley effect in 'Springtime for Hitler' is, of course, my little nod to *A Chorus Line*," added Wagner, "which I designed. I figure any time you line up 24 dancers in front of a mirror, you've got *A Chorus Line*."

"It was Robin who also pointed out that I didn't have enough cast members to make a dancing swastika," said Stroman. "Then I

remembered William Ivey Long had once done a show for those
Vegas magicians, Siegfried and Roy, where he created a whole army
coming at the audience; dancers with army men dummies on each
side of them. So I called William and said, 'What if we put storm
trooper puppets on either side of the dancers and make them goose
step, could you do that?' And he said, 'Sure I can do that.' So we
worked out how many dancers we would need. And it became a
perfect statement of what the Nazis were like actually, these indis-
tinguishable storm trooper puppets."

"Mel kind of turned the key in the ignition and then we were off,"
Wagner concluded. "'Hmm,' you think, 'maybe we can do that.'
And when you find out you can, well, Mel is so damn pleased!"

Stroman agreed. "It's just so great to make him laugh," she said.
"That became our litmus test in *The Producers*. Because, ultimately,
when Mel Brooks laughs, we all do."

Unfortunately, there was an unspoken (and in some cases out-
spoken) sense along Broadway that the tumultuous reception
accorded *The Producers* in 2001 was, in part, an expression of relief;
relief that the Broadway musical had somehow been spared from the
dour inroads made by young composers like Michael John LaChiusa
the previous season. Of course, much of this simply was about
laughter versus the limited box office appeal of filicide in a musical.
Certainly, Brooks and LaChiusa made audiences howl for entirely
different reasons. In fact, though, if the 2000–2001 Broadway season
had any unifying theme at all beyond the dawning of *The Producers*,
it actually was the continuing youthful tilt in the range of ages
among Broadway composers.

Some that year were neophytes like David Yazbek, whose lyrics and
music helped transform a hugely popular film, *The Full Monty*, into
a very solid Broadway musical that opened at the Eugene O'Neill

Theater in October. Yazbek was pushing 40 in the year 2000. Among the ancients of Broadway's musical theater fraternity this made him a veritable child. The same went for 40-ish Don Schlitz, a Grammy Award–winning country western cross-over composer, who helped turn Mark Twain's Tom Sawyer into *The Adventures of Tom Sawyer*, a very bland musical that opened at the Minskoff Theater in April and closed in May. It also applied to Paul Gordon, a 40-something writer of pop songs for Bette Midler and Amy Grant, among others, who helped bring another epic novel, *Jane Eyre*, to the stage of the Brooks Atkinson Theater in December. As a musical, this *Jane Eyre* stubbornly clung to vestiges of the British mega-model, with a set designed by *Cats'*, *Miss Saigon's*, *Les Miz's*, and *Sunset Boulevard's* notorious spectacle manufacturer, five-time Tony Award winner John Napier. It featured a Gothic pop-operetta score á la Andrew Lloyd Webber by Gordon. The gambit did not yield much success, though. The mega-model was now well past its prime.

Also represented on Broadway in 2000–2001 were youthful veterans Ahrens and Flaherty with *Seussical* (derived from the classic children's books by the late Theodor Seuss Geisel, a.k.a. Dr. Seuss). Another Livent-initiated musical, *Seussical* did not turn out well at all after it opened in November 2000 at the Richard Rodgers Theater.

No one from musical theater's younger generation had yet rivaled the success of Ahrens and Flaherty who, with their Tony Award–winning score for *Ragtime* and before that their Off-Broadway transfer, *Once On This Island*, truly had managed to make it on Broadway. The bankruptcy proceedings still engulfing Livent, however, also had singed Ahrens and Flaherty financially.

"It has been a really rough year," Ahrens acknowledged. "In terms of musical theater, I now know far more about bankruptcy law than I ever hoped to."

It could be argued that Livent's involvement in *Seussical* also had affected Ahrens and Flaherty from a creative point of view. As a

Drabinsky-originated project, *Seussical* had endured a four-week workshop in Toronto in August 1999, just as Drabinsky was being removed from Livent. The charming little musical that Ahrens and Flaherty had written was increasingly inflated into a very big musical by Livent's inheritor on the project, SFX Theatrical Group and Universal Studios. It was this latter bunch, abetted by the producers, Barry and Fran Weissler, who fired the show's costume designer and, for all intents, the director Frank Galatti, bringing in the director/choreographer Rob Marshall to "consult" after the show was poorly received in its subsequent September Boston tryout.[44]

The *Seussical* musical that reached Broadway was an unsprung disaster; confused about its proper scale and style, more than a little vulgar, and often quite tacky. By that point Livent was, in fact, no more. All of its remaining musicals in-progress, including *Seussical*, had become the bankruptcy-sale property of SFX.

Seussical was notably kept afloat for a time by the intense ministrations of Rosie O'Donnell, the effusive talk show hostess, who actually joined *Seussical's* cast for a time in a desperate effort to attract an audience to it. O'Donnell's six-year reign as "The Queen of Nice" on daytime television, from 1996 to 2002, was an extraordinary one for the Broadway musical. Proudly proclaiming her avowedly plebian (i.e., "suburban") appetite for all things Broadway, O'Donnell gave many new musicals and revivals a live shot on her program. Her avidity was matched by a serene lack of concern about quality. The O'Donnell factor proved a conflicted blessing for Broadway—wonderful for selling tickets but painfully retrograde in terms of taste. What was Broadway to do when its most visible champion often fell in love with lousy musicals? The answer was plain and simple: Please her.

"Still," said Ira Weitzman optimistically, "I think producers are at least wising up to the fact they're gonna run out of revivals. They're finally realizing musicals just don't get born somewhere where you can go shop for them; they're starting to develop them rather than merely buying up shows. And the coterie of writers has become larger and more varied in the kind of work they're doing. The more experimental composers are still around, but there's also a ground-swell of young people writing in a more pop vernacular. Despite the odds, a new generation has come into existence on their own; a sub-community of Broadway. It's been insulated and now it's coming out. There really was a healthy mixture of established and emerging artists who got shots this season, an intermingling of them. In fact, no one's even emerging anymore—everybody seems to have emerged. There's just a lot more receptivity."

It was easy to overlook "young" David Yazbek, as the composer and lyricist who had made *The Full Monty* a new musical. Not only was he an unknown Broadway novice, he also was laboring in the shadow of his own show's widely advertised male nudity.

Yazbek's clever pop/rock score for *The Full Monty* was, however, as fresh as Mel Brooks' music for *The Producers* was recycled. Yazbek was no great innovator. But he did have a feeling for the sound and sense of contemporary music and an unpretentious quick-wittedness as a lyricist. Together, these two qualities defined *The Full Monty*'s appeal as a musical.

So, who was David Yazbek?

"I'm just a guy with a wife and a kid and a band. I have a marginal career as a recording artist," said Yazbek, "these albums that no one buys: one called *The Laughing Man*, which didn't sell here but did in other countries, and the other called *Tock*, which didn't sell here and was never released in other countries. I have this little cult fan base of guys mostly, who all look, well...like me; chubby with glasses, in T-shirts. And I once wrote comedy for David Letterman."

How did that happen?

"He hired me.

"I hated it," Yazbek added. "I realized I really needed music."

Born and raised in New York City, the son of a clothing designer father and a mother "who was just my mother," Yazbek was, he said, "a rock music snob. I was interested in musical theater as a kid because my parents were. But that passed."

In college, as if anticipating his future Broadway debut, Yazbek had directed a revival of *Hair*, "just to see if I could get away with having people naked onstage."

Beyond his many rock and roll influences, though — particularly the band XTC and its primary songwriter, Andy Partridge — Yazbek nursed one guilty musical theater vice, a weakness for the songs of Frank Loesser. "I've always loved Loesser," he acknowledged. "That unbelievably catchy little counterpoint melody line he uses in 'Standin' on the Corner'? I've applied that kind of riff to everything I've ever written, in a way. I've just always thought that was way cool."

Recognizing Loesser's artistry was one thing, though. How did Yazbek wind up on Broadway?

"A garage band did it," he insisted. "Just after Letterman, I was in this band called Barn, with a bass player named Adam Guettel. Adam seems to have been the first person considered by the producers to write *The Full Monty* score. He turned them down but recommended me.

"I remember asking Adam whether I should go to one of those workshops, you know, to learn the basics of musical theater writing," Yazbek laughed. "And Adam started screaming at me: 'Whatever you do, don't do that! Just jump in, jump in over your head! Start writing!'"

Yazbek submitted his two poor-selling CDs as audition material, followed by two demonstration songs written specifically for the show. To his amazement, he got the gig.

Lindsay Law, *The Full Monty*'s lead producer, acknowledged the choice was a conscious gamble. "*The Full Monty* is a contemporary show," Law said. "The people onstage are dealing with real life today. So the idea was, could we find somebody whose music sounded that contemporary and that real? Which pretty much eliminated just about everybody writing for Broadway today. David's music immediately impressed me with its warmth and incredible sense of humor. But it was a bit scary betting it all on David. As things have turned out, I got much more than I'd bargained for."

Yazbek experienced his own initial doubts about the whole business. "What did I think at first? Honestly? I thought: Great, another cheesy Broadway adaptation of a popular movie."

And what did he think now?

Yazbek grinned. "Well, now I think: Hey, this is really good."

Though the Manhattan Theater Club had gotten badly burned producing its own *Wild Party* just a year before, it nevertheless returned with three new musicals over the course of 2000–2001. The first, *A Class Act*, which opened in November, used existing show music by the late Edward Kleban to tell Kleban's life story beyond *A Chorus Line*. The second, which opened in January, was a full-scale book musical based on the popular novel *Time and Again*, while the third, in March, was a revue called *The New Yorkers* with entirely original music by two relatively new musical theater writers, Glenn Slater and Stephen Weiner.

Of the three, *A Class Act* certainly traveled the furthest, moving to Broadway, where it reopened at the Ambassador Theater in March.

Some found *A Class Act* charming and even moving in its depiction of the egoistic and often insufferable Kleban tormenting himself and those who loved him until his tragic and untimely death from cancer. This sympathy for the show appears to have been unavoidably influenced by the unfortunate circumstances of Kleban's passing. The musical was a decidedly minor achievement that affectionately and altogether unintentionally managed to underline the limits of Kleban's gift as a frustrated composer, even as it reinforced his reputation as a very fine lyricist.

Time and Again, adapted from the popular Jack Finney novel, was an uninteresting work in almost every respect. Its presence at the Manhattan Theater Club was inexplicable except as an excuse to showcase a 21-year-old talent named Laura Benanti.

To dub her a "future star" would be presumptuous. Benanti, though, was more than just gifted. Her lustrous vocal ability and onstage presence ranked her alongside a new generation of charismatic musical theater performers, led by Audra McDonald, that now included Kristen Chenoweth, Heather Headley, Marc Kudisch, Melissa Errico, Sherie René Scott, Norbert Leo Butz, and Brian d'Arcy James. These kids no longer needed "a shot"; all of them were well past that. What they needed, and deserved, were substantive new musicals.

Benanti seemed too young to be so good, even while handling less than choice material. "I was kind of born 40-years-old," she insisted. "I was always a little adult—even as a little kid—one who just couldn't understand why she was surrounded by all these...kids. I took things very seriously."

But how did such a kid, even one with outsized intimations of maturity, come to give her heart, in this day and age, to Julie Andrews rather than, say, Britney Spears?

"You know I actually enjoy Britney Spears," Benanti conceded. "Not as a singer but as a performer. I just enjoy watching her. I think: You are *so* brave."

Where Spears' artistry roughly brought to mind, well, a Warhol soup can, Benanti, with her cascading dark curls and direct gray eyes, seemed drawn from another era.

"I've just always wanted to do this," she said. "My mom is a voice teacher—*my* voice teacher. I used to fall asleep under the piano while she gave lessons. Mom was also on Broadway when she was my age. It's definitely in my blood. My parents were in *Brigadoon* on Broadway when I was a couple of years old; my mom understudied Fiona—her name at the time was Linda Vidnovic—and my dad, Martin Vidnovic, played the lead. My parents are divorced," Benanti added. "My stepfather, who is my father, raised me. We moved to Jersey when I was four or five—Kinnelon—it's very beautiful there, but I was so bored. That's when I really knew I wanted to be on Broadway."

In rapid succession, Benanti moved from winning the Papermill Playhouse Rising Star Award at 16, as the lead, of course, in her high school *Hello Dolly*, to being cast at 17 as Rebecca Luker's understudy in the Broadway revival of *The Sound of Music*, to taking over from Luker at the age of 19 as Maria Von Trapp opposite Richard Chamberlain, to winning a Tony nomination at 20 for her work in the Broadway musical *Swing*.

Benanti's director in *Time and Again*, Susan Schulman, also directed *The Sound of Music*. "I'll never forget her audition," she recalled. "This kid walked in. And, yes, she was a very beautiful woman. And, yes, she sang beautifully. That's not so unusual. But Laura had a kind of emotional transparency that was just staggering. The way she connected to the material—the way she inhabited the lyrics. She was there to audition for one of the nuns, for heaven's sake. 'Lovely, lovely,' I said. 'Could you just wait outside for a minute?' And then I turned to the producers. 'I know you think I'm out of my mind, but we've got to read this kid for the lead.' And we did. Gave her some lines, a cold reading. And the same thing happened. The connection was so visceral. It's just there—a gift. Onstage is where she lives."

Of Manhattan Theater Club's three musicals, *The New Yorkers* actually was the most diverting. Like many revues, its score and sketches were terribly uneven. But at its best, the lyric work of young Glenn Slater was impressive. Unsurprisingly, Disney already had Slater's number, having hired him to work on a new animated feature called *Home on the Range*, as well as helping to adapt *The Little Mermaid* for the stage.

There was one more musical that slipped in Off-Broadway at the close of the 2000–2001 season. It's significance, though, was really not felt until the following year. *Urinetown: The Musical* was a stupid show written for smart people. In this sense, it set deep thinkers about musical theater, like the New York Shakespeare Festival's Wiley Hausam, on their collective ears.

"My personal belief is we are not going to be seeing serious, adult musicals on Broadway anymore, except as an aberration," Hausam had said as the 2000–2001 season ended. "In a way, last season was the most extraordinary we've seen, with new musicals by non-profits that were better than anything Broadway has done in a while. But audiences have become so much less sophisticated that I worry for the future."

The musical theater historian Ethan Mordden was even more blunt. "Writing smart shows is no good with stupid audiences and stupid critics. Lately, Off-Broadway, the shows have been too smart and people are too dumb. The music is too sophisticated—these are lazy, stupid people who just can't get a handle on the music in the theater because they don't want to work hard; they don't know *how* to work hard, intellectually. Most are not actually happy to be in a theater anyway. They've been told they should go, so they do and then they find that they have to think. Think? You mean I paid all that money and I have to think?"

No one was really too dumb for *Urinetown*. In contrast to bygone Broadway musicals, which had largely projected sophistication without making audiences think too much, *Urinetown* made audiences think just a little, while proclaiming a near total lack of sophistication. Like good television writing, *Urinetown* could be enjoyed, for better or worse, on virtually any level. Its music and lyrics were not especially complicated. But "lazy, stupid people" probably enjoyed them less. Ultimately, you didn't have to think at all to enjoy *Urinetown*. Still, it helped if you could.

CHAPTER 24

THIS IS URINETOWN

This is Urinetown!
Here we are in Urinetown!
—*Urinetown: The Musical*

The point is perhaps a subtle one. But it still should not be missed. *The Producers* was a musical about making a musical that laughed at itself for being a musical. This ironic self-reflexivity was, of course, what Seinfeld did to the sitcom, what Letterman does to the talk show, what reality programming has done, well, to the very act of watching television. It's what David Eggers did to the literary memoir in his solipsistic *A Heartbreaking Work of Staggering Genius*; what hip hop does to pop music every time it "samples." It was what the movie director Baz Luhrmann did to that all-American form, the movie musical, in *Moulin Rouge*, his self-consciously anachronistic film about bohemian love in fin-de-siècle Paris, with a score consisting almost entirely of 20th-century pop songs.

Musical theater arrived late to this game, but that was musical theater's inherent relationship to contemporary culture; it had, for a while now, been stupendously out of touch.

On Broadway and off, the 2001–2002 musical theater season turned out to be the season of irony. No new musical more overtly embodied this than *Urinetown*. From its name and subject matter (corrupt big business takes over a drought-stricken city's public restrooms and charges exorbitantly for the privilege to urinate) to its thematic substance and performance style, *Urinetown* tapped the same ironic currents of popular culture as *The Producers* but amplified them.

Where *The Producers* flirted with vulgarity, *Urinetown* sang about urinating. Where *The Producers* garnered laughs by occasionally acknowledging out loud what it takes to make a musical, *Urinetown* never stopped laughing at the fact that it was a musical.

Were younger audiences so inherently embarrassed by musical theater that only pre-emptive, reflexive laughter could induce them to listen? The creators of *Urinetown*—composer and lyricist, Mark Hollmann, 37, and book writer and lyricist, Greg Kotis, 35— certainly thought so. "I just figured this futuristic idea I had about corporations controlling where you could urinate was so bad it had to be a musical," Kotis said. "There's a ridiculousness about people breaking into song every few minutes that is both wonderful and terrible at the same time."

"During our development period," Hollmann added, "people would point out such profound problems with the show, flaws that we soon realized had no remedy, that our only avenue of escape was to say: 'We can't fix that, but maybe if we let the audience know we know, they'll let us off the hook.'"

Kotis and Hollmann had both graduated from the University of Chicago, entering Chicago's vibrant improvisational theater culture straight out of college. In 1995, Kotis was touring Europe with an improv group called the Neo-Futurists.

"The Neo-Futurists' defining aesthetic was and is that people don't play characters onstage, they play themselves and everything that they say onstage must be true and if it's not true they must point that out. So it was all about exposure, revealing the mechanics by which we were creating the show. Obviously a very Brechtian influence. Even though you're telling the audience that you're tricking them, the audience is willing to be tricked anyway."

Kotis performed at a theater festival in Paris with the Neo-Futurists, then got stranded there. "The festival we'd been in ended and I decided to stay on for two more weeks. I ran out of money almost immediately. I slept in parks and train stations. For 2½ francs there were these amenities where you could relieve yourself. I found myself budgeting my bathroom visits; 'If I don't go until tonight, I'll be uncomfortable but I can walk. That'll be a savings.' This idea came to me of an evil corporation owning all the bathrooms, not just publicly but privately as well. I knew it was a terrible idea. I tried to forget about it. But I couldn't.

"It had to be a musical," said Kotis. "A musical taking itself seriously is infinitely more funny than a straight play trying to take itself too seriously.

"Luckily for us," added Kotis, "writing musicals is not something people our age want to do much anymore."

Kotis brought his bad idea to Mark Hollmann in the spring of 1996.

"Greg takes musicals with a grain of salt," Hollmann laughed. "Or at least he used to. I never have. I started writing musicals right after I got out of college and I've always thought the form was a thrilling one. I learned the craft at the Lehman Engel BMI Workshop in 1993. Brecht, Weill, and Bernstein are my heroes. When Greg brought his idea to me it was like what we'd done before in Chicago, plots with something wrong in the community, a worm in the apple. Both of us had studied political science. Greg got his degree in it. These social themes of class conflict, with a love story, I thought: That's a musical."

Hollmann went away and wrote the song, "It's a Privilege to Pee." In the fall of 1997 the two then went to work, more or less, in earnest. By June of 1998 a first draft was complete. An ad was placed in *Backstage* magazine and actors found to make a demo, for free — recorded in the church where Hollmann worked as an organist. This demo was then sent, with a script, to roughly fifty agents and theaters. No one responded affirmatively except the Neo-Futurists out in Chicago, and they quickly changed their minds. A one-night reading was mounted in New York at Musical Theater Works before Kotis and Hollmann approached the New York International Fringe Festival.

"They said yes," Hollmann recalled. "We couldn't believe it. We put the show on in a converted garage on the Lower East Side. And it became the hit of the festival."

"People are much hungrier for this kind of material than we ever thought," Kotis concluded.

After its very successful 1999 Fringe Festival premiere, *Urinetown* found itself on an expedited, if thoroughly unlikely, ride straight to Broadway. First, the show was picked up by two sets of producers, the less-than-mainstream Araca Group, followed by the very mainstream Dodger Theatricals organization. Largely recast and with an entirely new production team, including the director John Rando and the choreographer John Carrafa, *Urinetown* then reopened in May 2001 Off-Broadway, at the American Theater of Actors, winning an Obie Award before transferring as a cult hit in September to Broadway's Henry Miller Theater (former home of the Roundabout Theater Company's grungy post-modernist revival of *Cabaret*). It turns out there really was quite an audience for a grossly ironic, post-modernist musical.

Surprising? Not really. America's most popular television cartoon, Matt Groening's *The Simpsons*, had long maintained a love-hate relationship with musicals, often singing of them ironically. Trey Parker and Matt Stone, creators of the irreverent *South Park* cable television cartoon, made *South Park*'s first feature-length film a musical. Before that, Parker had written the words and music for his own perverse movie musical, *Cannibal! The Musical*, which, in 2000, had a rude run Off-Off-Broadway in a stage adaptation.

"I watch *The Simpsons* religiously," said Kotis. "Part of our guiding thought was, when you see *The Simpsons* you get to see, like, one number from a bad musical. So, let's see the whole bad musical, from start to finish. That's what we'd thought about the film of *The Producers*, too. We only get to see a few numbers from *Springtime for Hitler*. We should write the whole thing—*Springtime for Hitler* from start to finish."

In 2000–2001, Kotis and Hollmann were not alone. First, *Reefer Madness*, a camp transplant from Los Angeles that broadly musical-ized the notorious 1936 marijuana fright film of the same name, opened at the Variety Arts Theater in October 2000, with out-landishly stylized choreography by MTV stalwart Paula Abdul. This was followed a month later by *The Rocky Horror Show* at the Circle in the Square Theater, an excessively obvious Broadway revival of the 1970s stage and, later, legendary film satire *The Rocky Horror Picture Show*.

Then there was *Bat Boy*, which opened Off-Broadway in March 2001 at the Union Square Theater. Derived from a tabloid newspaper story about a boy found in a cave who was supposedly half-bat, *Bat Boy* was the work primarily of a talented young composer-lyricist named Laurence O'Keefe, whose whacked-out tunes celebrated their own silliness while over-the-top production numbers poked fun at musical theater history and, of course, at the musical itself.

Filmmaker Baz Luhrmann certainly believed that the use of irony could multiply an entertainment's pleasures. "Irony, to me, in the cinema or in the theater means you can laugh and cry at the same time at the same thing. You can take something very trashy, turn it, and from another angle see it has another function entirely. I think ironic edge absolutely can be alive in the musical theater. Having said that, the requirements are quite different. Slap an ironic gesture on *La Bohème* and you're layering silliness upon silliness."

Too much silliness, of course, is entirely in the eye of the beholder. At least one contemporary cultural critic, novelist, and editor, Kurt

Andersen, found all this talk of irony in musicals pretty funny. "The fact that self-referential irony is only now reaching the musical theater just as it's receding in other media into some post-ironic something, strikes me as, well, amusing. Musical theater's lack of interest in post-modern irony is one of the ways it has always seemed quaint to me. I don't get musicals. My favorite moments in *Moulin Rouge* were when it kidded itself. In fact, I wish Luhrmann had gone further than he did. I bought *Moulin Rouge* though, mostly because I just wasn't bored. I mean *Show Boat* bored me silly."

Of course, musicals that laughed at themselves were hardly new. One of the first and the best had been Stephen Sondheim, Burt Shevelove and Larry Gelbart's *A Funny Thing Happened on the Way to the Forum* in 1962. "We can't take complete credit for breaking down the wall," Gelbart conceded, "but we did address the audience directly in a very George Burnsian way. More and more, though, I think that sort of stuff actually reflects a diminished interest on the part of the audience in anything other than show business and, by inference, celebrity. Everybody wants to go backstage now; to be inside."

Show business and celebrity were, in fact, the primary subject of the 2001 season's most anticipated musical, *Sweet Smell of Success*, which opened in March at the Martin Beck Theater. Adapted from the unflinching 1957 film noir about New York press agents and gossip columnists that had starred Tony Curtis and Burt Lancaster in memorably venal roles, *Sweet Smell of Success* aspired to be one very dark musical.

Only in an era as cynical yet ravenous for celebrity as our own could such a bleak, sublimely cynical movie have been considered suitable for song. Was it a coincidence that *Sweet Smell of Success* also had been a Garth Drabinsky, Livent-initiated project? With music by Marvin Hamlisch and lyrics by Craig Carnelia, a book by John Guare, and a return-to-Broadway star turn by John Lithgow as the Walter Winchell–surrogate, J. J. Hunsecker, under the direction of Tony Award winner Nicholas Hytner, *Sweet Smell of Success* clearly possessed one signature Drabinsky musical commodity: superb talent.

"It's a good time to do this," insisted Lithgow, whose just-canceled television series, *Third Rock from the Sun*, had itself been a quintessentially post-modernist sitcom exercise in irony. *"Sweet Smell of Success* was a movie years ahead of its time. It's a piece just dripping with irony. In our version every musical number has some sort of incredibly ironic undertow. It really makes the darkness gleam."

But *Sweet Smell of Success* barely registered at all. The show was not even impressively bad. Somehow the conjunction of all that creative talent seemed to cancel itself out, leaving *Sweet Smell of Success* a helpless waif of a musical; a fatal flaw in any show, but especially so for a musical derived from one of the tautest, nastiest films about America's entertainment business ever made.

As one would have expected, Marvin Hamlisch's score looked backward exclusively to the same age, roughly, that had provided Mel Brooks with his tunes for *The Producers*. "That driving New York sound," as Hamlisch characterized it. "The sound of nightclubs and Broadway and jazz."

Music still was the realm in which musical theater remained farthest out of the contemporary cultural loop. Not even *Urinetown* addressed this disconnection, its satirical musical palette falling conventionally along musical theater history's sardonic Brecht-Weill continuum. Of late, only David Yazbek's pop/rock score for *The Full Monty* had managed to inject the Broadway musical with even a hint of the contemporary, though a superb re-rendering of Jonathan Larson's *tick, tick...BOOM!* that opened at the Jane Street Theater in June 2001, with Larson's book effectively reworked by David Auburn, reconfirmed one tragic fact: No one wrote better rock and roll songs for the stage than the deceased composer of *Rent* had.

Lincoln Center Theater's *Thou Shalt Not* attempted to bridge this gap by engaging Harry Connick, Jr., a composer-lyricist plucked, if not directly from the pop cultural mainstream then definitely from a near tributary, in a high-profile collaboration with *The Producers'* Tony Award–winning director and choreographer, Susan Stroman. As a jazz pianist, pop singer, and screen actor, Connick had managed to straddle the mainstream without ever quite giving himself up to it. But *Thou Shalt Not*—a transplanting to New Orleans of Émile Zola's classic novel of murderous adultery, *Therese Raquin*—which opened on Broadway in October, could not synthesize its New Orleans jazz musical impulses with the dramatic story-telling requirements of musical theater. Its musical score swung nicely. But it rarely connected dramatically with the story it purported to tell.

Mamma Mia!, on the other hand, side-stepped the problem of music, story-telling, and irony shamelessly. A package of disco-era hits by the Swedish vocal group ABBA, draped around a wafer-thin book musical best characterized as a paternity whodunit set on a Greek island, *Mamma Mia!* had already been a massive hit in London when it opened in October at *Cats'* former Broadway residence, the Winter Garden Theater. With an advance sale that challenged *Miss Saigon's* $37 million Broadway record, *Mamma Mia!* also gave every indication that it would become, in terms of audience enthusiasm and critical vexation, *Cats'* commercial successor.[45]

Mamma Mia! deployed its own deconstructive spin with a lack of subtlety that any pop ironist would appreciate. By painstakingly reconstituting ABBA's ridiculously catchy pop singles down to the last sugary harmonic inflection (the group's co-founder Björn Ulvaeus personally had trained *Mamma Mia!*'s orchestra and cast to deliver the score "exactly how we sang it [and] played it"), the show invited audiences to see right through the musical they'd paid to attend (at a top ticket of $100) and just sing along, as if with their radios at home. Quite a post-modernist theatrical coup—though couched in kitsch. As the show's director Phyllida Lloyd acknowledged to the *Los Angeles Times*, "*Mamma Mia!* is actually quite Brechtian in calling attention to form and the relationship the audience develops with characters onstage."[46]

In other words, here was a musical that laughed at itself less overtly than *Urinetown* and *The Producers* did but just as decisively.

Even Broadway's best musical Tony Award–winner in 2002, a nominally straightforward remake of the 1967 film musical *Thoroughly Modern Millie*, traded heavily in irony. The film itself had been a thoroughly ironic spoof of Roaring Twenties–style Hollywood film musicals. The stage version, which opened in April at the Marquis Theater, further blurred the boundaries of authorship through a score that was a hybrid tangle. Original songs written for the film by Jimmy Van Heusen and Sammy Cahn (including the famous title tune) were mixed with a couple of authentic vintage standards, a bit of borrowed Gilbert and Sullivan (strictly inserted for laughs), plus many new "period" songs written by *Violet's* Jeanine Tesori and *Millie's* lyricist and co–book writer, Dick Scanlan.

"More commercial you cannot get," acknowledged Tesori. "Filling 1,700 seats a night, eight nights a week, though, is real pressure. *Crazy for You* was our model. *Millie* is a typical commercial Broadway musical."

But *Millie* was not typical. Though the results onstage were sporadically entertaining, *Millie*, as staged by the director Michael Mayer, was a hyperventilating cartoon that rarely slowed to take seriously Tesori's snappy tunes and Scanlan's well-crafted lyrics. Virtually every scripted line and song lyric was delivered in boldface, semi-ironic, quotation marks.

Moreover, there remained something very troubling about *Millie's* slippery bastardized content. Clearly, Tesori and Scanlan were capable of writing a very nice musical together. And clearly, *Thoroughly Modern Millie*, the movie, possessed some nice music on its own.

So why bother to shake the two together? It was as if *Thoroughly Modern Millie* had been constructed from sampled tracks.

Surprisingly, Baz Luhrmann, the cinematic champion of cut-and-paste musical scores and emotionally detached, pop-culturally ironic singing in *Moulin Rouge*, actually drew a sharp distinction between live musical theater and film musicals. Luhrmann, who would soon be bringing a post-modernist production of the opera *La Bohème* to Broadway, explained that "the pop cultural layering in my films is specific to my films. With *La Bohème* we're going to do the reverse. Where all of our steps in cinema have been to theatricalize cinematic language, we'll be trying to make *La Bohème* less theatrical and more cinematic. The performers will look very realistic; for one thing they'll actually be young. Plus, we've reset the story in 1957. Why? Because 1957 had all the social and economic realities we needed to match 1814. We're absolutely period strict to 1957, an accuracy so complete it will seem like a realistic 1957 movie. There is irony, of course, just in the whole notion of *La Bohème* being moved to this period, but not in the way we understand irony in the cinematic forms I've created. Because *they're* all about being in on the jokes. Here, rather than being pop-culturally layered, our production is a straight study in very traditional 1950s drama, a copybook of an Actors Studio production. Yet, it's told through a pure operatic voice. It's that clash that creates your irony."

But what was the need for that clash at all? Had irony become the chaser audiences required in order to swallow any sort of musical theater entertainment?

"Well, yes," Luhrmann replied. "Irony is one very good way to force an audience's engagement these days."

Larry Gelbart, in a sense, agreed. "I think the feeling is that a modern audience doesn't want to see people just break out into song anymore. Remember, an audience's idea of a musical number is no longer Fred and Ginger anyway. It's Britney."

John Cameron Mitchell, creator and star of *Hedwig and the Angry Inch*, believed there was room for anything. "Musicals are just songs and a narrative onstage," he said, "and there can be all kinds. The tradition is sturdy enough. I don't think there's anything bad about this. The only bad thing is if they're done badly. Ultimately, it's taste I'm more worried about."

One couldn't help feeling, though, that abject self-reflexiveness was the end of the line for musical theater history at least as we have known it. Perhaps the tradition had to finally laugh itself out before something new could be born.

"The well has run dry," Stephen Sondheim insisted. "Not just on Broadway but in movies, in television. The adolescent nature of this kind of easy irony is indicative of our culture, the dumbing down of Western culture."

Ira Weitzman didn't believe things were quite that dire. "I don't know that it's even a trend," he maintained. "I certainly don't think that the people who wrote *Urinetown* are doomed to a life of self-parody."

The people who wrote *Urinetown* were, however, not so sure. "When I start to think about writing a musical seriously," Greg Kotis confessed, "I think…"

Mark Hollmann finished the thought: "Why bother?"

Larry Gelbart understood. "You know what? Making fun of yourself is just easier than writing plot. It's easier than creating character. It's easier than creating situations. Still, it's hardly my place to talk about creating new anything, at least not in the context of *Forum*. Because, admittedly in our plot, characters and situations, we made sure that not only the author but the whole civilization we stole from was dead."

CHAPTER 25

MUSIC AND THE MIRROR

All I ever needed
Was the music and the mirror
And a chance to dance.

—*A Chorus Line*

In the summer of 2001, on the tiny stage of a little cabaret down on lower Park Avenue called Arci's Place (now defunct), one gritty survivor from a mostly deceased civilization just got up and danced. Certainly there was irony in Donna McKechnie's being confined to a stage that simply was not big enough to accommodate everything that McKechnie still could do in the summer of 2001, to say nothing of all the things that she had done. Irony, however, was not the point here. Arci's puny platform was simply the limited space McKechnie filled to overflow that summer with a retrospective of her life in musical theater.

"My career in a nutshell," McKechnie acknowledged, with no little bemusement. "I just have to be careful not to kick anybody."

Once, only Broadway stages could contain musical theater legends. Now those stages increasingly were reserved for musical-comedy novices from other media performing in an endless rerun cycle of revivals. Over the previous decade, Broadway producers had grown increasingly addicted to the public relations rush provided by the injection of stars and demi-stars from television and the movies into their retread musical productions. The popular acceptance of this practice had also encouraged yet another bad habit: dispensing with the search for *bona fide* musical theater talent altogether in favor of hiring non-singing (usually celebrity) actors who could act a song rather than sing it.

All of which left performers like Donna McKechnie...well, at Arci's. Not that Arci's was such a bad place to be. But Broadway it wasn't.

McKechnie remained philosophical. She had been the quintessential Broadway gypsy for more than 40 years now, since her debut at 16 in the original production of Frank Loesser's *How To Succeed in Business Without Really Trying*. Her choreographer on that show had been Bob Fosse. Throughout the 1960s and '70s, she'd been the muse of Michael Bennett, who'd enshrined for all-time McKechnie's cult status as Broadway's greatest chorus dancer by creating the role of Cassie in *A Chorus Line* with her and for her.

"Michael Bennett's dream of what musical theater could be was essentially limitless," McKechnie said. "Musical numbers that moved seamlessly from drama to music and back again were what Michael aspired to. And I kind of attached myself to that dream. It was one of the things that we believed together as young dancers in New York."

Did McKechnie believe Broadway would be a different place had Bennett survived? Or would Disney have swallowed up Michael Bennett as well?

"Michael would have eaten Disney for lunch."

The point, of course, was moot. Today McKechnie found herself marginalized on a Broadway musical landscape that the likes of Bennett and Fosse would find almost unrecognizable.

"There's no one in charge anymore, creatively," said McKechnie. "The people in charge are all about dollars. They've disturbed the balance. Great musical theater producers once knew how to involve themselves in the creative process and they also knew how to get out of the way, and when. That's a subtlety of enormous importance.

"Producers today, who are hiring people for musicals who've never done musicals and think they'll just be able to act it, I say to them: good luck. Doing a musical is not just acting. It's total theater. It's our Kabuki. It's a lifetime of devotion to build the craft, the confidence and the ability to sing and dance and act believably.

"The trick is to make the audience feel as if they are themselves singing and dancing without letting them be aware of it. It's a heightened reality, it's not naturalistic theater. Not that naturalistic theater isn't heightened reality, of course, but when you have to justify the enormous projection of energy that it takes to just go into song or dance, you realize why it's such a humbling experience every time. I'm still learning."

The act McKechnie presented at Arci's was actually an abridgement of a one-woman theatrical memoir she hoped to bring to a Broadway house one day. Titled *Inside the Music*, that show, directed by fellow *Chorus Line* alum Thommie Walsh, had a book written by McKechnie in collaboration with Christopher Durang.

And what was her show essentially about?

"A little girl from the Midwest in the 1950s who runs away to New York to be a dancer."

For years now, McKechnie had continued to work, largely on the road, away from New York, in practically any legitimate vehicle that would have her—from the ill-fated Broadway-bound *Annie II* of a few seasons back to the critically acclaimed 1998 Papermill Playhouse revival of *Follies*, in which she'd delivered what many regarded as the definitive portrayal of Sally Durant, the nostalgia-blinded former chorine.

"Being in theater is a brutal career choice, third maybe to boxing and prostitution," Ms. McKechnie laughed. "It is amazing that I'm still doing this. But it was always really important to me to be a creative artist. Not to be a star, not to be rich, not to be famous. My impulse as a dancer was never just to move but rather to interpret the music. I needed meaning. It completed me."

CHAPTER 26

CLIMBING UPHILL

I'm climbing uphill, Daddy,
Climbing uphill.
— *The Last Five Years*

And so, it had come to this.

In May 2001, at the Northlight Theater in Chicago, a new musical by Jason Robert Brown entitled *The Last Five Years* had opened to very favorable reviews. Written as a commission from Lincoln Center Theater, *The Last Five Years* had been conceived by Brown as a direct response to the super-sized Sturm und Drang that had engulfed the oversized *Parade* at Lincoln Center just three years before. Brown's new show was an intensely intimate chamber musical, a study of a marriage that falls apart, as told in reverse chronology, á la *Merrily We Roll Along*, by two solitary actors, abetted by an orchestra of six, including Brown himself on keyboard.

The Last Five Years already had been placed on Lincoln Center Theater's schedule for a September 2001 opening. A tentative deal had been reached with Bill Rosenfield at RCA to record the show. "I wanted to have everything in place this time, given what happened to *Parade*," explained Brown. "I wanted all the ducks in a row. I didn't want to worry about anyone going bankrupt."

But Lincoln Center suddenly bailed on the project for no overtly stated reason, but at least to avoid one major behind the scenes complication. Jason Robert Brown had received threats of litigation from his ex-wife, who objected to the parallels between the sad marital fable of *The Last Five Years* and her own nasty divorce from Brown. According to Ira Weitzman, Lincoln Center Theater was warned by its lawyers that it could be made a party to such litigation. And so, *The Last Five Years* was dropped from Lincoln Center's fall lineup. Shortly thereafter, Bill Rosenfield was eased out of his job at RCA. And just like that, Tony Award winner Jason Robert Brown's surefire little musical was an orphan.

The Last Five Years did ultimately open, scooped up by the producers Marty Bell and Arielle Tepper for a commercial run that commenced in March 2002 downtown at the Minetta Lane Theater. Brown's score proved to be by far the most original of the season, a wonderfully approachable blend of contemporary pop music with traditional show-tune style; well-crafted and filled with lyrics of wit and, often, unflinching pain. *The Last Five Years*, however, suffered a fate very much akin to that of *Merrily We Roll Along*. Telling a tragic story backward in time again proved a good way to rob it of all forward motion, as well as a good measure of its essential pathos. Brown's protagonists, moreover, were unsympathetic; the male insufferably cocky, yet somehow victimized; the female insufferably self-flagellating, yet also a victim. The endeavor, however, was audacious. And again, critics, for the most part, did not comprehend a truly original new musical's merits on-balance, confrontationally dismissing it out of hand. By May, *The Last Five Years* was history.[47]

If a musical opens in New York and no record company records it, does it still make a sound?

The Last Five Years was just the sort of worthy, needy new musical that Bill Rosenfield had liked to record at RCA. With the record industry reeling from corporate consolidation and the post-9/11 economic downturn, though, producing cast albums had become more of an extravagance than ever. The devotion of a small niche audience no longer was enough to justify such sustained losses. And, predictably, the major labels were cutting back.

Over the winter, BMG had downsized its RCA Victor cast album division, relegating senior vice president for shows and soundtracks, Bill Rosenfield, to a consulting job. The refrain among senior executives at most major labels (at least those who would speak on the record at all) focused on one word: "Selectivity." Meaning simply: "We will be recording less."

"The nurturing of young composers and their shows by big recording companies is no longer going to happen," Rosenfield himself stated flatly. "What they're telling us is they only want hits."

Not that the major labels had ever been interested in anything else. The list of musicals not recorded since the dawn of original cast albums was a litany of fascinating failures, including 2002's critically dismissed Lincoln Center Theater production of *Thou Shalt Not*, with a score by Harry Connick, Jr. Even Connick's own record company, Sony, had passed on preserving *Thou Shalt Not* on disc. Connick was so put out, he went ahead and recorded the show at his own expense. His self-produced CD was now on sale at Amazon.com.

Then there were the murky shenanigans surrounding the recording of another 2002 bomb, *Sweet Smell of Success*. Apparently Sony had tried to extricate itself from a signed commitment to record this show, after reading the withering out-of-town reviews from Chicago that presaged *Sweet Smell*'s disastrous opening on Broadway.[48] In the end, Sony chose not to exercise its contractual escape clause and a cast album was released. No one directly involved, however — from Sony CEO, Peter Gelb, to Marty Bell, one of the show's many producers, to the lyricist, Craig Carnelia — would discuss the matter.

The problem, of course, was that recording musicals had always been pre-eminently a labor of love. Yes, *Oklahoma!* and *My Fair Lady* had both sold staggeringly well at first and continued to earn handsomely today. The numbers for recording an average musical, though, had never added up.

"It is very difficult to record a new Broadway show for under $300,000, and quite frankly, it can be much more than that," observed Denis McNamara, senior vice president for Decca U.S., which included Universal Classics' Decca Broadway line. "You really have to sell in excess of 150,000 units for a fair return. Our *Mamma Mia!*—we're also one of the show's producers—is the most successful cast recording since *Rent*, which tells you something about the reality of original cast albums. *Mamma Mia!* will be a gold record by the end of the summer. And it's not just the cast album. *ABBA Gold* on our Polydor label has actually sold more during the same period."

Mamma Mia! was another example of ledger sheets legislating against Broadway cast albums. The CD referred to by McNamara was actually *Mamma Mia!'s* London cast recording. Despite the show's substantial Broadway box office, there were no plans to record the Broadway cast because Decca did not wish to dilute the public's ABBA appetite with another competing release.

Looking at recent original cast album sales was very much an eye opener. *Phantom of the Opera* was king, with more than fifteen million units sold. *Rent* followed far behind, at two million-plus. After almost five years, *The Lion King* had sold in excess of 800,000, which seemed impressive until one noticed that the movie's soundtrack had sold more than sixteen million.

Surprisingly, *The Producers*, which Sony had paid a king's ransom to record (Sony executives would not comment, but estimates ranged as high as $500,000), had sold about 200,000 copies so far. This was a very nice number but it paled by comparison with *Mamma Mia!'s* 340,000, to date. Obviously, the music of ABBA transcended the limited world of musical theater, while the music of *The Producers* did not. "We think that five, ten years from now *Mamma Mia!* will probably have outsold it five to one," McNamara quietly crowed.

Bill Rosenfield understood the math all too well. "Record companies will continue to overpay for hit Broadway shows," he said, "even as they phase out the rest, because overpaying is what the real record business is all about."

Surely there had to be a better way.

Rather than let *The Last Five Years* disappear unrecorded, Rosenfield opted to share the show with a three-year-old independent label founded by a 35-year-old actor named Kurt Deutsch, whose wife, Sherie René Scott, was one of the musical's stars.

The very enterprising Mr. Deutsch had created Sh-K-Boom (pronounced *Shik*aboom) Records in 1999 solely to produce and market his wife's first solo CD. He'd very quickly realized, though, that the label could fill a potentially lucrative niche.

"There are a lot of Broadway stars who don't want to make showtune records," said Deutsch. "They want to bridge the gap between rock 'n' roll and theater without being pigeon-holed. Major labels would never give these guys the time of day because they believe that you cannot be associated with Broadway if you're going to do a mainstream, crossover record; they think Broadway is corny, even cheesy, and appeals to older audiences. And you know what? They're right in a lot of ways. But there is this whole new generation of artists who are cool and are appealing to a much younger audience. I figured, if I branched out, I could build a community of young fans, composers and stars."

Deutsch first approached Adam Pascal, who'd made his name starring in *Rent* and was then playing in Disney's *Aida* opposite Deutsch's wife. He also signed up Alice Ripley from *The Rocky Horror Show*. Pascal and Ripley's respective albums wound up sharing one fundamental with Sherie René Scott's debut CD: each, in different ways, rocked.

"The records have all sold upward of my break-even figure—5,000 copies," said Deutsch, "with Adam's CD the leader at 12,000. Pretty good, considering we only got distribution in stores a few weeks before they came out. We're talking sales exclusively on the Net and in theaters where these guys were working."

The cost management problems inherent in recording a cast album, however, did bowl Kurt Deutsch over: "You have to pay to re-use everything. You have to re-license the orchestrations, you have to re-pay the music copyist, the press agent — they're unionized too — the company manager. The biggest obstacle, though, is Actors' Equity, which has this rule requiring each actor in a show, plus the stage manager, to be paid a week's salary for every eight hours in the studio. That's why all musicals are recorded in one desperate day."

Over the course of 2001–2002, actor Norbert Leo Butz had delivered a breakout, Tony Award–nominated performance in *Thou Shalt Not* before starring with Sherie René Scott in *The Last Five Years*. "It is funny that I did two original musicals, one small and one enormous, and only the small one made it officially to CD," Butz laughed. "But it's an ephemeral process. And, let's face it, those people who care are a stalwart few."

Only a few years before, during the flush '90s, original cast album action had reflected the inflated value of musical theater as a whole. So many were recorded — as the number, if not the quality, of new musicals briefly spiked.

By 2002, those days were over.

"Classical recordings and Broadway records are getting more expensive, while the audiences that purchase these records are getting smaller," observed Robert Hurwitz, the president of Nonesuch Records, "so it should not be surprising that companies are becoming more restrictive."

Denis McNamara at Decca ruefully concurred. "There are easier ways to have a hit. Boy, for that million dollars spent recording and marketing one show you could make an awful lot of pop records."

Yet, Deutsch remained eager. "Most producers simply don't understand how record labels work," he said.

Rocco Landesman was one producer who readily acknowledged this. "Of course we don't understand the record business. We're theater producers. Unfortunately, original cast albums have never made producers any money. Their sole value is as P.R."

Kurt Deutsch, however, believed producers could make money if they owned their cast albums outright. "They need that album to market their show and they don't want to pay for making it," he said. "Well, they should. If you're going to raise $12 million for a Broadway musical, what's another $300,000 for the record? Hey, the reason Sony has an entertainment division to begin with is so they can sell their electronics. Why shouldn't Broadway producers do the same thing for their product?"

The question was a good one. Even Landesman conceded, "it's something we should look at." The answer, however, remained elusive. All that was clear to everyone up and down the musical theater food chain in 2002, from producers to composers, performers and especially recording company executives, was that a new age for original cast albums must be dawning because yet another golden age was definitely gone.[49]

CHAPTER 27

DON'T CRY FOR ME, ARGENTINA

In person, Andrew Lloyd Webber is bigger than one might think. His apartment however is not—it is just as big as you would think. Perched near the summit of New York's Trump Tower, the Lloyd Webber manse has many throw pillows and spotlessly clean windows. The throw pillows are embroidered with personalized needlepoint samplers relating to the Lloyd Webber musical theater oeuvre; stitched lyric snatches and the like. The windows, at least in the living room, offer a panoramic view over Central Park, north-ward to the George Washington Bridge and beyond.

One afternoon, a month or so post–September 11, Lord Lloyd Webber hosted an informal midweek luncheon party at his Trump Tower home. The guest list was small: his longtime publicist, the musical theater division chief of his American record label, a top PBS arts programming executive, a local journalist and one of the pro-ducers behind Lloyd Webber's impending return to Broadway.

It was then nearly seven years since a new Andrew Lloyd Webber musical had reached Broadway. It is, as of this writing, now going on nine. The show opening later that week was not new. *By Jeeves* had been written in the '70s as just *Jeeves*, a collaboration with the playwright Alan Ayckbourn, adapting the much-beloved P. G. Wodehouse stories about the infallible butler, Jeeves, and his half-wit boss, Bertie Wooster. Numerous efforts to get *Jeeves* to Broadway had failed since the show's 1975 West End debut. Even this current attempt nearly had gone up in smoke. The smashing of planes into the World Trade Center also had frightened away two of *By Jeeves'* principal financial backers, resulting in the show's October opening being "indefinitely postponed," at least initially. At the eleventh hour, however, Lord Lloyd Webber himself had stepped in to pick up the slack. *By Jeeves* now would open as scheduled.

The 53-year-old host was in a jovial mood. Circulating among his guests, he smiled as cocktail glasses were liberally filled. A waiter emerged from the kitchen with tray after tray of succulent finger food. Sunlight shimmered across the many enormous Pre-Raphaelite canvases adorning the walls.

For a while now, America had not been especially kind to Lloyd Webber's creative efforts. His last new Broadway musical, *Sunset Boulevard*, had been a financial failure.[50] It was even revealed during the show's run that Lloyd Webber's Really Useful Group had inflated *Sunset Boulevard*'s reported box office grosses to hide this.[51] Meanwhile, *Sunset Boulevard*'s anointed Broadway successor, a Lloyd Webber musical derived from the movie *Whistle Down the Wind*, ignominiously was dying out of town, in Washington. Though *Whistle Down the Wind* eventually opened in London, it never did play Broadway. Nor, apparently, would Lloyd Webber's latest West End musical, *The Beautiful Game*, about a Northern Ireland youth soccer team playing in the shadow of Ireland's political troubles.

To what degree all of this professional misfortune actually impacted upon Lloyd Webber's personal fortune is impossible to say, though the composer did sell his London mansion and world-famous wine collection during this period. Loads of Really Useful employees also had been laid off. Some press reports even had it that Andrew Lloyd Webber was, in fact, retired.

"I'm delighted all of you could make it because I have a very lovely surprise to share with you," he announced that afternoon. A pianist had materialized at the buffed baby grand, framed by the living room picture window.

Was Lord Lloyd Webber about to present something new?

His guests hurriedly found seats.

A very willowy, very young, very blonde woman joined the host beside his piano. "This is my newest discovery," he announced, gripping the young woman's hand and introducing her by name. "We met in the most extraordinary way, at an open call for *Beautiful Game* held in Ireland. She was working at the time..." Lloyd Webber turned solicitously to the young woman for confirmation, "...you were a singing waitress at Balmoral Castle, yes?"

The young woman nodded.

Lloyd Webber smiled conspiratorially. "I took one look and just said to my casting director: '*Expedite* her.'"

His young discovery would be singing three songs today, Lloyd Webber explained: one by Rodgers and Hart, one by Rodgers and Hammerstein and one—Lloyd Webber actually blushed—"by the old man."

The blonde young woman looked more or less like any pretty blonde young woman who might just then have been wandering the city far below. Her voice, as it turned out, sounded no better or worse than any number of voices belonging to pretty blonde young women who might just then have been auditioning in far smaller rooms all over town. The worldly drollery of Rodgers and Hart eluded her in the first song, though she did hit all the basic notes. The simpler Rodgers and Hammerstein optimism was easier for her to grasp in the second. Nothing, however, could match her rendering of "Don't Cry for Me, Argentina" directed to the composer himself, as he gazed up avidly from his sofa, cushioned by piles of needlepoint pillows, conducting her with his eyebrows.

There was wine, both white and red, at lunch. Also chicken. The host held forth from the head of the table.

"We must find her a record deal first," he began. "Don't you think so?" he added quite rhetorically in the direction of his record company functionary before going on. "Once she's had a hit, then she can do a show. Not before. We don't want her getting stuck in musical theater, pigeon-holed like that Audra McDonald woman. First a hit, then the stage. People will be amazed she can do that sort of thing at all."

"When I began in television," the PBS executive interrupted suddenly. Ten minutes later, he was still deeply engrossed in his own career retrospective. The host attempted to wrestle the conversation back, but to no avail.

More wine was poured.

"...and many of my programs get shown again and again particularly at pledge time, Andrew," the PBS executive was saying. "Do you know what pledge time is, Andrew?"

"Yes," Lloyd Webber replied. "My 50th birthday special must be one program that gets done a lot."

"No," mused the man from PBS heedlessly. "Not so much. Our Stephen Sondheim Carnegie Hall Concert. That's a big one."

Spoons, forks, and knives seemed suddenly to suspend their motion in horror, all around the table. For a moment there was only silence, a muted, group-marveling at the *faux pas* of Lloyd Webber's prime rival being named at Lloyd Webber's own luncheon table.

"What kind of music do you like to sing most?" a hesitant voice inquired finally, shifting the focus back toward Lloyd Webber's protégé.

The young woman thought about this.

"Music that makes me feel," she answered at last, then went on: "Andrew, is it alright if I go? I've got some shopping to do."

"My wife absolutely adores her," insisted Lloyd Webber, as the young woman exited. "She's out shopping herself right now."

Someone asked if Lloyd Webber was working on a new musical.[52]

"Yes," he answered excitedly. "I've discovered this absolutely marvelous composer. He's the most famous composer in India, he's scored dozens and dozens of Indian movies. His name is A. R. Rahman. Thoroughly hypnotic. Marvelous stuff."

Lloyd Webber proceeded to explain how, as a businessman, he was certain that Rahman's "Bollywood" sound was the next big thing. Enunciating the bottom line aspect of his own genius, not as a composer, *per se*, but as a sniffer of populist musical taste, Lloyd Webber also outlined his already advanced plans for capitalizing on this trend.

"*Bombay Dreams*," announced Lloyd Webber proudly. "A Bollywood musical, scored by Rahman. I'm going to produce it in London first," he said. "Then I imagine we'll bring it here.[53] I really, really believe Rahman could carry the torch of musical theater in a completely different direction. As a producer that just thrills me.

"I love new sounds in the theater," concluded Andrew Lloyd Webber, rising to indicate this lunch was at an end. "I mean, how can there be a future for musicals," he asked, "without something that is truly new?"

BUT WHO CALLS THAT LIVIN'?

But who calls that livin'
When no gal'll give in
To no man what's nine-hundred years?
—"It Ain't Necessarily So"
Porgy and Bess

As of this writing the mega-musicals are all gone from Broadway, save for *The Phantom of the Opera*. In their stead, *The Producers* reigns along with *Hairspray*, the Tony Award–winning high-octane adaptation of John Waters' over-the-top 1988 cult film classic. After opening in August 2002, *Hairspray* dominated a 2002–2003 Broadway season that was nearly bereft of original new musicals.

Set in the early 1960s, *Hairspray* riotously celebrated the transformative power of Top 40 pop music. Propelled by a pastiche score full of hormonal *American Bandstand* energy — the slick work of composer (and lyricist) Mark Shaiman, with lyricist Scott Wittman — and staged as one continuous '60s dance party by the director Jack O'Brien and the choreographer Jerry Mitchell, the show incited a kind of delirium in audiences akin to that inspired by *The Producers*.

Delirium, though, is, by definition, an *over*-reaction. Even history's greatest Broadway musicals rarely triggered delirium, nor did they hope to. Delirium is not about discernment. Delirium is, however, a response that today's Broadway musicals seem to be actively aiming for.

The reasoning behind this is obvious enough. Broadway audiences

257

are no longer trusted by Broadway musical creators. Viewed as an attention-deprived breed, they are increasingly smacked into alertness with eardrum rattling over-amplification and dervishlike onstage freneticism.

In *A Chorus Line*, Michael Bennett exposed the automaton factor underlying so much traditional Broadway dance dazzle with "One," his chilling yet thrilling deconstruction of an eleven o'clock number. Recent big musicals—like *Hairspray* and *The Producers, Thoroughly Modern Millie*, or Twyla Tharp's *Movin' Out*—have ratcheted up this empty-eyed roboticism into mach-speed overkill, apparently trying to drive audiences...well, out of their minds.

To a degree, it is hard to blame the creators. They are battling, after all, for hearts and minds attuned to the addling rhythms of video games and the sonic levels of the cineplex. In such a vacuum of overstimulation only the aesthetics of an arena rock concert may seem to have any chance at prevailing.

Take *Movin' Out*, which opened at the Richard Rodgers Theater in October 2002. Danced to a score of reconstituted Billy Joel hits performed by a Billy Joel impersonator, the show boasted phenomenally athletic dancers whom Tharp kept in nearly constant motion at a pace that left dancers and audiences both breathless. Which would have been fine if *Movin' Out* simply was a twitchy piece of movement. Unfortunately, Tharp felt compelled to tell ticket buyers a story for their hundred bucks, and so her choreography madly mimed a fatuous Vietnam War interpretive dance. The results were a travesty of both the war itself and the decade that was torn apart by it. Still, the hysterical hurry-up of it all could be blinding. How else to explain the delirium with which many critics received *Movin' Out?*[54]

De-evolution is a funny thing. It can happen with the best of intentions. Back in the 1970s, musical theater was unmistakably in trouble. What had once worked, somehow no longer mattered. And so, musical theater mutated. The more creative artists, for the most part, retreated, writing smaller, more intimate, more personal musicals—musicals that were in many ways the antithesis of the classic Broadway model. Conversely, the more commercial artists let their work balloon, writing bigger and bigger, anything but intimate, far less personal musicals—musicals that in their unsubtle way were also the antithesis of the classic Broadway model.

Over time, the smaller-scale musicals grew ever more solipsistic. *Balancing Act*, which opened Off-Broadway at the Westside Theater in June 1992, had one character, "The Main Character," played by five actors portraying: "Ambitious Side," "Sensitive Side," "Optimistic Side," "Skeptical Side," and "Humorous Side." *Fallen Angels* in 1994, with book, music and lyrics by the convicted corporate raider Ivan Boesky's son, Billy, told the epic story of a songwriter's efforts to hold his rock band together. That same season, *Hysterical Blindness* sang of a lone Tennessee Baptist coping with his mother's psychosomatic illness while trying to break into show business.

Enough already. It's not that small-scale musicals came to be discredited, so much as their intimate size was abused. In the '90s, many younger creators, like Ahrens and Flaherty, Michael John LaChiusa, and Jeanine Tesori, who'd largely made their initial reputations writing chamber musicals, began to try working on a grander scale. But their attempts yielded very mixed results. *My Favorite Year*, *Seussical*, and even *Ragtime* by Ahrens and Flaherty seemed more pumped up than organically grand. LaChiusa's *Marie Christine* and *The Wild Party* alienated far more mainstream critics and theatergoers than were captivated by LaChiusa's audacity, while Tesori's *Thoroughly Modern Millie* seemed, in its cynical blurring of old and new music, something of a sell-out.

The most successful mega-musical makers—namely Andrew Lloyd Webber and his imitators—meanwhile grew increasingly complacent. Their work, never especially inventive to begin with, grew staler. And audiences began to abandon them.

So, where does that leave us?

In an age of anxiety, unfortunately. Broadway producers and musical creators alike may have dropped the crutch of spectacle and bombast for the moment but their insecurity remains, now expressed in nervous onstage hyperactivity. At least *Hairspray* and *The Producers*, with their antics, also restored a sense of humor to serious musical theater ambitions.

But is that enough? Is the future of musical theater assured solely by the return of musical comedy?

Of course not. This was rather dishearteningly spelled out on Broadway by the 2002–2003 season's two biggest financial disasters. *Dance of the Vampires*—based on the 1967 Roman Polanski film, *The Fearless Vampire Killers*—was a bloated horror show that tried to prop up the doddering remnants of the mega-musical tradition by laughing at its own bloated expense. There was very little pleasure or even irony, however, in witnessing a $12-million, crudely written, hideously outfitted musical monstrosity. After opening in December at the Minskoff Theater, the show ignominiously departed after 56 performances, taking its star, *The Phantom of the Opera*'s original Phantom, Michael Crawford, along with it.

Where *Dance of the Vampires* trafficked in jocular vulgarity, *Amour*, which opened at the Music Box in October, endeavored to seduce Broadway theatergoers with whimsy. Whimsy, however, is a very perishable comedic commodity. Though cleverly adapted by Jeremy Sams from Marcel Ayme's *Le Passe-Muraille*, and scored with offhand wit by Michel Legrand, this $6-million musical concoction sank within days of opening. Critics yawned.[55] At 90 intermission-less minutes, the whole enterprise seemed, to many, sadly undernourished. *Amour*'s confoundingly dreary set design didn't help matters, but the show also was blessed with lovely lead performances by Malcolm Gets and Melissa Errico. *Amour* deserved better, but fared worse than even *Dance of the Vampires*. So much for selling understatement and semi-cerebral humor in a contemporary Broadway musical.

Another victim of Broadway's taste for frenzy in 2002–2003 was *A Year with Frog and Toad*, a charming little children's diversion derived from the *Frog and Toad* children's book series by Arnold Lobel. *A Year with Frog and Toad*, which opened in April at the Cort Theater and closed there in June, exhibited a lot of guts rolling the dice on Broadway but absolutely no sense. The show was filled with very simple pleasures geared perfectly to its very young target audience, particularly in the deceptively smart score supplied by Robert and Willie Reale. It might have enjoyed quite a run in a suitable Off-Broadway location. Tossed into Broadway's $100-plus ticket environs and the accompanying climate of noisy desperation that those prices have engendered, the modest *Frog and Toad* (undercut by its immodest $90 top ticket) seemed hopelessly inflated.

Off-Broadway, the 2002–2003 musical season produced further dismaying developments and one critical downshift in taste.

At Second Stage Theater in February, Michael John LaChiusa returned to the more intimate musical scale at which he particularly excelled, with *Little Fish*, a dyspeptic yet not unaffectionate look at a neurotic, 30-something young woman living in New York right now. Directed and cleverly choreographed by Graciela Daniele, with vividly contemporary orchestrations by Bruce Coughlin, *Little Fish* had an invigorating score that managed to pay frequent homage to Stephen Sondheim's *Company* while remaining rooted in the musical currency of our own urban moment. Coming down the stretch, though, the book surrendered uncharacteristically to sentimentality and bathos. Perhaps, stung by so much criticism in the past, LaChiusa felt compelled to soften his aesthetic just slightly. He needn't have bothered. Again, far too many critics reacted to the mixed blessings of *Little Fish* with undifferentiating disdain.[56]

In March at Playwrights Horizons, Ricky Ian Gordon tackled a far grander subject, Marcel Proust's *Remembrance of Things Past*—at least a fragment of it—in *My Life with Albertine*. With a book by Richard Nelson, who also directed, *My Life with Albertine* proved even more disjunctive than *Little Fish*. The show was beautiful to look at, with sumptuous scenic designs by Thomas Lynch, costumes by Susan Hilferty, and eloquent lighting by James Ingalls. Gordon's score reveled in Gordon's justly celebrated compositional strengths: a lyrical melodic gift and bittersweet harmonic sense. But the show failed to animate its wistfully evanescent Proustian tale. A very difficult task, to be sure, but *Albertine*, as theater, proved indefensibly inert.

Still, what remained exciting about both of these musicals was their ambition. And what again proved so dispiriting was not just the varying success with which those ambitions were realized but the wide-scale critical indifference to the ambitions themselves.

In this there was nothing particularly new. What set the 2002–2003 season apart, however, was a singular change in critical sensibility. This change was announced by the hosannas with which two strikingly unambitious Off-Broadway musicals were received: *Avenue Q* by Robert Lopez and Jeff Marx, and *Zanna, Don't!* by Tim Acito.

A not even thinly veiled *Sesame Street* lampoon, *Avenue Q* spun very familiar stories of stunted growth among aging Generation Xers via the onstage interaction between human characters and Muppet-like puppets. The tone was stupefyingly juvenile. And that was the point. Underachievement *was* achievement for the authors of *Avenue Q*, making it the first musical to aim for mediocrity—not campy, self-reflexive badness but transparently middling, sing-song doggerel—and succeed as a result. Critics "got" *Avenue Q*.[57] Audiences got it. Even the puppets could get it. The show was so simple-minded it seemed, to some, sophisticated; a true expression of our culture. Opening in February at the Vineyard Theater, *Avenue Q* found itself an overnight, counterintuitive hit, the season's biggest after *Hairspray*, and on its way to a Broadway transfer.

Zanna, Don't!, which reached the John Houseman Theater in April, was even more dunderheaded. A slack-jawed variation on *Grease* for the politically correct, *Zanna, Don't!* was a one-joke fairy tale about, literally, a high school fairy, complete with magic wand, who helps bring love and understanding to his schoolmates. With inane lyrics that almost never scanned properly and a bubblegum pop score so primitive it made *Avenue Q* sound sophisticated, *Zanna Don't!* was objectively, empirically, Musical Theater 101 bad.

Yet critics loved it.[58]

Why?

Perhaps *Zanna Don't!* and *Avenue Q* allowed critics to relax. There was little or no work involved in absorbing either show. And, for these critics, easy absorption led to easy approbation.

But there remains an even more insidious possible explanation. Champions of both shows seemed relieved to be able to conform at last with a pop culture that has long prized adolescent, anti-intellectual *un*pretensions. *Avenue Q* and *Zanna Don't!* gave critics and audiences their blessing to be lame-o pinheads too; to fancy themselves finally ushered past the velvet rope and into the kiddy club; to be hip and, yes, cool; to get the joke and still remain unimpeachably stupid.

Tapping into this pop cultural vein, though, does not require that the musical theater itself actually *be* stupid. At the Public Theater in March 2003 a new musical called *Radiant Baby*, while not nearly a success, nevertheless suggested how this might be accomplished.

Directed by George Wolfe and scored by a pop music veteran named Debra Barsha, *Radiant Baby* attempted to tell the life story of Keith Haring, the subway graffiti artist who attained both widespread celebrity and serious regard as an artist before dying of AIDS in 1990 at the age of 31. In this attempt, *Radiant Baby* largely failed. Its story-

telling technique—centered around a Greek chorus of pre-pubes-
cent Haring art students grilling the artist in song about his many
sexual and pharmacological transgressions—seemed disingenuous
at best and, at worst, self-serving and manipulative. Haring, the
musical theater character, wound up a sanitized shadow of Haring,
the wildly contradictory original.

Still, there were moments in *Radiant Baby* when Barsha's score
succeeded in integrating an awful lot of the pop music that, since
the 1960s, has eroded the Broadway musical's former pop pre-
eminence—rock and roll, soul, funk, R&B, rap, and especially disco.
In those moments *Radiant Baby* did seem to sweep audiences into
an inner sanctum of hipness (in *Radiant Baby*'s case, literally a
disco called the Paradise that Haring frequented). However fleeting,
the moments managed to capture Haring's uniting of high and low
art authentically, without resorting to simply being dim.

Stupidity is an enormous hurdle for musical theater to overcome
while engaging with today's pop culture. Pop culture has never before
been so barren. And yet, this has long been musical theater's challenge in America; to elevate the present day by reinventing it
musically. Jerome Kern, P.G. Wodehouse, and Guy Bolton did this
in the 1910s with their Princess Theater series of musicals. George
and Ira Gershwin did it in the Roaring Twenties beginning with
Lady Be Good. Cole Porter encapsulated the Depression-era 1930s
with *Anything Goes*. Though the 1940s were destined to be the decade
of Rodgers and Hammerstein, it could be said that Rodgers and
Lorenz Hart's *Pal Joey* in 1940, along with Bernstein, Comden, and
Green's *On the Town* in 1944, actually best captured the spirit of the
'40s, just as *West Side Story* did in the '50s, *Hair* in the '60s, *Company*
and, yes, *A Chorus Line* in the '70s. The '80s? Well, *March of the
Falsettos* came close, while *Rent* and *Noise/Funk* in the '90s hit the nail
right on the head.

So, what is musical theater to make of a decade and a new century
thus far ruled by hip-hop?

"The best thing about musical theater today," Stephen Sondheim has observed, "is that there's no one direction it's going in. It's going in many directions, some of which I approve of, some of which I deplore, but it is not a concentrated direction the way it was in the '50s, when everyone pursued the Rodgers and Hammerstein banner in their own way."

A nice out, then, would be to suggest that this multi-directionalism *already* reflects the cut and paste ideology of the hip-hop sampling aesthetic.

But that really would be stretching a point.

There is no doubt that hip-hop speaks with a very theatrical voice. Can this voice make a great hip-hop musical? To date, none have appeared. The sloppy rhymes and gerrymandered cadences of lingua hip–hop are diametrically opposed to the rigorous standards of poesy that have long governed musical theater's songwriting essence. Of course, shaking up those standards might be a good thing. But it will take both revolutionary imagination *and* rigor to make a hip-hop musical that is a leap forward for musical theater, rather than yet another de-evolutionary step backward.

Far more important than merely engaging with contemporary culture is musical theater's need to develop original voices, voices that are not just new and gifted, but heartfelt and individual.

"You rarely hear a composer's voice today," notes Sondheim. "We all start out writing pastiche, imitating others, satirizing what came before. The trick is to find your own voice within that. Sure, Leonard Bernstein is an amalgam, you hear his music and you say, yeah, that's Copland, yeah, that's Bowles, yeah, that's Barber. But it's still always Bernstein, above and beyond."

So, is there any reason to be optimistic?

"I keep in my bathroom a book by Nicolas Slonimsky called *Lexicon of Musical Invective*," says Sondheim. "It's a compendium of all these terrible reviews throughout musical history, from Beethoven to Shostokovich. The reviews are all about one thing: How dare they? How dare they? How dare they? Anything that's new is dismissed. Guess what, though? Progress is made anyway. Look at my career. Suddenly when I was 40-years-old, some people began to say, hey, this is pretty good. And now I'm considered an icon. *And* old fashioned!"

"Don't underestimate audiences," insists Harold Prince. "They *are* interested in change, they are interested in new material, they are interested in new voices, they're interested in all these things. But everyone does so much handicapping. It's like we were in a horse race or some damned thing. It isn't about that. It's about creating things and hoping people want to see what you put out there. And that, really, honestly, hasn't changed.

"When I produced *West Side Story*, there were a lot of long faces around our rehearsals," Prince recalled. "And I remember vividly Leland Hayward, who was Broadway's pre-eminent producer at that time, running into me on the street and saying, 'Well, you had a lot of hits, it's time you had a flop.' And I thought that was a pretty hostile thing to say. On the other hand, there were no stars in *West Side Story*. It sounded different, it looked different, it moved differently. The point is, it was fresh. And everybody turned out to be grateful for the change. So, I think tomorrow you can open a show with an unknown composer and a subject about anything—My Lord, a musical about *that*?!—and find you've handed audiences precisely what they're ready for. Because they're tired of the same old diet. That's always been true in the theater. I'm not being disingenuous. I know what I'm saying."

It is inescapably true that—with the exceptions of *Sweeney Todd* and *Rent*—the last 25 years of musical theater have not produced ground-breaking hits on a par with *West Side Story* or even

Oklahoma! Was this the fault of an inferior class of creators? Perhaps. Once upon a time, the cream of American creative talent aspired to write for Broadway. Now, the most promising young writers and composers head for pop music, movies, and television. Was it the fault of undiscerning producers? No doubt. While theater in America has always been a business, this generation of producers largely embraced the lowest common denominator greediness of the mass marketplace with pathetic gusto. Was it the fault of audiences? Obviously. They continue to settle far too easily for less and less.

What the last 25 years did give us, though, were musicals for our moment in time. Not equivalents of past achievements. Parables for our imperfect present. Yes, this period will always be the era that came after musical theater's glory days. Ever after. But it also was a time of innovation, an age when off-beat experimentation competed with conformity and in many instances won. Clearly, this art form still matters to a great many people. So long as it does, so long as passion, craftsmanship, and irreverence conjoin to tell stories in song, there is the potential for that next musical to be the one that changes everything once again.

CURTAIN CALL

As the 2003 Tony Award season in New York hurtled toward its inevitable televised ending, Adam Guettel was out in Seattle. Four years of angst over his next full-length musical had at last brought Guettel to Seattle's Intiman Theater where *The Light in the Piazza*, his musicalization of a 1958 story by Elizabeth Spencer, finally was about to sing before its first paying audience.

It had not been an easy journey but, then, nothing that Guettel tackled in musical theater seemed to come easily. His initial collaborator on this project had been the respected Alfred Uhry, a Pulitzer Prize winner for his 1988 play, *Driving Miss Daisy*, and a veteran librettist. But that partnership had proved unsustainable, and Guettel next had turned to an old family friend, Arthur Laurents; perhaps the musical theater's most respected book writer. Once they, too, parted, Guettel for a time had tried writing his own libretto. Finally, after just about giving up on *The Light in the Piazza*, he'd been persuaded to work with Craig Lucas, another prize-winning playwright, the author of *Prelude to a Kiss* and *The Dying Gaul*, among many admired works. It was this last teaming that had dragged Adam Guettel and his long-birthing new musical across the finish line.

Lucas was also the main reason Guettel now was in Seattle. Lucas, who also would direct *The Light in the Piazza*, had a relationship with the Intiman as its associate artistic director. But Guettel's own long-range plan for his musical actually made Seattle a perfect destination.

"The theory has been to stay as far from New York as possible," he explained, "to work in a non-profit theater where we can shape the show based on what it needs—*not* on what the biggest money-making venue might ask of it—so that *The Light in the Piazza* can be pretty much formed and on its feet before it is subjected to the forces that the commercial world exerts."

Guettel's earnest desire to lie low had already been subverted by his music. Those who'd managed to hear *The Light in the Piazza*, including a number of Broadway producers, were entranced. This musical was a love story—with a twist, of course, but still a love story—and set in Florence, no less. Guettel's music was romantic in the extreme and, as ever, anointed with his signature poignancy of spirit. The commercially barren caverns of *Floyd Collins* seemed very far away.

"We have had an offer from somebody in London," Guettel acknowledged. "And Roger Berlind [the producer] has said he would open it on Broadway pretty much immediately. Lincoln Center Theater has also expressed interest, though they haven't offered us a production yet. And Playwrights Horizons *has* offered us a production. I told them all that we just wanted to keep developing it, though, and see what we have before turning *The Light in the Piazza* over to anyone.

"My ideal, dream scenario," Guettel said, "is to raise enough money ourselves and find a space in New York that's mid-sized enough— keep the production lean enough, which right now means a cast of eight with orchestrations for four musicians—to just run for a year, say, and let word-of-mouth build. Better to come in the backdoor after having time with it out of town, instead of blowing our money on commercials and full-page ads in the *New York Times*. That's my idea, anyway. More like a prayer, I guess.

"I don't rule Broadway out," Guettel added, "if we could find the right theater and get the right breaks from the unions. I just have a strong instinct, though, about how this show can be flushed right down the toilet."

And what would that be?

"To present it to New York," Guettel replied, "as some kind of savior of musical theater."

It is sobering, though hardly surprising, that among the younger composers who've enjoyed the greatest measure of attention, if not success, over the previous few years in musical theater, Guettel, Michael John LaChiusa, and Jason Robert Brown seem bruised rather than blessed by their experience, allowing themselves little more than taciturn circumspection about their own futures. "Right now I'm writing a musical based on the Kurosawa film, *Rashomon*, for Audra McDonald," LaChiusa would only say, for example, when asked about his immediate plans. "I don't really think about the future. I'm living hand-to-mouth doing what I love to do. That's better than most people, no?"

Brown encountered big-time commercial Broadway failure in 2003, though the show in question barely even involved him as a composer. After working many months on the road as musical director helping to develop *Urban Cowboy* into a musical molded from the 1980 film, Brown had watched *Urban Cowboy* open at the Broadhurst Theater in March to scathing reviews.[59]

Given that most movie-to-musical transfers tend to be pretty corrupt enterprises, *Urban Cowboy* had not, in fact, been so very bad. Certainly its tale of rocky, white-trash romance had been more sincere and even more grown-up than, say, *Avenue Q*'s. The grab bag score of new and familiar country tunes also had included five tangy originals by Brown, who'd led a kicking onstage honky tonk band. The chemistry between the show's self-effacing leads, Matt Cavenaugh and Jenn Colella, had been perfectly, crudely believable and both had sung just the way their characters should have sung. A foolish decision to assault audiences with relentless profanity had proven self-defeating. Overall, though, the show's almost unanimous critical pasting seemed more a reflection of New York condescension to Texans two-stepping on Broadway than an accurate response to *Urban Cowboy's* fundamental flaws.

"I took the gig because it promised to be a nice paycheck," said Brown without hesitation. "I thought it would be fun to be a part of. And at the end of the day, it was a very nice paycheck and a hell of a lot of fun. I don't think we fooled ourselves into thinking that we were creating *Sweeney Todd* or even *Hairspray*. We were just trying to make an evening as enjoyable as we could within the parameters that were set for us. I'm glad I did it."

Brown had no answer at all, though, to the question: What was he doing next?

"I've been pretty dispirited about the current market for musicals," he said. "The way that shallowness is getting rewarded with alarming regularity while artistic ambition is generally derided as pretension and ignored. I've been trying to determine how to weather the vagaries of this particular climate and I can't say I've come up with a real answer yet. In terms of what really gets me fired up and excited about writing, I'm keeping to myself these days until I get the sense that someone really wants that from me. Until then, I'll be doing concerts and recordings and some corporate work, trying to get the bills paid any way I can."

Could this gloom just be a guy thing? Kirsten Childs, while working on an original new musical commissioned by the Vineyard Theater called *Miracle Brothers*—"a sort of magical realism adventure tale about two Brazilian brothers bound by blood and separated by race"—readily confessed that she was "hopeful" about the future.

"I'm mainly hopeful because the alternative is unacceptable," said Childs. "But also because I see a lot of new work that's interesting. I've been challenged, thrilled, shocked, angered, and awed by writers who are unafraid to try new approaches to musical theater form and by writers who are unashamedly embracing traditional musical theater to explore new themes. What excites and encourages me about these writers is their increasing numbers, their diversity, the passion they have for musical theater and the certainty that, because of them and others yet to come, musical theater will continue to flourish. Maybe it'll take a while before a lot of Broadway producers take the kinds of chances on new shows that they used to. Or maybe those days are gone for good. That just means that Broadway's not going to be where you go to see great, interesting, cutting-edge musical theater. I think everybody's pretty much made their peace with that, and it's not going to stop good new writers from doing what they have to do to get their shows up. The musical theater mine is not tapped out. There is a wealth of creativity yet to be discovered.

"I'm a mentor in the Theater Development Fund's Open Doors program," added Childs, "which means I take high school students to the theater and we discuss the shows afterwards. My students this year went crazy over *Cabaret* and *Avenue Q* (the latter being their favorite show). At *Avenue Q*, students who I know would normally be squirming in their seats or snoring or extremely jaded and stone-faced were beaming, exclaiming, 'I love this show!' These works reached them; they articulated with great enthusiasm and eloquence how the shows were relevant to their lives. That's another reason I'm hopeful. Young people are starved for good musical theater. Now if we could only get those damned ticket prices down so we can culti-vate a more youthful audience, how great would that be?"

Jeanine Tesori's view was similarly optimistic but grounded in a very particular pragmatism. "I have to believe in the future," Tesori said, "I'm the mother of a six-year-old."

Her newest musical, *Caroline, or Change*, with a book and lyrics by the Pulitzer Prize winning author of *Angels in America*, Tony Kushner, would soon open at the Public Theater under the direction of George Wolfe. Tesori and Kushner had been writing *Caroline, or Change* for about three years now. A nearly sung-through piece ("but not an opera," insisted Tesori), the show told the story of a young Jewish boy and his relationship with a black maid working in his family's home, a couple of weeks before and after the assassination of John F. Kennedy.

"I've learned to just concentrate on writing and let go of the rest," said Tesori. "It's the gift of parenting; you focus and you work. Between the ages of 40 and 60 it has to be that. You ignore the backstory and just produce as much material as possible, hopefully of the greatest quality."

As Tesori spoke, Stephen Sondheim was in Chicago preparing for the premiere of his nineteenth new musical, a show called *Bounce*, at the Goodman Theater.[60]

Bounce had taken a route even more serpentine than Adam Guettel's *Light in the Piazza* to its own first appearance before paying ticket holders. Commissioned by the Kennedy Center in 1996, *Bounce*'s original title had been *Wise Guys*. The show was (and still is) a musical about the raffish Mizner brothers—Addison, the architect, and Wilson, the dissolute wit, who among other things, had helped develop and hype Florida real estate during the early part of the last century.

With a libretto by John Weidman, *Wise Guys* had been expected to reach Broadway in April of 2000, directed by Sam Mendes and starring Nathan Lane and Victor Garber. A month-long workshop with this dream team held at New York Theatre Workshop in November 1999 had been treated by the media virtually as the show's Broadway preview period. But things had not gone well.

"What happened in the workshop," Sondheim said, "was Sam Mendes wanted to emphasize the relationship between the two guys and their mother, which seemed to us at the time to be a good idea and which turned out to be a bad idea."

Simple as that sounds, the ensuing complications were endlessly entangling. After Sondheim and Weidman parted ways with Mendes, a dispute blew up between the two creators and the show's lead producer, Scott Rudin, over who owned the rights to *Wise Guys*. Then things turned really ugly. In November 2001, Sondheim and Weidman filed a $5 million lawsuit against Rudin. In December, Rudin countersued. The resulting out-of-court settlement, in February 2002, gave Sondheim and Weidman their musical back and Rudin his $160,000 investment back. It was at this point that Sondheim's former collaborator and longtime friend, Harold Prince, stepped in.

"Hal agreed to direct," said Sondheim.

The two had not worked together in more than 20 years, not since the debacle of *Merrily We Roll Along*.

"It's great to be back with him," acknowledged Sondheim, adding, "the reason he and I work so well together is, Hal sees to it that the truck keeps going and I see to it that the truck doesn't go off the cliff. He's the positive force and I pull back on the reins.

"Hal pointed out that what this show lacked was sex," Sondheim continued, "meaning that there should be some female interest, particularly since Wilson was a well-known womanizer. So that's the essential change we've made. I had an idea back in 1952 for a female character and now we've expanded her into a leading character. Plus, we've reverted to the musical that we intended to do before the workshop, which was a bouncy, fast musical comedy, as opposed to the rather serious, even lugubrious, one that the workshop turned into. We're back to musical comedy with a capital *M* and a capital *C*. The only thing I'm worried about is that after all these years everybody's expecting some sort of Götterdämmerung and in fact it's just a musical comedy—song, scene, song, scene, song—not because at this moment I want to do a musical comedy, but because that's just what this show demands."

It is, in fact, one of the wonders of musical theater to hear Stephen Sondheim, at 73, speak about his latest musical with the same intensity and undiminished enthusiasm that he surely brought to his first more than 50 years ago. No one in musical theater today has less to prove than he does and yet no one keeps coming back again and again so tenaciously with something new.

"I'm also working on *The Frogs*," Sondheim added, "which I won't even call a rewrite; it's an expansion into a full-length musical of a one-act based on Aristophanes' play that I first wrote with Burt Shevelove in 1974. It requires five or six new songs as well as a revamping of some others. Nathan Lane's written the book—he got exposed to *The Frogs* when he did a recording of it a couple of years ago for Nonesuch. I'd say when we're through, maybe an eighth of the show will be Burt's book and the rest will be Nathan. We go into rehearsal a year from now at Lincoln Center with Susan Stroman directing. And I can't wait."

In all probability, Ira Weitzman will be there. After his years in part-time limbo, Weitzman is back at Lincoln Center Theater full-time as associate producer of musical theater. "André Bishop asked me to come back," Weitzman said simply. "I welcomed having a home base again."

During the 2003 season, Weitzman had worked on Lincoln Center Theater's *A Man of No Importance*, a new musical by Lynn Ahrens and Stephen Flaherty based on the 1994 film, with a book by Terrence McNally, directed by Joe Mantello. Though critics gave the show short shrift,[61] many others found its understated voice quite charming. Weitzman, meanwhile, continued to consult at Playwrights Horizons. Early in 2003, he'd helped Playwrights open a spectacular new theater on the renovated site of its former–massage parlor home by organizing celebratory reunion concert performances of two musicals that he'd worked on, William Finn's *Falsettos* and Jeanine Tesori's *Violet*, along with one that he hadn't Adam Guettel's *Floyd Collins*. Shortly after that, he'd worked on a limited engagement at Lincoln Center Theater of *Elegies: A Song Cycle* by Finn.

Talk about coming full circle.

"The concerts, for me, were a way of acknowledging some of the things I've done in the past and closing those chapters," Weitzman said. "With a great deal of luck, I've managed to develop at least one new musical a season that I've been excited about, and sometimes more than one. Not that they've all succeeded in a traditional way.

"But," he noted bemusedly, "I've learned not to measure my own success in those terms."

Success, on the most traditional terms, of course, remained very much the domain of the Disney Company, where the two "Disney guys" now were down to one. In June 2001, after ascending to the summit as chairman of Walt Disney Studios, Peter Schneider rather abruptly had resigned.

"That had nothing to do with theater," said Schneider. "It had to do with the Disney business. As you get higher up in a company of this size, overseeing more and more divisions—live-action movies, home video, the music company, feature animation, TV animation, theater—you are, I found, involved less and less in the creative process and the creative decision making. You're forced to delegate that. And I missed it. I am still involved in theater. I'm helping to develop five or six different projects, I have my own production company and invest in various Broadway shows. I dabble. I still have my hand in. What am I doing otherwise? Basically, I'm a man of leisure and having a fantastic time."

Schneider's exit had left Tom Schumacher in charge of the Disney Theatrical Organization.

"I'm working on three musicals at the moment," Schumacher said, "two pulled from animated movies and one from our live-action library. There's *Tarzan*, with music by Phil Collins—we're deeply into that; and *Little Mermaid*, which we've done a lot of writing on but haven't got a schedule for yet. *Tarzan* will be directed *and* designed by Bob Crowley, and Phil Collins has written about ten new songs already. The ideal plan would be the 2004–2005 season."

It is Schumacher's third musical project that is the wild card in the Disney portfolio: a stage version of the beloved Julie Andrews film *Mary Poppins*, originally released by Disney in 1964. What makes *Mary Poppins* something more than just another non-revival revival—if only from a business point of view—is the fact that Disney actually has a producing partner for the project, and an altogether surprising one, at that—none other than the former-maestro of mega, Cameron Mackintosh.

"When P. L. Travers, who wrote *Mary Poppins*, was still alive," Schumacher said, "she sold the theatrical rights to Cameron. However, when Walt Disney had done his deal with her for the movie, there did exist this notion that the Disney Company would have to give permission if *Mary Poppins* ever were to be done onstage. Over the years, if anyone wanted to do a play of *Mary Poppins*, Travers would check with us and we would always say no.

"Then the theatrical division got going, after *Beauty and the Beast* in 1995. Suddenly, doing *Mary Poppins* became a priority for everybody here, from Michael Eisner on down. There *we* were, though, without theatrical rights but *with* so-called 'blocking' rights. And there was Cameron with *his* theatrical rights but without the music, which Walt Disney does own. This resulted in a stalemate that went on for years and years. Still, after Peter left I kept thinking *Mary Poppins* was *the* big idea for our immediate future in theater. Because it's new and old, it's classic, it's books, it's film. It seemed like a natural."

Schumacher had met Mackintosh just once before, in the south of France over lunch the summer after *Lion King* had opened on Broadway. "I didn't really know him," Schumacher said. "Still, I decided, without telling anybody, to just make an appointment and go see Cameron in December of 2001.

"I said to him, 'You think this a great idea, we think this a great idea, so what if for just a moment we say out loud what we would do if it did happen.' By the following December the deal was virtually done to produce *Mary Poppins* together, 50/50. It will be: 'Walt Disney Productions and Cameron Mackintosh Present *Mary Poppins*, based on the book by P. L. Travers and the Walt Disney film.'"

The all-Anglo team that Schumacher and Mackintosh have assembled for the job is impressive: Richard Eyre, director; Matthew Bourne, musical staging and choreography; Bob Crowley, sets and costumes.

"In May I heard both acts for the first time, at Cameron's house, with all of the songs and most of the underscoring," said Schumacher. "We'll have one more meeting of what Richard calls 'The Coven.' We're then scheduled to go into rehearsal in July of 2004 for the 2004–2005 season in London."

Even when Cole Porter walked the earth there were corporate musicals.[62] Today, though, only corporate musical makers like Disney and "Cameron Mackintosh, Inc." have the means to *work* on musicals (if not actually *make* them) in the rarified Cole Porter manner.

"I drove down to Cameron's house, this 12th-century priory of his, on a Friday," Schumacher recalled. "We did some business stuff and then about seven, eight o'clock, everyone started arriving. By nine, Cameron was cooking and we were all just drinking and eating. We were then handed the revised version of act one and sent to bed to read it. In the morning, people were jogging, swimming, eating, until by eleven everyone had gathered at the piano. We stayed there until eight. Then we woke up the next morning and did the same thing again, but breaking up into smaller groups, until luncheon was served. It was truly, 'A Weekend in the Country.'

"I suspect that there are a number of projects we will now do in partnership with other people," Schumacher concluded, describing

Disney's long-term musical future. "We never partnered before but it does open up the kind of material we can do. I want people to know when they come to one of our shows that they are getting a Disney show. But there's also a lot of other good stuff out there that we would like to be involved in. I'm even licensing shows from our catalogue to other producers, not the animated catalogue, but live-action Disney films. It all allows me to broaden the Disney footprint."

To raise money for the first production of *The Light in the Piazza*, and for the Intiman Theater itself, Adam Guettel also agreed to appear at a fancy private home or two. Once, so many years ago, all aspiring new musicals gave backers' auditions—going hat in hand to deluxe residences. Now, in Seattle, Guettel and company took this quaint old route once again.

"We hit the houses of five different really rich people," said Guettel, "where there were anywhere from 20 to 50 other really rich people. And we kind of told them the story, or rather Craig told them the story and I played four or five songs on the guitar and at the piano, and I sang. Some of these people had money from the computer world, some of them had money from lumber, one of them was in root beer. And these folks were generous. I don't know the exact numbers, how successful we were, but I enjoyed it a lot. For me, it's how I grew up—wearing my Dr. Dentons and coming into the living room of my parents' apartment to meet the company before going to bed. It sort of felt like my default setting."

Perhaps the most intriguing aspect of these Seattle house calls was that Guettel's audiences often were comprised of young people— young people with an awful lot of money but next to no exposure to, or interest in, musical theater.

"Some of them were really young Microsoft guys," Guettel said, "your basic, run of the mill Silicon billionaires. One house was a few doors down from Bill Gates' place and it reminded me of this Roald Dahl short story where the entire house is so completely automated that they forget how to do anything, they can't even make toast, and then they go into one room and get eaten by lions. *That* kind of a house."

According to Guettel, Bill Gates himself was persuaded to give money, even though Gates never actually made it to any of the events. "Gates gave us over $100,000, I think. He's never invested in the arts before like this, and he gave the Intiman, like, 100 and Microsoft co-founder Paul Allen gave 25. It was kind of our seed money and it got a lot of people excited. So, I think it worked."

It's a nice image to close a book with, especially one about musical theater: Adam Guettel as an emissary, serenading disinterested strangers in their homes, singing to them of musical theater's mysteries and hoping, just maybe, to strike a chord. And succeeding.

ACKNOWLEDGEMENTS

Thank you to the musical theater community for your time and your talent.

Heartfelt thanks to Andrea Stevens for getting this whole business started, for always believing that this was, in fact, a book, and for editorial assistance beyond the call of duty.

Thank you Glenn Young for making this book a book.

Thank you Michael Messina for keeping this book together.

Thank you Sara Krulwich for the superb cover photograph that wasn't, and to Adam Guettel.

Thank you Amy Asch, Nancy Kassak Diekmann and, especially, (note the commas) Allan Larson.

Thank you Larry Gelbart.

Thank you Robert Kimball.

For photo generosity, thank you Mary Bryant, Michal Daniel, Paul Kolnik, Tim Sanford, and Tom Schumacher.

Thank you John Barlow and Chris Boneau for the infinite number of things that you both do so well. Also thanks to Erin Baiano, Bill Coyle, Anne Love, Aaron Meier, Kallie Shimek, John J. O'Sullivan, and Elizabeth Wehrle for all your legwork. And thank you John Greenleaf, for keeping the hard drive running.

A special thank you to Stephen Sondheim.

I'd also like to acknowledge the Really Useful Group and the Mel Brooks office for their respective refusals to grant permission to reprint even two lyric lines each from their bosses' songs.

A loving thank you to Judy and Iz Singer for introducing me to musicals. And to Elisa and Mark Singer for your stellar, dizzying work in our living room productions of *Fiddler on the Roof.*

Lastly, thanks to Loretta and Leah. For everything.

NOTES

1   Composer/lyricist Randy Courts wrote a number of musicals with book writer and lyricist Mark St. Germain that were produced Off-Broadway throughout the 1990s. These musicals included *Gifts of the Magi* (December 1989/Lamb's Theater Company); *Johnny Pye and the Foolkiller*, winner of AT&T's New Play of the Nineties Award (October 1993/Lamb's Theater Company); and *Jack's Holiday* (Playwrights Horizons/March 1995).

We're Bitching

2   "Broadway history was made at the end of the first act of Michael Bennett's beautiful and heartbreaking new musical, *Dreamgirls*," wrote Frank Rich in his *New York Times* review on December 20, 1981. "…*Dreamgirls* is the same kind of breakthrough for musical stagecraft that *Gypsy* was."

All It Has to Be Is Good

3   *Forum*'s original (and still-credited) director is George Abbott.

Music of the Night

4   For a fuller understanding of Broadway's inflationary equation see: *The Numbers*, page 315.

5   It must be noted that *Romance Romance* received the Outer Critics Circle award for Best Musical of 1987–1988 and was also nominated for a Best Musical Tony Award.

Somethin' More

6   *Crazy for You*'s score was anchored by five of *Girl Crazy*'s biggest hit songs: "Embraceable You," "I Got Rhythm," "Could You Use Me?," "Bidin' My Time," and "But Not for Me," along with a less significant number called "Bronco Busters." *Crazy for You*'s remaining fifteen or so songs were an assortment borrowed from the Gershwin catalogue. The original book for *Girl Crazy* was by Guy Bolton and John McGowan. The credited bookwriter on *Crazy for You* was Ken Ludwig, as "inspired by" Bolton and McGowan.

Maybe It Better Soon No

7 Drabinsky and his partner Myron Gottlieb would be indicted in January 1999
by a New York City federal grand jury on sixteen counts of criminal fraud and
conspiracy. The U.S. alleged that the pair had led an eight-year scheme to fake
earnings or hide financial losses and siphon off some $4.6 million from Livent.
In a separate civil complaint, the SEC charged the two with securities fraud.
Drabinsky denied the charges and has since remained in Canada, avoiding a
return to the United States that would bring him to trial.

In October 2002, in Canada, Drabinsky and Gottlieb were charged with
nineteen counts each of fraud following a four-year investigation into Livent's
books. "We are alleging that the accused defrauded creditors and private and
public investors of approximately one-half a billion dollars between Dec. 14,
1989 and June 23, 1998," RCMP Detective Inspector Craig Hannaford of the
commercial crime unit told reporters during a news conference in Toronto."
(*Canadian Broadcasting System*, October 23, 2002). See also endnotes 25 and 33.

8 *New Musicals* had expressly forbidden critics to review performances at
Purchase, claiming a kind of "in-progress" exemption for its productions. *New
York Times* drama critic Frank Rich flouted this ban, bought a ticket and wrote
a negative (and not inaccurate) review.

The Red Shoes

9 Though one hates to question Jule Styne's memory, according to theater historian Mary Henderson in her book, *The City & the Theatre*, the Mark Hellinger
Theater opened in 1930 as the Hollywood Theater, a movie house owned by
Warner Brothers. In 1934 the Hollywood became a legitimate theater and in
1936 the principal entrance was moved from Broadway to 51st Street, with the
name of the theater then changed to the Fifty-First Street Theater. In 1949, its
new owner re-christened the Fifty-First Street Theater in honor of the Broadway
columnist Mark Hellinger.

10 Sondheim insists that Styne misremembers this too. "I had exactly one dinner at
Jule's home, which was in Ruth Dubonnet's mansion," Sondheim recalls. "I used
to walk over and drop my lyrics off, which included the musical rhythms written
out. He had a spinet piano downstairs. I don't think I even made it upstairs to
the rest of the house more than once. And there was never any lunch."

A KIND OF HAPPINESS

11 "What is the best Broadway musical comedy score of 1991?" wrote Frank Rich in the *New York Times* on November 13, 1991. "Make no mistake about it, it is the score that Alan Menken and Howard Ashman wrote for *Beauty and the Beast*, the animated Walt Disney movie that opened this week…Their goose-bump-inducing accomplishment in *Beauty and the Beast*…accentuates what is missing from the Broadway musical scene."

In his year-end summation *Theater/1991* (*NYT* 12/29/91), Rich reiterated this opinion under the header: "The Hit That Got Away."

12 "The greatest of all Disney magic is the magic of copyright," wrote William A. Henry III in his *Time* magazine review on May 2, 1994. "More remarkable than Mickey or Dumbo or any other creation, pre- or post-Walt, has been the company's success in exploiting established franchises and accumulating new ones. Perhaps the most cunning Disney trick is to take fairy tales in the public domain and reinvent them as corporate property. A billion-dollar example is *Beauty and the Beast*, which has metamorphosed from a bedtime story known to every child into a mega-hit animated film (and an even bigger hit on video), a sound track, a theme-park attraction, an ice show, a lunch-box and T-shirt decoration and, as of last week, a Broadway musical. Actually, not just a Broadway musical but the costliest and most complex ever, not to mention maybe the most vapid, shallow and, yes, cartoonish."

The review in *Variety* by Jeremy Gerard on April 19, 1994 summed things up: "Disney arrives on Broadway with a bang, a boom, a roar, plenty of fireworks, and a fistful of lovely songs. The show will almost certainly be met with varying levels of derision by Broadway traditionalists, many critics among them, and there's plenty in the $12-million production to fuel their ire. The complaints, however, will be meaningless where it counts, which is at the Palace Theater box office and at the *Beauty and the Beast* bazaar that used to be the Palace lobby. Disney's first Broadway show will be packing them in—and thumbing its nose at the naysayers—for a very long time."

13 "The Broadway production has earned back, at best, 80 percent of the initial $13 million [investment]," reported the *New York Times* on March 24, 1997.

Glory

14 Larson did also write his first full-length musical at Adelphi, *Sacrimoral-immorality*, about the Christian Right. Retitled *Saved*, the show later ran for two weeks at a 42ⁿᵈ Street Off-Off-Broadway theater.

15 A draft of this letter was discovered among Larson's personal papers after his death. It is unclear whom it was addressed to. It is included here courtesy of the Larson family.

16 *Theater Forum*. "*Rent* Uptown and Downtown — An interview with director Michael Greif," by Theodore Shank (Winter/Spring 1997, University of California, San Diego), p. 11.

17 Ibid.

How Glory Goes

18 To achieve this sound, Guettel was abetted by the brilliant orchestrations of Bruce Coughlin and the superb musical direction of Ted Sperling.

This Is the Moment

19 The York Theatre Company, a very enterprising, small Off-Broadway company with a history of reviving worthy old musicals, also began in 1995 to produce new musicals on a regular basis. These shows have since come to include: *The IT Girl, Little by Little, Suburb, After the Fair, No Way to Treat A Lady, The Last Sweet Days, Fermat's Last Tango, The Show Goes On, Prodigal, Roadside,* and *Exactly Like You*, among others.

20 "There is an anthem-like lyricism here — good stuff for ice-skating and the like." Clive Barnes. *The New York Post*, April 29, 1997.

21 "[*Jekyll & Hyde*] doesn't require your undivided attention, since it keeps saying the same things, with the slightest variations, over and over again," wrote Ben Brantley in his *New York Times* review on April 29, 1997. "The overall effect is like having the television and the radio (set to a "lite" station) on at the same time... [A] synthetic fog... creeps on and off the stage, rather like a wandering attention span. It is easy to sympathize with the fog."

"*Jekyll & Hyde* has half the personality of its title character, and it's the dour, humorless half," wrote Greg Evans in his *Variety* review on April 29, 1997. "...[T]his much-traveled and revised musical quickly settles into a self-serious sameness that pretty much drains the well-known horror tale of whatever guilty pleasures lurk within."

22 *Jekyll & Hyde* ultimately ran for four years, a total of 1,543 performances.

Pure and Blameless

23 Weitzman did have a nominal title at Playwrights Horizons as musical theater program director but generally he received program credit under the rubric: Playwrights Horizons Staff.

24 "Violet isn't quite as different as her creators intend her to be. Nor, for that matter, is the musical itself," wrote Ben Brantley in his *Times* review on March 12, 1997. "...*Violet* integrates a number of [musical] styles into a consistently pretty aural tapestry...What the show fails to do is to provide any compelling sense of character.... This show, unfortunately, lets you wrap your mind around its message nearly from its inception. That's not a good thing when the musical is, for the most part, the message."

Hakuna Matata

25 As the *New York Times* reported in an article entitled, "A Bit of Barnum on Broadway," dated August 21, 1998: "That company [Cineplex Odeon] was also criticized for its aggressive accounting methods. In 1989, Mr. Drabinsky was ousted in a fierce battle with MCA, one of Cineplex Odeon's largest shareholders."

Saturn Returns

26 "*Triumph* is largely propelled by a crude, anything-for-a-laugh avidity," wrote Ben Brantley in his *Times* review on October 24, 1997. "Heidi Ettinger's wonderfully inventive set...does indeed shimmer with theatrical wit. But ten minutes into the production, it's obvious that little else, Ms. Buckley aside, is going to rise to that level."

27 [B]e warned: if it's pulse-racing suspense and derring-do you're after, you would

be better off watching tourists crossing against the light in Times Square," wrote Ben Brantley in his *New York Times* review on November 10, 1997. "*Pimpernel*...has a pulpy pop score by Frank Wildhorn and a wooden book and lyrics by Nan Knighton."

"Seek him here, seek him there, just don't expect to really care, wrote Greg Evans in his *Variety* review on November 10, 1997. "Nan Knighton and Frank Wildhorn's middlebrow *The Scarlet Pimpernel* is B-movie melodrama set to an Adult Contemporary format."

28 See endnote 34.

29 *Capeman* went through three directors, officially: Susana Tubert, Eric Simonson and Mark Morris, who wound up receiving formal program credit for the show's direction and choreography. Uncredited as director was Jerry Zaks, who "edited and restructured" *Capeman* during its final pre-opening weeks, together with the choreographer Joey McKneely.

"We wanted to do it our way, and we wanted a director whose thinking was compatible with ours," said Simon in a February 2, 1998 interview with *Time* magazine. "...We wanted to work with a good director, but we didn't want to work for a good director."

30 "Simon, one of pop's great songwriters, has lent Broadway a collection of great songs," wrote Greg Evans in his *Variety* review on January 30, 1998. " His music for *The Capeman* ranks among the best Broadway scores of this or any recent season...Scrap the irredeemable book, make peace with the static nature of the show and dispense with any foolhardy attempt to flesh out one-note characters or raise the barely-a-footnote real-life tale to the stature of social significance."

31 "[I]t would take a hard-core sadist to derive pleasure from the sad, benumbed spectacle that finally opened last night at the Marquis Theater, three weeks behind schedule," wrote Ben Brantley in his *New York Times* review on January 30, 1998. "[*The Capeman*] may be unparalleled in its wholesale squandering of illustrious talents..."

32 *Myths and Hymns* premiered in a concert staging at the New Lyric Festival in Northampton, Massachusetts in the summer of 1996. The New Lyric Festival

was an ambitious, if short-lived, summer festival for new musical theater founded and run by Wiley Hausam.

ELABORATE LIVES

33 "Livent...announced yesterday that an internal investigation had found serious accounting problems involving millions of dollars. The company's new managers, led by Michael Ovitz...said that they were 'virtually certain' that the company's financial results dating back to the beginning of 1996 would have to be restated...The company suspended Garth H. Drabinsky, Livent's chief creative director." (*The New York Times*, "Broadway Producer Has Big Accounting Woes," August 11, 1998.)

YOU DON'T KNOW THIS MAN

34 "Broadway producers are selling their shows directly to the public when they are savaged by the critics," reported the *New York Times*' Robin Pogrebin in an article headlined, "The Magic Is in the Marketing; Theaters Go Around the Critics and Straight to the People," on November 19, 1998. "Among the poorly reviewed shows benefiting from aggressive marketing are *Footloose, Jekyll & Hyde, Sound of Music*, and *The Scarlet Pimpernel*."

35 See note 27.

36 *The Scarlet Pimpernel*'s tenacity extended to a mid-run revamping of the entire show under the direction of Robert Longbottom. This "new" *Pimpernel* opened in November 1998 to more respectable reviews. "Restructured, rewritten, restaged and significantly recast," wrote Ben Brantley in his *New York Times* review on November 5, "...what was once a frozen lump of a production is on its feet and moving...*The Scarlet Pimpernel* still isn't, by any stretch of the imagination, a *My Fair Lady* or even a *Phantom of the Opera*. But on its own terms...it works."

37 "Why are we here at the St. James Theater?" asked Ben Brantley in his *New York Times* review on April 23, 1999. "What is the point in remaining for more than two hours?...Mr. Wildhorn's songs for *The Civil War* blend into one bland current of generic pop. The overall effect is of being imprisoned not in some theme-appropriate cell in Andersonville but in a jukebox stocked entirely with B-side selections."

Dream True

38 "Sweet of spirit, beguilingly old-fashioned and, alas, utterly unexciting, the musical *Captains Courageous* sails into the unlikely port of the Manhattan Theater Club after a long voyage that dates back almost a decade," wrote Charles Isherwood in his *Variety* review on February 17, 1999. "...Clearly the show has many admirers, but...it's hard to see what inspired such enthusiasm for this nicely behaved but rather plain child."

"The director, Lynne Meadow, dreams up an endless checklist of tasks for her actors, and as *Captains Courageous* progresses, the reason becomes clear," observed Peter Marks in his *New York Times* review on February 17, 1999. "She is desperately trying to create the illusion of something happening. For all its handsome rigging, for all the muscular chanteys, and wistful sailing songs by the songwriting team of Frederick Freyer and Patrick Cook, the show itself is rather static and pale."

Wild Party

39 "The worst aspect of Michael John LaChiusa's new musical, *Marie Christine*, at Lincoln Center's Vivian Beaumont Theater, is Michael John LaChiusa's new music," wrote Clive Barnes in his *N.Y. Post* review on December 3, 1999.

"What LaChiusa ain't got is a particular affection for the kind of melodic charm that most audiences expect from a Broadway musical," insisted Charles Isherwood in his *Variety* review on December 3, 1999. "His lyrically dense, musically spare songs...contain few memorable tunes and nary a hummable chorus."

One contrarian critic was Fintan O'Toole of the *Daily News* who raved in his December 3, 1999 review, "Michael John LaChiusa's *Marie Christine* is a triumphant contradiction. It's a stark, severe, but successful musical."

40 "*The Wild Party*...on Broadway...is a cause for sorrowful head-shaking," wrote Ben Brantley in his *New York Times* review on April 14, 2000. "...What has wound up on the stage is a portrait of desperation that itself feels harshly, wantonly desperate.... Even singing the jauntier examples of Mr. LaChiusa's vaudeville and jazz pastiches (with Stravinsky hovering in the background, (natch), [the cast] tend[s] to be as whiny and overstimulated as a party of two-year-olds with no videos to watch."

What Sings

41 Ironically, the founding artistic director of *Encores!* was, of all people, Ira Weitzman, who quit after the first season. "I was a little ambivalent about working on concert versions of old shows," he explained. "Obviously, my whole life has been devoted to the production of new musicals."

A Showbiz Mausoleum

42 *Variety*, "Broadway Says Bye to 'Phantom' Funk," May 28, 2001.

43 *Cats* closed on September 10, 2001 after 7,485 performances (nearly eighteen years), the longest running musical in Broadway history. *Miss Saigon* closed on January 28, 2001 after 4,092 performances (nearly ten years). *Les Misérables* closed on May 18, 2003 after 6,680 performances, second behind *Cats*.

44 All of this information — though no secret — was confirmed by Lynn Ahrens in an interview with the author.

This Is Urinetown

45 "[I]f you take apart *Mamma Mia!* ingredient by ingredient, you can only wince," wrote Ben Brantley in his *New York Times* review on October 19, 2001. "It has a sitcom script about generations in conflict that might as well be called *My Three Dads*. The matching acting, perky and italicized, often brings to mind the house style of *The Brady Bunch*.

"The choreography is mostly stuff you could try, accident-free, in your own backyard. And the score consists entirely of songs made famous in the disco era by the Swedish pop group ABBA, music that people seldom admit to having danced to, much less sung in their showers. Yet these elements have been combined, with alchemical magic, into the theatrical equivalent of comfort food."

46 *The Los Angeles Times*, "What Would Muriel Think?" February 18, 2001.

Climbing Uphill

47 "...As a post-mortem of a relationship *The Last Five Years* is pretty tedious," wrote Ben Brantley in his *New York Times* review on March 4, 2002. "...Mr. Brown's lyrics only rarely achieve...depth."

"Jason Robert Brown...gives both players less than they deserve," wrote Donald Lyons in his *N.Y. Post* review on March 4, 2002. "While the lyrics are clever and occasionally sad, they never probe deeply; the music is glib and generic."

48 This information was confirmed in interviews with a number of individuals closely involved with *Sweet Smell of Success*, none of whom would go on the record for attribution.

49 Perhaps a herald of that next cast album golden age was the arrival in 2002 of PS Classics, a new company run by Nonesuch alumnus Tommy Krasker and his partner Philip Chaffin. PS Classics has since gone on to record a Los Angeles production of Michael John LaChiusa's *First Lady Suite*, the 2003 Broadway revival of *Nine*, and the Off-Broadway musicals *My Life with Albertine*, and *Zanna, Don't!*, among other projects.

Don't Cry for Me, Argentina

50 "*Sunset Boulevard*...has proved to be a major financial headache," reported *Reuters* in an article on June 16, 1997, quoting Lloyd Webber himself as acknowledging that, '*Sunset* has lost money massively overall.'"

51 "In April 1995, it was reported that the Really Useful Group, Lord Lloyd Webber's American production company, had provided *Variety* with inflated figures for the period when Ms. [Glenn] Close was on vacation, apparently in an attempt to minimize Ms. Close's impact on the show." *The New York Times*, February 4, 1997.

52 Lloyd Webber has since begun work on a new musical of his own, *The Woman in White*, based on the Wilkie Collins novel.

53 Though Lloyd Webber did ultimately produce *Bombay Dreams* in London, he disengaged from the show as producer before its arrival on Broadway.

Finale: But Who Calls That Livin'?

54 "You can waste a lot of time trying to decide exactly what to call *Movin' Out*," wrote Richard Zoglin in his *Time* magazine review on November 4, 2002. "It's

not a traditional musical because none of the main characters say a word — or even sing. You're getting warmer if you think of a choreographed rock concert for which the star hasn't shown up but a lot of really good dancers have. Or maybe just compare it with previous dance pieces Tharp has done to popular music.... But then what's it doing on Broadway? Setting a new standard for the rock musical, that's what."

Ben Brantley in his *New York Times* review on October 25, 2002 observed rather obliquely: "Ms. Tharp and her vivid team of dancers unearth the reasons certain clichés keep resonating and, more important, make them gleam as if they had just been minted."

55 "Even charming is too weighty a word to describe the wispy appeal of *Amour*," wrote Ben Brantley in his *New York Times* review on October 21, 2002. "Americans...may be disappointed by the production's exceedingly mild taste."

Wrote Charles Isherwood in his *Variety* review on October 20, 2002: "This head-scratcher of a musical aims for whimsical charm — not an easy target to hit, for sure — but mostly comes across as just odd."

56 "For readers who do not immerse themselves in musical theater," wrote Howard Kissel in his *Daily News* review on February 14, 2003, "you should know that LaChiusa has had seven musicals produced in New York in the last decade, including three on Broadway...

"All of these shows, as well as his Off-Broadway musicals, were produced by subscription theaters. LaChiusa is a favorite of such theaters because his music, with its mildly unexpected harmonic turns, gives the impression of 'pushing the envelope.' Thus, theaters that produce his shows seem to be doing something significant in the development of musical theater...You could say it pushes the envelope. But who cares?"

57 "This canny toy chest of a show...is the first mainstream musical since *Rent* to coo with such seductive directness to theatergoers on the fair side of 40 in their own language," wrote Ben Brantley in his *New York Times* review on March 20, 2003. "...*Avenue Q*, the inspired brainchild of the songwriting team of Robert Lopez and Jeff Marx, may apply the coaxing, learning-is-fun attitude of children's educational television to the R-rated situations of post-collegiate life in

the big city. But theatergoers who grew up from the late 1960s onward will instantly grasp the show's wistful and affectionate sincerity as well as its thorny humor."

58 "Happily oblivious to everything else happening in the world, a chirpy new Off-Broadway musical, *Zanna, Don't!* arrived at the John Houseman Theater last night with a pop score that aims to be nothing but catchy and a message that says nothing but that people should love each other," wrote Bruce Weber in his *New York Times* review on March 21, 2003. "And gee whiz, wouldn't you know it? Something about its pure, sugary hopefulness satisfies a sweet tooth that many of us may have forgotten we have."

Wrote Marilyn Stasio in her *Variety* review on March 30, 2003: "For a show that panders so shamelessly to its audience, this 'musical fairy tale'...is just clever enough to get away with being so cute...Credit Tim Acito with a terrific concept for an upbeat pop musical. There are endless opportunities for his sweet brand of satiric humor."

Curtain Call

59 "Broadway disaster cultists may be disappointed to learn that *Urban Cowboy*, directed with a hand of lead by Lonny Price, does not eclipse the now departed *Dance of the Vampires* as the season's worst musical," wrote Ben Brantley in his *New York Times* review on March 28, 2003. "...*Urban Cowboy* doesn't have the imagination to be so extravagantly bad. Instead, it exudes the mechanical air of a show dutifully assembled according to a low and specific assessment of audience expectations."

Wrote Howard Kissel in his *Daily News* review on March 28, 2003, "The whole thing is as mechanical as the bull."

60 In fact, *Bounce* was not well received in Chicago, nor during a subsequent autumn 2003 run at the Kennedy Center in Washington, D.C. As of this writing, its future remains in doubt.

61 "...Bursting with cliches that have always raised lumps in susceptible throats, *Man* never really delivers on its premise that ordinary souls harbor extraordinary feelings," wrote Ben Brantley in his *New York Times* review on October 11, 2002. "It's as if the entire enterprise had been muffled in gray wool."

"The score is largely wan," wrote Howard Kissel in his *Daily News* review on October 11, 2002. "...*Man* has many virtues, but it neither crystallizes nor transforms the material."

62 In Cole Porter's time the corporate powers behind Broadway musicals often were film studios. MGM, for example, in 1935, agreed to finance Porter's new musical before the show even had a title. The musical turned out to be *Jubilee*, which Porter wrote with his collaborator Moss Hart during the course of a four-and-a-half-month cruise around the world.

THE SEASONS

(A Broadway Chronology)

CHAPTER 1: WE'RE BITCHING (1977–1982)

1977–1978

Original Broadway book musicals referenced in chapter: *The Act* (opened October 1977 at the Majestic Theater), book by George Furth, music by John Kander, lyrics by Fred Ebb; *On the Twentieth Century* (opened February 1978 at the St. James Theater), book and lyrics by Betty Comden and Adolph Green, music by Cy Coleman; *Runaways* (opened May 1978 at the Plymouth Theater), book, music and lyrics by Elizabeth Swados; *Working* (opened May 1978 at the 46th Street Theater), book by Studs Terkel, adapted by Stephen Schwartz, music by Craig Carnelia, Micki Grant, Mary Rodgers, Schwartz and James Taylor; lyrics by Susan Birkenhead, Carnelia, Grant, Schwartz and Taylor.

Other original Broadway book musicals: *A History of the American Film*, book by Christopher Durang, music by Mel Marvin; *Angel*, book by Ketti Frings and Peter Udell, music by Gary Geld, lyrics by Udell.

Revivals: *Man of La Mancha*; *Hair*; *Jesus Christ Superstar*; *Timbuktu!* (*Kismet*); *Hello, Dolly!*

Other: *Beatlemania*; *Elvis: The Legend Lives!*; *Dancin'*; *Ain't Misbehavin'*.

Off-Broadway, the one new musical to make a mark was *I'm Getting My Act Together and Taking It on the Road*, a midlife crisis revue for newly liberated women that was very much of its time, with music by Nancy Ford, book and lyrics by Gretchen Cryer. After opening at the Public Theater in May 1978, the show ran for nearly three years (1,165 performances).

1978–1979

Original Broadway book musicals referenced in this chapter: *The Best Little Whorehouse in Texas* (opened June 1978 at the 46th Street Theater), book by Larry L. King and Peter Masterson, music and lyrics by Carol Hall; *Ballroom* (opened December 1978 at the Majestic Theater), book by Jerome Kass, music by Billy Goldenberg, lyrics by Alan Bergman and Marilyn Bergman; *A Broadway Musical* (opened December 1978 at the Lunt-Fontanne Theater), book by William F. Brown, music by Charles Strouse, lyrics by Lee Adams; *The Grand Tour* (opened January 1979 at the Palace Theater), book by Michael Stewart and Mark

299

Bramble, music and lyrics by Jerry Herman; *They're Playing Our Song* (opened February 1979 at the Imperial Theater), book by Neil Simon, music by Marvin Hamlisch, lyrics by Carole Bayer Sager; *Sweeney Todd* (opened March 1979 at the Uris Theater), book by Hugh Wheeler, music and lyrics by Stephen Sondheim; *Carmelina* (opened April 1979 at the St. James Theater), book by Alan Jay Lerner and Joseph Stein, music by Burton Lane, lyrics by Lerner; *I Remember Mama* (opened May 1979 at the Majestic Theater), book by Thomas Meehan, music by Richard Rodgers, lyrics by Martin Charnin, additional lyrics by Raymond Jessel.

Other original Broadway book musicals: *King of Hearts*, book by Joseph Stein, music by Peter Link, lyrics by Jacob Brackman; *Platinum*, book by Will Holt and Bruce Vilanch, music by Gary William Friedman, lyrics by Holt; *Saravà*, book and lyrics by N. Richard Nash, music by Mitch Leigh; *My Old Friends*, book by Mel Mandel and Norman Sachs; *The Utter Glory of Morrissey Hall*, book by Clark Gesner and Nagle Jackson, music and lyrics by Gesner.

Revivals: *Stop the World—I Want to Get Off*; *Whoopee!*

Other: *Eubie!*

1979–1980

Original Broadway book musicals referenced in this chapter: *Evita* (opened September 1979 at the Broadway Theater), book by Tim Rice, music by Andrew Lloyd Webber, lyrics by Rice; *Barnum* (opened April 1980 at the St. James Theater), book by Mark Bramble, music by Cy Coleman, lyrics by Michael Stewart; *A Day in Hollywood/A Night in the Ukraine* (opened May 1980 at the John Golden Theater), book and lyrics by Dick Vosburgh, music by Frank Lazarus.

Other original Broadway book musicals: *Got Tu Go Disco*, book by John Zodrow, music and lyrics by an assortment of ten different writers; *But Never Jam Today*, book by Vinnette Carroll and Bob Larimer, music by Bert Keyes and Larimer, lyrics by Larimer; *King of Schnorrers*, book, music, and lyrics by Judd Woldin; *Comin' Uptown*, book by Philip Rose and Peter Udell, music by Gary Sherman, lyrics by Udell; *Reggae*, book, music, and lyrics by a whole host of different folks; *Musical Chairs*, book by Barry Berg, Ken Donnelly, and Tom Savage, music and lyrics by Savage.

Revivals: *Peter Pan*; *The Most Happy Fella*; *Oklahoma!*; *West Side Story*.

Other: *Broadway Opry '79*; *The 1940's Radio Hour*; *Sugar Babies*; *A Kurt Weill Cabaret*; *Bette! Divine Madness*.

1980–1981

Original Broadway book musicals referenced in this chapter: *Woman of the Year* (opened March 1981 at the Palace Theater), book by Peter Stone, music by John Kander, lyrics by Fred Ebb.

Other Broadway musicals: *It's So Nice to be Civilized*, book, music, and lyrics by Mikki Grant; *Fearless Frank*, book and lyrics by Andrew Davies, music by Dave Brown; *Charlie and Algernon*, book and lyrics by David Rogers, music by Charles Strouse; *Onward Victoria*, book and lyrics by Charlotte Anker and Irene Rosenberg, music by Keith Herrmann; *Bring Back Birdie*, book by Michael Stewart, music by Charles Strouse, lyrics by Lee Adams; *Broadway Follies*, music and lyrics by Walter Marks; *Copperfield*, book, music, and lyrics by Al Kasha and Joel Hirschhorn; *The Moony Shapiro Songbook*, book by Monty Norman and Julian More, music by Norman, lyrics by More.

Revivals: *Your Arms Too Short to Box With God*; *42nd Street* (technically from the Warner Bros. film); *The Music Man*; *Camelot*; *Brigadoon*; *The Pirates of Penzance*; *The Five O'Clock Girl*; *Can-Can*.

Other: *Tintypes*; *Perfectly Frank*; *Shakespeare's Cabaret*; *Sophisticated Ladies*; *Oh Me, Oh My, Oh Youmans*; *Lena Horne: The Lady and Her Music*.

Off Broadway, *Really Rosie*, a children's musical of modest charm, ran (274 performances) after opening in October 1980 at the Chelsea Theater Center, with book and lyrics by Maurice Sendak and music by Carole King.

One "living composer" revue, *I Can't Keep Running in Place*, also enjoyed a decent run (208 performances) after opening in May 1981 at the Westside Arts Theater. It featured some nice, knowing songs (music and lyrics) by Barbara Schottenfeld.

1981–1982

Original Broadway book musicals referenced in this chapter: *Merrily We Roll Along* (opened in November 1981 at the Alvin Theater), book by George Furth, music and lyrics by Stephen Sondheim; *Dreamgirls* (opened in December 1981 at the Imperial Theater), music by Henry Krieger, book and lyrics by Tom Eyen; *Nine* (opened in May 1982 at the Ethel Barrymore Theater), book by Arthur Kopit, music and lyrics by Maury Yeston.

Other original Broadway book musicals: *Marlowe*, book by Leo Rost, music by Jimmy Horowitz, lyrics by Rost and Horowitz; *Oh, Brother!*, book and lyrics by Donald Driver, music by Michael Valenti; *The First*, book by Joel Siegel with

Martin Charnin, music by Bob Brush, lyrics by Charnin; *Waltz of the Stork*, book, music and lyrics by Melvin Van Peebles, with additional music and lyrics by Ted Hayes and Mark Barkan; *Is There Life After High School?*, book by Jeffrey Kindley, music and lyrics by Craig Carnelia; *Do Black Patent Leather Shoes Really Reflect Up?*, book by John R. Powers, music and lyrics by James Quinn and Alaric Jans.

Revivals: *Fiddler on the Roof*; *My Fair Lady*; *Camelot*; *Little Me*; *Joseph and the Amazing Technicolor Dreamcoat*; *Little Johnny Jones*.

Other: *This Was Burlesque*.

It should also be noted that the marvelous *Forbidden Broadway* series of satirical revues written by Gerard Alessandrini was inaugurated in May 1982 at Palsson's Supper Club.

1982–1983

Original Broadway book musical referenced in this chapter: *Cats* (opened October 1982 at the Winter Garden Theater), music by Andrew Lloyd Webber, lyrics by T. S. Eliot based on "Old Possum's Book of Practical Cats" by T. S. Eliot, additional lyrics by Trevor Nunn and Richard Stilgoe.

Other original Broadway book musicals: *Cleavage*, book by Buddy and David Sheffield, music and lyrics by Buddy Sheffield; *Play Me a Country Song*, book by Jay Broad, music and lyrics by John R. Briggs and Henry Manfredini; *A Doll's Life*, book and lyrics by Betty Comden and Adolph Green, music by Larry Grossman; *Merlin*, book by Richard Levinson and William Link, music by Elmer Bernstein, lyrics by Don Black; *Dance a Little Closer*, book and lyrics by Alan Jay Lerner, music by Charles Strouse.

Revivals: *The Best Little Whorehouse in Texas*; *Seven Brides for Seven Brothers* (technically, from the MGM film); *Your Arms Too Short to Box With God*; *On Your Toes*; *Porgy and Bess*; *Show Boat*.

Other: *Blues in the Night*; *Rock 'n Roll! The First 5,000 Years*; *My One and Only*.

CHAPTER 2: ALL IT HAS TO BE IS GOOD (1983–1984)

1983–1984

Original Broadway book musicals referenced in this chapter: *La Cage aux Folles* (opened August 1983 at the Palace Theater), book by Harvey Fierstein, music and lyrics by Jerry Herman; *Baby* (opened December 1983 at the Ethel

Barrymore Theater), book by Sybille Pearson, music by David Shire, lyrics by Richard Maltby, Jr.; *The Tap Dance Kid* (opened December 1983 at the Broadhurst Theater), book by Charles Blackwell, music by Henry Krieger, lyrics by Robert Lorick; *Sunday in the Park with George* (opened May 1984 at the Booth Theater), book by James Lapine, music and lyrics by Stephen Sondheim.

Other original Broadway book musicals: *Amen Corner*, book by Philip Rose and Peter Udell, music by Gary Sherman, lyrics by Udell; *Marilyn*, book by Patricia Michaels, music and lyrics by an assortment of five different writers; *Doonesbury*, book and lyrics by Gary Trudeau, music by Elizabeth Swados; *The Rink*, book by Terrence McNally, music by John Kander, lyrics by Fred Ebb; *The Human Comedy*, book by William Dumaresq, music by Galt MacDermot.

Revivals: *Mame*; *Zorba*; *Oliver!*; *The Wiz*.

Other: *Shirley MacLaine on Broadway.*

One Off-Broadway musical curiosity was the revue *A... My Name Is Alice*, which opened in February 1984 at the American Place Theater, conceived by Joan Micklin Silver and Julianne Boyd. It featured song contributions by a number of semi-unknowns who later would make names for themselves, including the lyricist David Zippel (*City of Angels*), the songwriting team of Lucy Simon and Susan Birkenhead (*The Secret Garden*), and Marta Kauffman and David Crane (co-creators of the television show *Friends*).

CHAPTER 3: OH, THERE'S A CAST OF THOUSANDS (1984–1987)

1984–1985

Original Broadway book musicals referenced in this chapter: *Grind* (opened April 1985 at the Mark Hellinger Theater), book by Fay Kanin, music by Larry Grossman, lyrics by Ellen Fitzhugh; *Big River: The Adventures of Huckleberry Finn* (opened April 1985 at the Eugene O'Neill Theater), book by William Hauptman, music and lyrics by Roger Miller.

Other original Broadway book musicals: *Quilters*, book by Molly Newman and Barbara Damashek, music and lyrics by Damashek; *André De Shields' Haarlem Nocturne*, book by André De Shields and Murray Horwitz, music and lyrics by an assortment of writers; *Harrigan 'n Hart*, book by Michael Stewart, music by Max Showalter, lyrics by Peter Walker.

Revivals: *The King and I* and *Take Me Along*.

Other: *Leader of the Pack*.

1985–1986

Original Broadway book musicals referenced in this chapter: *Song & Dance* (opened September 1985 at the Royale Theater), music by Andrew Lloyd Webber, lyrics by Don Black, additional lyrics by Richard Maltby, Jr.; *The Mystery of Edwin Drood* (opened December 1985 at the Imperial Theater), book, music and lyrics by Rupert Holmes; *Big Deal* (opened April 1986 at the Broadway Theater), book by Bob Fosse, music and lyrics by an assortment of writers.

Other original Broadway book musicals: *Mayor*, book by Warren Leight, music and lyrics by Charles Strouse; *The News*, book by Paul Schierhorn, David Rotenberg, and R. Vincent Park, music and lyrics by Schierhorn; *Wind in the Willows*, book by Jane Iredale, music by William Perry, lyrics by Roger McGough.

Revivals: *Sweet Charity* and *Singin' in the Rain* (technically, from the MGM film).

Other: *Tango Argentino*; *Jerry's Girls*; *Jerome Kern Goes to Hollywood*; *Uptown...It's Hot!*

1986–1987

Original Broadway book musicals referenced in this chapter: *Rags* (opened August 1986 at the Mark Hellinger Theater), book by Joseph Stein, music by Charles Strouse, lyrics by Stephen Schwartz; *Smile* (opened November 1986 at the Lunt-Fontanne Theater), book and lyrics by Howard Ashman, music by Marvin Hamlisch; *Les Misérables*, book by Claude-Michel Schönberg and Alain Boublil, music by Schönberg, lyrics by Herbert Kretzmer, French text by Boublil and Jean-Marc Natel; *Starlight Express*, music by Andrew Lloyd Webber, lyrics by Richard Stilgoe.

Other original Broadway book musicals: *Honky Tonk Nights*, book and lyrics by Ralph Allen and David Campbell, music by Michael Valenti; *Raggedy Ann*, book by William Gibson, music and lyrics by Joe Raposo; *Into the Light*, book by Jeff Tambornino, music by Lee Holdridge, lyrics by John Foster.

Revivals: *Me and My Girl*; *Oh Coward!*; *The Mikado*.

CHAPTER 4: MUSIC OF THE NIGHT (1987–1988)

1987–1988

Original Broadway book musicals referenced in this chapter: *Into the Woods*, book by James Lapine, music and lyrics by Stephen Sondheim; *The Phantom of the Opera*, book by Richard Stilgoe and Andrew Lloyd Webber, music by Lloyd Webber, lyrics by Charles Hart; *Sarafina!*, book, music and lyrics by Mbongeni Ngema, additional numbers by Hugh Masekela; *The Gospel at Colonus*, book and lyrics by Lee Breuer, music by Bob Telson; *Chess*, book by Richard Nelson, music by Benny Andersson and Björn Ulvaeus, lyrics by Tim Rice; *Romance Romance*, book and lyrics by Barry Harman, music by Keith Herrmann; *Carrie*, book by Lawrence D. Cohen, music by Michael Gore, lyrics by Dean Pitchford.

Other original Broadway book musicals: *Roza*, book and lyrics by Julian More, music by Gilbert Becaud; *Late Nite Comic*, book by Allan Knee, music and lyrics by Brian Gari; *Mail*, book and lyrics by Jerry Colker, music by Michael Rupert.

Revivals: *Dreamgirls*; *Anything Goes*; *Cabaret*.

Other: *Oba Oba*.

CHAPTER 5: YOU'RE NOTHING WITHOUT ME (1988–1990)

1988–1989

Original Broadway book musicals referenced in this chapter: *Legs Diamond* (opened December 1988 at the Mark Hellinger Theater), book by Harvey Fierstein and Charles Suppon, music and lyrics by Peter Allen; *Chu Chem*, (opened March 1989 at the Ritz Theater), book by Ted Allen, music by Mitch Leigh, lyrics by Jim Haines and Jack Wohl; *Welcome to the Club* (opened April 1989 at the Music Box Theater), music and lyrics by Cy Coleman, book and lyrics by A. E. Hotchner; *Starmites* (opened April 1989 at the Criterion Center Stage Right), book by Stuart Ross and Barry Keating, music and lyrics by Keating.

Other: *Jerome Robbins' Broadway*; *Black and Blue*.

Revival: *Ain't Misbehavin'*.

1989–1990

Original Broadway book musicals referenced in this chapter: *Grand Hotel*, book by Luther Davis, music and lyrics by Robert Wright and George Forrest; *City of Angels*, book by Larry Gelbart, music by Cy Coleman, lyrics by David Zippel; *Aspects of Love*, book and music by Andrew Lloyd Webber, lyrics by Don Black and Charles Hart.

Other original Broadway book musicals: *Dangerous Games*, book by Jim Lewis and Graciela Daniele, music by Astor Piazzolla, lyrics by William Finn; *Prince of Central Park*, book by Evan H. Rhodes, music by Don Sebesky, lyrics by Gloria Nissenson; *Truly Blessed*, book, music and lyrics by Queen Esther Marrow, additional music and lyrics by Reginald Royal; *A Change in the Heir*, book by George H. Gorham and Dan Sticco, music by Sticco, lyrics by Gorham.

Revivals: *Shenendoah*; *Sweeney Todd*; *Meet Me in St. Louis* (technically, from the MGM film); *3 Penny Opera*; *Gypsy*; *The Sound of Music.*

Other: *Mandy Patinkin in Concert: "Dress Casual."*

CHAPTER 6: WHY WE TELL THE STORY (1990–1991)

1990–1991

Original Broadway book musicals referenced in this chapter: *Once on This Island*, book and lyrics by Lynn Ahrens, music by Stephen Flaherty; *Shogun: The Musical*, book and lyrics by John Driver, music by Paul Chihara; *Miss Saigon*, book by Alain Boublil and Claude-Michel Schönberg, music by Schönberg, lyrics by Boublil and Richard Maltby, Jr.; *The Secret Garden*, book and lyrics by Marsha Norman, music by Lucy Simon; *The Will Rogers Follies*, book by Peter Stone, music by Cy Coleman, lyrics by Betty Comden and Adolph Green.

Revivals: *Oh, Kay!*; *Fiddler on the Roof*; *Peter Pan.*

Other: *Buddy.*

CHAPTER 7: SOMETHIN' MORE (1991–1992)

1991–1992

Original Broadway book musicals referenced in this chapter: *Nick & Nora*, book by Arthur Laurents, music by Charles Strouse, lyrics by Richard Maltby, Jr.; *Metro*, original book and lyrics by Agata Miklaszewska and Maryna Miklaszewska/English book by Mary Bracken Phillips and Janusz Józefowicz, music by Janusz Stoklosa; *Jelly's Last Jam*, book by George C. Wolfe, music by Jelly Roll Morton, lyrics by Susan Birkenhead, additional music by Luther Henderson.

Revivals: *Peter Pan*; *The Most Happy Fella*; *Guys and Dolls*; *Man of La Mancha*; *Falsettos*. (This total does not include the revival of *Brigadoon*, mounted by the New York City Opera.)

Other: *Catskills on Broadway*; *Crazy for You* (see footnote 20); *Five Guys Named Moe.*

CHAPTER 8: MAYBE IT BETTER SOON NO (1992–1993)

1992–1993

Original Broadway book musicals referenced in this chapter: *Anna Karenina*, book and lyrics by Peter Kellogg, music by Daniel Levine; *My Favorite Year*, book by Joseph Dougherty, music by Stephen Flaherty, lyrics by Lynn Ahrens; *The Goodbye Girl*, book by Neil Simon, music by Marvin Hamlisch, lyrics by David Zippel; *Blood Brothers*, book, music and lyrics by Willy Russell; *The Who's Tommy*, book by Pete Townshend and Des McAnuff, music and lyrics by Townshend, additional music and lyrics by John Entwhistle and Keith Moon; *Kiss of the Spider Woman*, book by Terrence McNally, music by John Kander, lyrics by Fred Ebb.

Other original Broadway book musicals: *The Song of Jacob Zulu*, book and lyrics by Tug Yourgrau, music and lyrics by Ladysmith Black Mambazo; *Ain't Broadway Grand*, book by Thomas Meehan and Lee Adams, music by Mitch Leigh, lyrics by Adams.

Other: *Gypsy Passion*; *Tommy Tune Tonite!*; *Tango Pasión*.

CHAPTER 9: THE RED SHOES (1993)

CHAPTER 10: TURN THE BLOOD TO BLACK AND WHITE (1993–1994)

CHAPTER 11: A KIND OF HAPPINESS (1993–1995)

1993–1994

Original Broadway book musicals referenced in these chapters: *Cyrano: The Musical*, book and lyrics by Koen Van Dijk, music by Ad Van Dijk, additional lyrics by Sheldon Harnick; *The Red Shoes*, book by Marsha Norman, music by Jule Styne, lyrics by Norman and Paul Stryker; *Beauty and the Beast*, book by Linda Woolverton, music by Alan Menken, lyrics by Howard Ashman and Tim Rice; *Passion*, book by James Lapine, music and lyrics by Stephen Sondheim.

Other original Broadway book musical: *The Best Little Whorehouse Goes Public*, book by Larry King and Peter Masterson, music and lyrics by Carol Hall.

Revivals: *She Loves Me*; *Camelot*; *Joseph and the Amazing Technicolor Dreamcoat*; *My Fair Lady*; *Damn Yankees*; *Carousel*; *Grease*.

Other: *A Grand Night for Singing*.

1994–1995

Original Broadway book musical referenced in these chapters: *Sunset

Boulevard, book and lyrics by Don Black and Christopher Hampton, music by Andrew Lloyd Webber.

Revivals: *Show Boat*; *How to Succeed in Business Without Really Trying*; *Gentlemen Prefer Blondes*.

Other*: Nanci Griffith on Broadway*; *Basia on Broadway*; *Lamb Chop on Broadway*; *Smokey Joe's Café*; *Laurie Anderson on Broadway*.

CHAPTER 12: GLORY (1994–1996)

CHAPTER 13: HOW GLORY GOES (1995–1996)

1995–1996

Original Broadway book musicals referenced in these chapters: *Chronicle of a Death Foretold*, book adapted by Graciela Daniele and Jim Lewis, additional material by Michael John LaChiusa, music by Bob Telson; *Bring in 'da Noise, Bring in 'da Funk*, book by Reg E. Gaines, music by Daryl Waters, Zane Mark and Ann Duquesnay; lyrics by Gaines, George C. Wolfe and Duquesnay; *Victor/Victoria*, book by Blake Edwards, music by Henry Mancini and Frank Wildhorn, lyrics by Leslie Bricusse; *Big*, book by John Weidman, music by David Shire, lyrics by Richard Maltby, Jr.; *Rent*, book, music and lyrics by Jonathan Larson.

Revivals: *Company*; *Hello, Dolly!*; *Cinderella* (NYCO); *State Fair*; *The King and I*; *A Funny Thing Happened on the Way to the Forum*.

Other: *Swinging on a Star*.

CHAPTER 14: THIS IS THE MOMENT (1996–1997)

CHAPTER 15: PURE AND BLAMELESS (1997)

1996–1997

Original Broadway book musicals referenced in these chapters: *Titanic*, book by Peter Stone, music and lyrics by Maury Yeston; *Steel Pier*, book by David Thompson, music by John Kander, lyrics by Fred Ebb; *The Life*, book by David Newman, Ira Gasman and Cy Coleman, music by Coleman, lyrics by Gasman; *Jekyll & Hyde*, book and lyrics by Leslie Bricusse, music by Frank Wildhorn.

Other original Broadway book musicals: *Play On!*, which inserted Duke Ellington songs into an updated version of Shakespeare's *Twelfth Night* (book by Cheryl West); *Juan Darién*.

Revivals: *Chicago*; *Grease*; *Once Upon a Mattress*; *Annie*; *Candide*.

Other: *Dream*.

Off-Broadway, *I Love You, You're Perfect, Now Change* opened in August 1996 at the Westside Theater. A boy-girl "relationships" revue of impressive banality, by Joe DiPietro (book and lyrics) and Jimmy Roberts (music), the show, as of this writing, continues to run.

The Green Heart, which opened in April 1997 at the Variety Arts Theater under the auspices of the Manhattan Theater Club was a sweet book musical with a charming score (music and lyrics) by Rusty Magee, a broad, buffoonish libretto by Charles Busch, and a delightful lead performance by Karen Trott.

CHAPTER 16: HAKUNA MATATA (1997–1998)
CHAPTER 17: SATURN RETURNS (1997–1998)

1997–1998

Original Broadway book musicals referenced in these chapters: *King David*, book and lyrics by Tim Rice, music by Alan Menken; *Side Show*, book and lyrics by Bill Russell, music by Henry Krieger; *Triumph of Love*, book by James Magruder, music by Jeffrey Stock, lyrics by Susan Birkenhead; *The Scarlet Pimpernel*, music by Frank Wildhorn, book and lyrics by Nan Knighton; *The Lion King*, book by Roger Allers and Irene Mecchi, music by Elton John, lyrics by Tim Rice, additional music and lyrics by Lebo M, Mark Mancina, Jay Rifkin, Julie Taymor and Hans Zimmer; *Ragtime*, book by Terrence McNally, music by Stephen Flaherty, lyrics by Lynn Ahrens; *The Capeman*, book by Paul Simon and Derek Walcott, music by Simon, lyrics by Simon and Walcott.

Revivals: *1776*; *The Sound of Music*; *Cabaret*; *High Society* (technically, from the MGM film).

CHAPTER 18: ELABORATE LIVES (1998)
CHAPTER 19: YOU DON'T KNOW THIS MAN (1998–1999)
CHAPTER 20: DREAM TRUE (1999)

1998–1999

Original Broadway book musicals referenced in these chapters: *Parade*, book by Alfred Uhry, music and lyrics by Jason Robert Brown; *The Civil War*, book by Frank Wildhorn and Gregory Boyd, music by Wildhorn, lyrics by Jack Murphy.

Revivals: *Little Me*; *On the Town*; *Peter Pan*; *You're a Good Man, Charlie Brown*; *Annie Get Your Gun*.

Other: *Footloose*; *An Evening with Jerry Herman*; *Mandy Patinkin in Concert: "Mamaloshen"*; *Fosse*; *The Gershwins' Fascinating Rhythm*; *Band in Berlin*; *It Ain't Nothin' But the Blues*.

Off-Broadway, one notable failed new musical was a direct follow-up to *Rent* — *Bright Lights, Big City*, produced by the New York Theatre Workshop in March 1999, adapted from the hipster 1980s novel by Jay McInerny, with book, music, and lyrics by Paul Scott Goodman.

CHAPTER 21: WILD PARTY (1999–2000)

CHAPTER 22: WHAT SINGS (2000)

1999–2000

Original Broadway book musicals referenced in these chapters: *Kat and the Kings*, book and lyrics by David Kramer, music by Taliep Petersen; *Marie Christine*, book, music and lyrics by Michael John LaChiusa; *James Joyce's The Dead*, book by Richard Nelson, music by Shaun Davey; *Aida*, book by Linda Woolverton, Robert Falls and David Henry Hwang, music by Elton John, lyrics by Tim Rice; *The Wild Party*, book by Michael John LaChiusa and George C. Wolfe, music and lyrics by LaChiusa.

Revivals: *Kiss Me, Kate*; *Putting It Together*; *Porgy and Bess*; *Jesus Christ Superstar*; *The Green Bird*; *The Music Man*.

Other: *Saturday Night Fever*; *Swing!*; *Squonk*; *Tango Argentino*; *Contact*; *Riverdance*.

Off-Broadway, the musical *Running Man*, about the life and death of a troubled black youth, opened in November under the auspices of Music-Theater Group and ultimately was nominated for a Pulitzer Prize. The jazz influenced score by Dierdre Murray was challenging and original, though Cornelius Eady's densely poetic book often seemed willfully oblique.

CHAPTER 23: A SHOWBIZ MAUSOLEUM (2000–2001)

2000–2001

Original Broadway book musicals referenced in this chapter: *The Full Monty*, book by Terrence McNally, music and lyrics by David Yazbek; *Seussical*, book by Lynn Ahrens and Stephen Flaherty, music by Flaherty, lyrics by Ahrens; *Jane Eyre*, book and additional lyrics by John Caird, music and lyrics by Paul

Gordon; *A Class Act*, book by Linda Kline and Lonny Price, music and lyrics by Edward Kleban; *The Producers*, book by Mel Brooks and Thomas Meehan, music and lyrics by Brooks; *The Adventures of Tom Sawyer*, book by Ken Ludwig, music and lyrics by Don Schlitz.

Revivals: *The Rocky Horror Show*; *Follies*; *Bells Are Ringing*; *42ⁿᵈ Street*.

CHAPTER 24; THIS IS URINETOWN (2001–2002)

CHAPTER 25: MUSIC AND THE MIRROR (2001)

CHAPTER 26: CLIMBING UPHILL (2001–2002)

CHAPTER 27: DON'T CRY FOR ME, ARGENTINA (2001)

2001–2002

Original Broadway book musicals referenced in these chapters: *Urinetown*, book by Greg Kotis, music by Mark Hollmann, lyrics by Hollmann and Kotis; *Mamma Mia!*, book by Catherine Johnson, music and lyrics by Benny Andersson and Björn Ulvaeus, some songs with Stig Anderson; *Thou Shalt Not*, book by David Thompson, music and lyrics by Harry Connick, Jr.; *By Jeeves*, book and lyrics by Alan Ayckbourn, music by Andrew Lloyd Webber; *Sweet Smell of Success*, book by John Guare, music by Marvin Hamlisch, lyrics by Craig Carnelia; *Thoroughly Modern Millie*, book by Dick Scanlan and Richard Morris, new music by Jeanine Tesori, new lyrics by Scanlan, old music and lyrics by James Van Heusen and Sammy Cahn, Sir Arthur Sullivan and W. S. Gilbert, Jay Thompson, Victor Herbert and Rida Johnson Young, Walter Donaldson, Sam M. Lewis and Joe Young.

Revivals: *One Mo' Time*; *Oklahoma!*; *Into the Woods*.

Other: *Bea Arthur on Broadway*; *Elaine Stritch At Liberty*.

Off-Broadway, *The Spitfire Grill*, adapted from the popular 1996 film about a young female ex-con's quest for a new life, found itself unexpectedly confronting a real-life twist of fate both tragic and ironic. Nurtured by two institutional theaters—first the George Street Playhouse in New Brunswick, New Jersey, which premiered the show in 1999, joined shortly thereafter by Playwrights Horizons, at the instigation of Ira Weitzman—*The Spitfire Grill*'s composer-bookwriter, James Valqua, and lyricist-bookwriter, Fred Alley, were experienced but still relatively unknown musical theater journeymen. One week before a scheduled May 21ˢᵗ, pre-rehearsal, final reading at Playwrights, Alley went out jogging at his home in Wisconsin and was found on the side of the road the next morning dead at 38 of an undiagnosed congenital heart condition.

The parallels to the fate of the late Jonathan Larson were overwhelming. "Of course it's shocking and sad when anyone dies so young, but Fred was the most warm-hearted, embraceable person I'd practically ever met," observed Weitzman. "It was just devastating. The wonderful thing, what I call the miracle of the timing of this tragedy, is that Fred had already done so much good work on the piece, we found that we had a draft that was produceable.

The Spitfire Grill opened in September 2001 at Playwrights Horizons' temporary home at The Duke on 42nd Street.

FINALE: BUT WHO CALLS THAT LIVIN'? (2002–2003)

2002–2003

Original Broadway book musicals referenced in this chapter: *Hairspray*, book by Mark O'Donnell and Thomas Meehan, music by Marc Shaiman, lyrics by Scott Wittman and Shaiman; *Amour*, French libretto by Didier van Cauwelaert, English adaptation by Jeremy Sams, music by Michael Legrand; *Dance of the Vampires*, book by David Ives, Jim Steinman and Michael Kunze, music and lyrics by Steinman, additional lyrics by Don Black; *Urban Cowboy*, book by Aaron Latham and Phillip Oesterman, music by Bob Stillman, Jeff Blumenkrantz, Ronnie Dunn, Jason Robert Brown, Danny Arena, Sara Light, Marcus Hummon, Martie Maguire, Wayland D. Holyfield, Bob Lee House, Carl L. Byrd, Pevin Byrd-Munoz, Roger Brown, Luke Reed, Lauren Lucas, Jerry Chesnut, Jerry Silverstein, Clint Black, James Hayden Nicholas, Tommy Conners, Skip Ewing, Rebekka Bremlette, Dorsey Burnette III, Annie L. Roboff, Charles Daniels, Tom Crain, Fred Edwards, Taz DiGregorio, Jim Marshall, Charlie Hayward, Wanda Mallette, Patti Ryan and Bob Morrison; *A Year with Frog and Toad*, book and lyrics by Willie Reale, music by Robert Reale.

Revivals: *The Boys from Syracuse*; *Flower Drum Song*; *Man of La Mancha*; *La Bohème*; *Nine*; *Gypsy*.

Other: *Movin' Out*; *The Look of Love*.

THE MUSICALS

A...My Name Is Alice

The Act

The Adventures of Tom
    Sawyer

After the Fair

Agnes

Aida

Ain't Misbehavin'

Alice in Concert

Amen Corner

Amour

Angel

Anna Karenina

Aspects of Love

Assassins

Avenue Q

Avenue X

Baby

Balancing Act

Ballroom

Barnum

Bat Boy

The Beautiful Game

Beauty and the Beast

Bed and Sofa

Bella, Belle of Byelorussia

The Best Little
    Whorehouse Goes
    Public

The Best Little
    Whorehouse in Texas

Big

Big Deal

Big River: The Adventures
    of Huckleberry Finn

Blood Brothers

Blues in the Night

Bombay Dreams

Bounce

Break

Bring Back Birdie

Bring in 'da Noise, Bring
    in 'da Funk

Broadway Follies

A Broadway Musical

The Bubbly Black Girl
    Sheds Her
    Chameleon Skin

But Never Jam Today

By Jeeves

The Capeman

Captains Courageous

Carmelina

Caroline, or Change

Carrie

Cats

A Change in the Heir

Charlie and Algernon

Chess

Christina Alberta's Father

A Christmas Carol

Chronicle of a Death
    Foretold

Chu Chem

City of Angels

The Civil War

A Class Act

Cleavage

Comin' Uptown

Contact

Copperfield

Crazy for You

Cyrano: The Musical

Dance a Little Closer

Dance of the Vampires

Dangerous Games

A Day in Hollywood/A
    Night in the
    Ukraine

Diamonds

Dispatches

Do Black Patent Leather
    Shoes Really Reflect
    Up?

A Doll's Life

Doonesbury

313

Dream True: My Life
    with Vernon Dexter
Dreamgirls
Eleanor Sleeps Here
Elegies: A Song Cycle
Eubie!
Evita
Exactly Like You
Fallen Angels
Falsettoland
Falsettos
Fearless Frank
Fermat's Last Tango
The First
First Lady Suite
Five Guys Named Moe
Floyd Collins
Footloose
Forbidden Broadway
Fosse
Four Jews in a Room
    Bitching
The Full Monty
Goblin Market
God Bless You, Mr.
    Rosewater
The Goodbye Girl
The Gospel at Colonus
Got To Go Disco
Grand Hotel
The Grand Tour
The Green Bird
The Green Heart
Grind
The Haggadah: A
    Passover Cantata

Hairspray
Harrigan 'n Heart
Hedwig and the Angry
    Inch
Hello Again
Herringbone
Honky Tonk Nights
Howard Crabtree's
    Whoop-De-Doo!
The Human Comedy
Hysterical Blindness
I Can't Keep Running in
    Place
I Love You, You're Perfect,
    Now Change
I Remember Mama
I'm Getting My Act
    Together and Taking
    It on the Road
In Trousers
Into the Light
Into the Woods
Is There Life After High
    School?
The IT Girl
It's Better With a Band
It's So Nice to be
    Civilized
J. P. Morgan Saves the
    Nation
James Joyce's The Dead
Jane Eyre
Jekyll & Hyde
Jelly's Last Jam
Jerome Robbins'
    Broadway

jon & jen
Juan Darién
Just So
Kat and the Kings
King David
King of Hearts
King of Schnorrers
Kiss of the Spider Woman
La Cage aux Folles
The Last Five Years
The Last Sweet Days
Late Night Comic
Legs Diamond
Les Misérables
The Life
The Light in the Piazza
The Lion King
Little by Little
Little Fish
Little Shop of Horrors
Lucky Nurse
Lucky Stiff
Mail
Mamma Mia!
A Man of No Importance
March of the Falsettos
Marie Christine
Marilyn
Marlowe
Mayor
Merlin
Metro
Miss Saigon
The Moony Shapiro
    Songbook
Movin' Out

Mr. Hamm

My Favorite Year

My Life With Albertine

My Old Friends

My One and Only

The Mystery of Edwin
    Drood

A New Brain

The New Yorkers

The News

Nick and Nora

Nine

No Way to Treat A Lady

Nunsense

Oh, Brother!

Olio

On the Twentieth
    Century

Once on This Island

One Mo' Time

Onward Victoria

Over Texas

Parade

Paradise!

Passion

The Petrified Prince

The Phantom of the
    Opera

Platinum

Play Me a Country Song!

Prince of Central Park

Prodigal

The Producers

Pump Boys and Dinettes

Quilters

Radiant Baby

Raggedy Ann

Rags

Ragtime

The Red Shoes

Reggae

Rent

Roadside

The Rocky Horror Show

Romance Romance

Roza

Runaways

Sarafina!

Sarava

Saturday Night Fever

Saturn Returns

Saved

The Scarlet Pimpernel

The Secret Garden

Seussical

Shogun: The Musical

The Show Goes On

Side Show

Smile

Sophisticated Ladies

Song & Dance

Songs for a New World

Starlight Express

Starmites

Steel Pier

Stomp

Suburb

Sugar Babies

Sunday in the Park with
    George

Sunset Boulevard

Superbia

Sweeney Todd

Sweet Smell of Success

The Tap Dance Kid

They're Playing Our Song

Thoroughly Modern
    Millie

Thou Shalt Not

Three Postcards

tick, tick... BOOM!

Time and Again

Tintypes

Titanic

Triumph of Love

Truly Blessed

Urban Cowboy

Urinetown: The Musical

The Utter Glory of
    Morissey Hall

Victor/Victoria

Violet

Waltz of the Stork

Welcome to the Club

Where's Mamie?

Whistle Down the Wind

The Who's Tommy

The Wild Party (2)

The Will Rogers Follies

Wind in the Willows

Wings

Woman of the Year

Working

A Year With Frog and
    Toad

Zanna, Don't!

THE NUMBERS

In terms of dollars grossed, Broadway has been setting records almost yearly during the period covered by this book. Yet, during this same 25-year stretch the sum total of actual ticket buyers on Broadway has only increased nominally, fluctuating between 8 and 11 million persons. It is sobering to study the numbers (taken from *Variety* and The League of American Theatres and Producers). Where total attendance has risen 33% overall since the 1977–1978 season, total box office *receipts* have risen 600%. This economic imbalance simply confirms what we already know. The price of a Broadway ticket—even with all inflationary factors considered—is indefensibly disconnected from reality. It remains one of the greatest impediments to the future evolution of adventurous theater (musical or otherwise) on Broadway.

	Total Box Office Sales (in millions)	Total Attendance (in millions)		Total Box Office Sales (in millions)	Total Attendance (in millions)
1977–1978 ($25 top ticket)	$103	8.6	1990–1991 ($100 top ticket)	$267	7.3
1978–1979	$128	9.1	1991–1992	$293	7.3
1979–1980	$143	9.4	1992–1993	$328	7.8
1980–1981 ($50 top ticket)	$194	10.8	1994–1994	$356	8.1
			1994–1995	$406	9.0
1981–1982	$221	10.7	1995–1996	$436	9.4
1982–1983	$203	8.1	1996–1997	$499	10.5
1983–1984	$226	7.9	1997–1998	$558	11.5
1984–1985	$209	7.3	1998–1999	$588	11.6
1985–1986	$190	6.5	1999–2000	$603	11.3
1986–1987	$208	7.7	2000–2001	$666	11.8
1987–1988	$253	8.1	2001–2002 ($480 top ticket)	$643	10.9
1988–1989	$262	8.0			
1989–1990	$282	8.0	2002–2003	$721	11.4

INDEX